THE TOON

Roger Hutchinson was born to a Tyneside family in 1949. He is a former British Weekly Newspaper Sportswriter of the year.

THE TOON

Roger Hutchinson

BIRLINN

This edition first published in 2010 by
Birlinn Limited
West Newington House
10 Newington Road
Edinburgh
EH9 1QS

www.birlinn.co.uk

ISBN: 978 1 84158 915 2

British Library Cataloguing-in-Publication Data
A catalogue record for this book is available from the British Library

Designed and typeset by Iolaire Typesetting, Newtonmore
Printed and bound by JF Print Ltd, Somerset

To Rosie and Ben

CONTENTS

PREFACE TO THE 2010 EDITION

❖

This history has been written and published independently of the proprietors of its subject matter, Newcastle United Football Club. Indeed, past and present owners of the club would certainly prefer that *The Toon* had never been produced at all, not only for the criticisms of them contained within, but also because they consider that every one of its modest sales – the few pounds that you the reader may have paid to hold it in your hands right now – nibbles at their profit margins.

Rather than being a defect, that independence is one of this book's greatest strengths. There is very little to be said in favour of 'authorised' biographies of either people or institutions. Authorisation always comes at a price, and that price is the denial of independence and the blunting of authorial judgement by whoever is doing the authorising – which will be whoever 'owns' the institution at the time of writing.

This book, *The Toon*, is written in the understanding that nobody owns Newcastle United. Millionaires will come and go, and their time in charge of the operation at St James's Park will be marked by success or mediocrity or – more commonly in recent years – by disaster. They will make money from the institution, or they will lose money.

But whatever their dreams, profits and pretensions, they will never hold personal copyright of the immense historical creation of Newcastle United Football Club. The hopes and prayers and embedded memories of millions of people have created that club, and will sustain it in the future, and those people's intense emotions are beyond ownership or copyright.

So this book is not for the temporary owners and their even more temporary placemen. It is not for the millionaires, but for the millions who always have been and always will be there, in person and in spirit.

Roger Hutchinson
June 2010

PREFACE TO THE 1997 EDITION

It is impossible to spend any time researching the history of Newcastle United Football Club without coming to realise that, all about you, thousands of others are engaged in the same pursuit. These are the Geordie fans. Very few of them are doing it for publication. But they are all, in one way or another, experts.

One afternoon in the late 1990s I was huddled by the microfiche printer in Newcastle City Library, running through the press coverage of (I think) the 1924 cup campaign, when I became aware of a kindred spirit. Behind me a man was laying open, page by careful page, the bound volumes of the *Evening Chronicle* from the 1880s – the editions which are too old to be put on microfilm and must be treated with immense care.

He was searching, he told me, among the late-Victorian advertisements and share prices (there were no sports pages back then), for accounts of Newcastle East End and Newcastle West End, the two clubs which eventually amalgamated to form Newcastle United. He was engaged in this labour of love to a specific end. He was interested not only in the workaday results of their matches, their goalscorers and such commonplace detail. He wanted to record what the weather had been like during every football match ever played at the Gallowgate. Often a careful study of the press could offer him this information. Where it was not available in print, he told me with proper satisfaction, he had discovered an alternative. A man at the local weather centre was able to give him meteorological print-outs. With these he was able not only to pin down the state of the climate on any given afternoon – if it was wet or dry, cloudy or sunny, that sort of thing – but also what time a shower fell on St James's Park on any Saturday since the 1880s.

That is dedicated history. There was not much room for weather in the following pages: Newcastle United's turbulent life took care of that. But every time I have stumbled upon an item of choice material from the past, my acquaintance from last winter has sprung to mind, and I have felt suitably humble. When the likes of Harvey, Milburn, Keegan and a score of others stated to the world that these fans deserve the best, they spoke from the heart. They were thinking not only of the match-winning roar of the people of one of the world's great football cities. They were thinking, although they did not know it, of the man researching the weather.

Roger Hutchinson
1997

CHAPTER ONE

ALMOST THE DOUBLE: FOURTEEN DAYS IN APRIL 1905

❖

Such an extraordinary seesaw of a fortnight, such a bittersweet 14 days: it might have been an omen of the century which lay ahead.

It began at the low ebb. At 3.25 p.m. on 15 April 1905, 11 footballers of Newcastle United FC walked out into the great open shallow bowl of Crystal Palace stadium in Sydenham to the rumbling roar of 101,117 spectators. It was the second-biggest FA Cup final attendance to date (it would eventually prove to be the fourth-biggest in history). It was comfortably the largest crowd that any of those 11 footballers – who were representing Newcastle in the club's first attempt at winning a major honour – would ever perform before. And it turned out to be the biggest gate ever attracted to watch Newcastle United Football Club in the whole of its long and distinguished life.

The 11 footballers posed awkwardly for a photograph: arms crossed over their black-and-white chests, an inch of knee-flesh showing between the hem of their shorts and the white band at the top of their bulging padded stockings, their Manfield Hotspur boots carefully laced from ankle to instep, goalkeeper Jimmy Lawrence also in black and white stripes and distinguishable from his colleagues only by his gloves and flat cap.

At 3.29 p.m. their opponents, three-time cup-winners Aston Villa, having lost the toss, kicked off with the sun in their faces.

At 3.31 p.m. Newcastle were a goal behind. Harry Hampton, Villa's centre-forward, collected a rebound to hit the ball low and hard to Lawrence's left from six yards out.

The Tynesiders fought back, of course – every side has its chances in an FA Cup final. But they failed to take them. Shortly before half-time United's centre-forward Bill Appleyard, the scorer so far that season of a respectable 13 league and cup goals, collected the ball from a free-kick and unleashed a typically fierce shot. Villa's keeper George was beaten, but it slammed against the square wooden post, leaving the upright – and 5,000 travelling Geordie fans – quivering.

That, in retrospect, was that. Newcastle's half-backs continued to play well but their cautious balls upfield were met by a forward line which leaked confidence by the minute. Villa, on the other hand, could feel the cup in their grasp. Their defenders were hard and uncompromising and their forwards were fast and carefree, and with just eight minutes left Harry Hampton poached his and his side's second goal.

There was no return, and they knew it. Newcastle had lost their first cup final by 2-0.

But they had discovered a ravenous appetite for the big event – which was as well, because 15 April 1905 would be by no means their last taste of sorrow in Sydenham. For days previous to the final, Euston, St Pancras and King's Cross stations had disgorged hordes of laughing, singing men wearing black-and-white hats, umbrellas and rosettes (scarves were to be a later development).

On the Friday evening before the final Newcastle Central Station played host to 4,240 travelling fans. A song had been composed for the occasion. (It was prophetic. 'Wi' colours wavin', black and white, Thor gannin' up to London strite, To gie th' Cockney folks a fright,' was the chorus, and the lines 'When Appleyard bangs in the baall, He myeks th' goalposts shivver' featured in one of the verses.) The trains south were bedecked with black and white. At York the bar was beseiged, and Geordie fans staged races and wrestling matches on the platform.

They decamped in London between four and half nine in the morning. Some headed off to see Buckingham Palace, some went straight to Crystal Palace, and others wandered about the 'arid wastes' of Grays Inn Road and Euston Road exchanging banter with the greater number of Villa supporters . . . 'Aston Villa for a thousand', challenged one Brummie.

The Geordie stopped and gazed at him. 'What d'ye say?'

'Aston Villa for a thousand.'

'Wey, aa hev nay mair a thousand than ye hev yersel. But aa'll tell ye what aa'll dee. Aa'll lay six pounds t' fower on Newcassel.'

There were no takers. United had already that season done the double over Villa, and on the morning of the final Newcastle were placed second in the league, five places and six points above Aston Villa, having scored seven more league goals and conceded 11 less. Newcastle United were the hot favourites. Six to four against Villa were, in fact, generous odds. The Brummie, in hindsight, should have taken them.

Back in Newcastle, in those days before popular radio or television, the streets were unusually busy that Saturday afternoon. 'A spirit of agitation' was in the air, and crowds of men, boys and even women wearing black-and-white neckties gathered outside the offices of the *Evening Chronicle*. Rosemary Lane and St John's Street filled with a small army of expectant souls as half past three approached. Minutes after Hampton's first goal an edition of the *Evening Chronicle* bearing the dismal news issued from the office. 'If it took,' the paper reported later, 'as much out of the team as it took out of those who watched its progress in the north it did more than can be expressed in a sentence.'

Rumours swept the streets of Newcastle as the afternoon wore on. United were pressing . . . Jim Howie had scored an equaliser . . . it seemed, said one observer, as if everybody had a telephone receiver at their ear, connected to a wild variety of different sources of information. People stood about town ignoring the Saturday afternoon shops, unfolding the latest editions of the evening press and frantically inquiring of all who passed for the latest news from the Crystal Palace.

'In the last quarter,' read the evening final, 'the Villa scored another goal.'

On Wearside the newsboys bawled with evident joy: 'Terrible defeat of Newcastle!' On Tyneside, they pulled themselves together and prepared for the team's Monday morning homecoming. It was naturally raucous: the players had to fight their way off the train, and wondered aloud what their reception would have been if they had won.

They had not played well, the North-east's first representatives at an FA Cup final. 'The United men were disappointing in every department,' said one commentator. 'Whatever the reason, whether it was staleness as some say, or nervousness as others contend, not one man came up to expectation, and the side as a whole was slow and listless.

'I am inclined to the theory of nervousness, because when they found the game going so much against them they persisted blindly in sticking to the ball and playing the short passing game without variation until the end of the match. Had they only given us a glimpse of their form in league matches the result might have been different . . . Having once found their way to the Crystal Palace, however, Newcastle United may be expected when next they get there to do themselves credit.'

That last comment would turn out to be a hostage to cruel fortune. But Newcastle's 'form in league matches' was something else, as the remaining 13 days of that see-saw fortnight would prove.

The season of 1904–05 was Newcastle United's 12th in the Football League, and their seventh in the First Division. They had never finished higher than third in the league, but had developed a comfortable habit of winding up in the top quarter of their division – and St James's Park had already achieved the reputation of a formidable ground to visit.

The 1904–05 season had begun much like any other. It kicked off at home with a nice 3-0 win – Jackie Rutherford and Ronald Orr (2) – over newly promoted Woolwich Arsenal (who had entered the league with Newcastle 12 years before) in front of 21,897 fans.

By 3 December, following straight away wins at Wolverhampton and Birmingham, and a home win over Blackburn Rovers, Newcastle were top of the First Division. Jackie Rutherford had scored six in 14 games, Colin Veitch five, and Orr, Howie and Appleyard four apiece.

Newcastle United, the world agreed, had got there by playing 'scientific' football. This was nothing more or less than the possession and short-ball game to which they so stubbornly adhered throughout the losing cup final. It came from Scotland. It was in fact the basis of the Scottish national squad's series of demolitions of their English opponents throughout the early years of that home international fixture.

This system arrived at St James's Park with a Scottish boss, Frank Watt; a Scottish trainer, James McPherson; and with a large sackful of extremely influential Scottish players. Throughout the late-Victorian and Edwardian period it seemed at times almost as though Newcastle United were a Scottish team playing in the English league.

Out of the 11 cup finalists in 1905, six were Scots. Four of those were already internationals: the full-back Andrew McCombie, captain and centre-half Andy Aitken, left-half Peter McWilliam, and inside-right James Howie. Of the other two, Glaswegian goalkeeper Jimmy Lawrence (who set an all-time United appearance record of 496 games) would gain his Scottish caps at a later date, and right-half Alec Gardner would serve the club for no fewer than 313 matches. The number of Scots in the team would have been seven if the free-scoring Ronald Orr – another international – had not been out through injury. (Of the minority Englishmen, incidentally, three were Geordies.)

So, the goalkeeper, one full-back, the trainer, the captain, the entire half-back line and half of the goalscoring forward line was Scottish. They played the thoughtful, steady, short passing game of their country; they rarely embarked on mazy individual runs; they kept their pattern through thick and thin . . . they were, in short, a side which was always likely to be rattled out of a helter-skelter cup-tie, but which was admirably equipped to withstand a long and rigorous league campaign.

5

And in the December of 1904 they sat, for the first time in Newcastle United's history, on top of the English league. They were, after 14 of the 34 matches, one point clear of Small Heath (who would become Birmingham FC at the end of that season, and Birmingham City in 1945), Sunderland and Preston North End.

By the end of the month, despite three good wins and just one defeat, they were third. Sheffield United and Everton stormed through a series of games in hand to leapfrog from halfway down the table to first and second respectively, while Newcastle travelled to Sunderland on Christmas Eve (taking with them 7,000 supporters) and lost 3-1.

And then came the cup. In the first round Newcastle were drawn at home to non-league Plymouth Argyle. They drew 1-1, and had to replay in Plymouth. Forty years later a stalwart of southern football, Alec Whitcher, would write a vivid account from personal memory of just such a cup-tie on the south coast against a big team from the north in 1905. Whitcher could have been summoning from his childhood this very game; it certainly provides a view of the sight and smells and sounds which would have greeted the travelling Geordie support in January 1905 . . .

'The great day dawns at last,' he recalled, 'and the weather glass is consulted for perhaps the first time in your young life . . . The whole timetable has been planned, and having quite a distance to travel, an early start is essential. Seldom are provincial grounds readily accessible [it should be stressed that, at St James's Park as well as on the south coast, football grounds which would soon find themselves surrounded by the burgeoning estates of expanding English towns, were originally built in green fields on their outskirts], and this is no exception, for we have to travel to the centre of the city and thence to the Ground, either by train, packed like sardines, by brakes or cabs.

'Tramcars do not go as far as the Ground, and there are dozens of every conceivable type of horse-drawn vehicle plying for hire, all marked "Football Ground".

'The cup-tie enthusiasm is at fever pitch, and after jostling, squeezing and the like we eventually get to the Ground's entrance by way of a road totally inadequate for the traffic . . . If it's wet, well, you get pretty muddy, and also enjoy showers of slush from passing vehicles. But who worries? We are going to the blankety cup-tie whatever happens. *En route*, hawkers are doing a brisk trade, especially with the favours. We notice that the visitors want to display to all and sundry that they have travelled probably through the night to support their favourites . . .

'In one corner we easily recognise the visitors' supporters, all bursting with enthusiasm and decked in their team's colours. Our attention while waiting is attracted by a supporter's performing dog, which causes great amusement as it runs round the pitch with a ball at its nose, and if the football was made to bounce the dog would jump in the air, heading the ball in the most acknowledged style. When the dog succeeds in running the ball into the goal there is a great shout of joy.'

And so, after a rural brass band had attempted a haphazard version of 'A Farmer's Boy'; after the crowd had been ordered by a man with a megaphone to 'pack up in front and allow others to see the match'; after the chocolate men and programme sellers had been round; the teams came out to 'the ringing of bells, the noise of rattles, and the waving of coloured umbrellas and top hats', and the game got under way.

When a goal was scored 'we invariably see carrier pigeons released to take home the good tidings, or otherwise, of the visiting side'. After the game the winning team's favours were sold outside, along with 'memorial cards, one penny each, the death of poor old——' (insert the losing team).

The carrier pigeons would twice have been released during Newcastle's cup-tie at Plymouth, to record a 1-1 draw. United won the second replay 2-0, and went on to beat Spurs in a second-round replay by 4-0.

As the New Year matured, United's successful cup run ensured that they always had games in hand over the league leaders, but they failed to top the table. By early March, after goals from Rutherford, Appleyard and McWilliam had sent the Wolves home from Tyneside with their tails between their legs,

Newcastle sat two points behind the joint leaders – Everton and Manchester City – with a game in hand over each of them, and eight to play.

By the end of March they had reached the cup semi-final and dragged themselves up to second spot in the league. 'How happy I shall be,' the local paper's Magpie cartoon character said, addressing the league and cup trophies, 'with either.'

Then, on All Fool's Day, 1 April 1905, disaster struck. Newcastle, having qualified for the FA Cup final for the first time, visited lowly Blackburn in a run-of-the-mill league game. The Tynesiders had released five key players to an England v Scotland international (chiefly the Scots McCombie, Aitken, Howie and McWilliam) – and they lost 2-0. Leaders Everton had the Saturday off, and so the substance of United's failure was that they had used up their one game in hand, but were still two points adrift, with just six games left. And Manchester City had sneaked back into second place.

The week before the final Everton dropped a point at Stoke, and Newcastle hammered Nottingham Forest 5-1. One point in it, Manchester City out of the race once more, four games to play.

And then the débâcle at Crystal Palace. The question was not, after that stunning cup final dismissal of Newcastle United's scientific game, were they good enough, but did they have the nerve?

Oddly, it was Everton who cracked. Searching their second league title, and already locked in mortal local combat with Liverpool FC, they played three league games between 8 April and 22 April, and lost two of them. Newcastle entertained Sunderland at St James's Park on 22 April knowing that victory would achieve two things: it would kill the cup final ghost, and it would put them at least one point clear at the top of the league with two games left to play – and a game in hand.

Thirty thousand packed into the stadium, and fully 90 minutes before kick-off the gates were closed on thousands more. But there could not have been a less sympathetic visiting team to the beaten cup finalists. Two years earlier, at the end of the 1902–03 season, Sunderland had visited Newcastle needing two points to win their second successive league title. United had won that day, and the league trophy had gone to Sheffield Wednesday by just one point.

Sunderland were out for revenge, and they got it. Holley and Buckle put them two up before Bill Appleyard tried to swing the game back single-handedly. He found the net from a Gosnell cross, but was declared offside. Undeterred, the centreforward immediately homed in on the Sunderland goal once more. Rhodes chopped him down, and Veitch converted the penalty.

After 25 minutes Newcastle, 2-1 down, were reduced to ten men when Alec Gardner was carried off with a small bone broken in his left leg. There were no substitutes and, with the home players and support baying for offside, Holley ran through the reduced United defence to make it 3-1.

It could have been worse, much, much worse. The fans trickling out of St James's Park picked up their evening sporting pink to discover that Everton had lost 2-1 at Woolwich Arsenal.

United had two games left to play. With a superior goal difference to both Everton and Manchester City, winning both matches would almost certainly mean winning the league title. On the following Wednesday afternoon they travelled to Yorkshire and beat Sheffield Wednesday 3-1, despite being nervous and outplayed for 75 of the 90 minutes.

And so that extraordinary fortnight, that extraordinary season, came to an end on 29 April 1905 with a game just down the road, at Ayresome Park, Middlesbrough. The home side had not beaten Newcastle since February 1903, and they sat fifth from the bottom of the First Division. They were, in short, no Sunderland. And it showed.

Before just 12,000 people on a warm and hazy afternoon, United went 1-0 up after six minutes. Howie hurtled down the right and whipped in a cross which Appleyard missed, but Orr did not. The team settled. They knew about being in the lead. Eight minutes after half-time Jackie Rutherford from Percy Main took the ball for a walk from the halfway line and beat Williamson gloriously. Sixty seconds later Appleyard made it 3-0, and that was the way it stayed.

United's players walked off Ayresome Park to the news that Aston Villa had repaid a favour by beating Manchester City 3-2. (City were famously later accused of offering huge inducements to the players of both sides to get the desired result in this game. If so, it was an extraordinarily stupid thing to do – if Newcastle won at Middlesbrough, as they were always likely to, a six-goal difference in goal average needed to be overturned by City before any bribe could be repaid.) The United players caught a special train out of Middlesbrough at 7 p.m., and arrived back in Newcastle Central Station 80 minutes later as champions of the Football League. They took an open-topped omnibus via Clayton Street to receive their fans at the Palace Theatre, Haymarket.

Newcastle United had come, just 12 seasons after joining the Football League, to within a couple of goals of winning the double. Preston had won both trophies in 1889, the first season of the Football League, and Villa had done it in 1897. But the 20th-century game was to be a different animal. Nobody did the 20th-century double until Tottenham in 1961. Until then, nobody had come as close as Newcastle United had in 1905.

Curiously, few people at the time paid much attention to the achievement. The celebrations of the league win were, after the cup final, strangely subdued. There was a reason for this, and it was not that people's energies had all been expended a fortnight earlier. It was, simply, that most would have traded the league title for the cup. For many decades the FA Cup remained the main trophy in England. It was the oldest by far, dating back to 1871, a full 17 years before the league kicked off, and comfortably the most prestigious. When, in the 1950s, Stanley Matthews was approaching the end of his playing career, it didn't much bother the best winger in the world that he had never played in a championship-winning team. But it tore at his heart that he had never won the cup – it burned away so fiercely inside him that eventually, in 1953, he just picked himself up off the Wembley turf and won the damned thing single-handedly.

As it was for Matthews in the 1950s, so it was for Newcastle United in the 1900s. The league was nice, but they lusted after the cup. It would be, had they only known, a painful infatuation.

The close of that fortnight in April 1905 marked two things of immense significance. It indicated the arrival of a great football team, probably one of the greatest club sides that Europe has seen, a team so good that it would dominate the remainder of the Edwardian era, and would only finally be killed by the outbreak of the First World War . . . and it posted notice of the presence in Britain of a magnificent football club. A club which, despite buffets and setbacks, lousy managers and worse directors, bad players and shoddy teams, would never for one moment after 1905 look like being killed off by anything – a club which, time and again, would rise triumphantly from the ashes of its past and stir the whole of Tyneside into song.

CHAPTER TWO

THE BIRTH OF A GIANT:
1893–1904

❖

April 1905, was not, of course, the month of the actual birth of Newcastle United Football Club. The club had been born 12 years earlier, when Newcastle East End and Newcastle West End FCs amalgamated.

It was something of a shotgun wedding. Essentially, West End had the ground (the 'Gallowgate enclosure', so called because it had been the site outside the old city walls of public hangings, which would be better known before long as St James's Park) and the support, but East End had the players and the organisation.

Professional football was legalised in England in 1885 (although with the proviso – which lasted a further four years – that that the FA Cup was open only to professionals who had been born within six miles of the club, or who had lived for two years within six miles of the club). Professionalism would not become legitimate in Scotland until 1893, and so most English clubs, Newcastle as much as any, attracted an early influx of Caledonian footballers. As one writer would put it, 'the sight of ten golden sovereigns for signing was not easily ignored'.

But East End and West End, despite entering the Northern League upon its inauguration in 1889, could not draw sufficient crowds to pay their wages. Gates were frequently less than a thousand, and rarely more than 1,500. Committee members were obliged to pay wages and subsidise travelling expenses from their own pockets. It was fairly assumed that the city of Newcastle could not support two football teams.

East End temporarily solved their problems by putting out a share issue in 1890. But within two years matters had come to a head. East End were easily the more successful team on the field, and they applied for membership of the Football League – which up until that summer had consisted of only one division.

The League's AGM was held that year in the Queen's Hotel, Fawcett Street, Sunderland, in recognition of the Wearsiders having won their first championship in 1892. The League considered East End's application, but understandably insisted upon them entering the newly created Second Division (there had been, between 1888 and 1892, just one division, and there would be, between 1892 and 1919, just two divisions). According to the recollections of an official of the time, 'through the delegates of the club not carrying out their instructions' the League was told that Newcastle East End insisted upon immediate access to the First Division – or nothing.

They got nothing. The League had formed a Second Division for the very purpose of blooding new sides in its ranks, and they were not about to make exceptions for stroppy North-easterners. The mule-headed delegates returned to Newcastle having condemned the city to at least another season of provincial football and friendly matches with the major clubs.

Over at the Gallowgate, meanwhile, things had become desperate. West End lacked money and success, and in May 1892 their executive decided to give up the unequal struggle and fold the club. In the course of doing so, they offered to Newcastle East End the remainder of the lease on St James's Park, and this was gratefully accepted. The ground itself was far from perfect. It had been grazing land owned on a 14-year lease by a West End stalwart, William Neasham, and the pitch had a drop of no less than 18 feet to the Gallowgate end goal. The 'Gallowgate enclosure' consisted of little more than a fence and a wooden cabin for changing-rooms (although the players usually preferred to change in the Lord Hill public house on

Barrack Road). But it was a comparatively permanent football pitch – the lease was renewable – and its location was good.

East End's problems were far from over. The Northern League programme offered just 16 matches, and not with the most glamorous opposition. In order to attract big sides such as Glasgow Celtic to St James's Park for friendlies, East End had to foreswear them large sums of money before they would travel to Newcastle, and 'the first season at St James's, owing to the heavy guarantees agreed to be paid to the visiting clubs, and the lukewarm support of the public, nearly landed the club into the Bankruptcy Court', according to one official.

It was decided that something must be done about that 'luke-warm support'. Newcastle East End, it was considered, was probably too parochial a name to attract the whole of Tyneside, and so on 9 December 1892 'a meeting of persons interested in Association football in Newcastle and district was held in the Bath Lane Hall, Newcastle, for the purpose of considering the advisa-bility of changing the name of the East End Football Club'.

Professional soccer clubs in the 1890s had inherited a host of – to modern ears – weird and wonderful titles. Leicester City was still Leicester Fosse (nickname: the Fossils); Burton Swifts were still in the league, as were Walsall Town Swifts. Others, such as Small Heath (later Birmingham City), Newton Heath (Manchester United) and Ardwick (Manchester City) still be-trayed their localised origins. Some of those distinctive Victorian names, such as Plymouth Argyle, Brighton and Hove Albion, and Sheffield Wednesday survive to this day.

But the more prosaic Newcastle East End would not survive. Three new names were proposed to that meeting in 1892: Newcastle, Newcastle City and Newcastle United. Perhaps mindful of the words of Councillor Henderson that 'The sup-porters of the East End and the old West End would have to sink any little jealousies they had, and be united', the latter won a decisive majority of the votes. Newcastle United FC was born on 9 December 1892 (although the FA would not formally ratify the change until 1895, which caused some small book-keeping confusions).

The effect was far from dramatic. East End's old supporters in Byker and Heaton – many of whom had underpinned the 1890 share issue – felt geographically and terminologically deserted, and most of them refused to take the trip over to the Gallowgate, where West End's former supporters were equally apathetic about paying to see their old team's usurpers.

So the second part of the plan was put into action. In the close season of 1893 – when Sunderland were once more runaway champions, having scored a record 100 goals in their 30-game programme – Newcastle United applied to join the Second Division of the Football League. This time their delegates quelled their unease about entering a lower division with such luminaries as Bootle and Burslem Port Vale, and Newcastle United's application was accepted – along, coincidentally, with those of Liverpool, Rotherham Town, Woolwich Arsenal (the league's first London club), and Middlesbrough Ironopolis.

The final card had been played. It is too much to say that if this plan had failed, if the single professional team left on Tyneside had not achieved solvency within the Football League, then league football in Newcastle would have died. Somebody else would have sprung up eventually to meet the demand, some other club would have risen – but that club would not, in name, in character, and possibly in situation, have been Newcastle United.

And it was a close-run thing. On the field, Newcastle were successful enough. Their first game was also the first league game to be played in the capital: at the Plumstead ground of Woolwich Arsenal. It was an expensive trip, which was once again subsidised from a director's pocket, but he may have considered the outlay worthwhile – Newcastle drew 2-2, and won their next game, at home to Arsenal, 6-0. The entire midfield, or half-back line, and two of the forward line were Scots. Newcastle's first league goal, scored in the second half at Plumstead, was credited to a local boy, inside-right Tom Crate.

Newcastle United urgently needed promotion. Their circumstances were similar to those which would be faced by the club 100 years later, in the early 1990s, when it was realised that the future of top-flight football lay in the newly formed Premiership.

Only First Division matches with Sunderland, Bolton, Villa and Everton would bring the gates to assure the future of the club. Access from the Second Division to the First was relatively straightforward. There was no automatic relegation or promotion – that was not introduced until 1899. Instead the Football League operated a play-off system. This at first involved the bottom three from Division One and the top three from Division Two, and in 1896 was reduced to the bottom two and top two. They were known as 'test matches', and were played immediately after the end of the league programme. Two seasons later, in 1896, they would take the form of a small league, but at the end of Newcastle United's first league season of 1893–94 just three test matches were played: the third team in Division Two played the third-from-bottom in Division One; the second in Two played the second-from-bottom in One; and the Division Two champions played the bottom club in Division One.

Newcastle finished fourth in the Second Division. They missed a play-off with Preston North End by two points. (Notts County had that third place, and were drubbed 4-0 by Preston. Liverpool and Small Heath beat their First Division opponents, however, and went up.)

It could have been disastrous. Newcastle United had hobbled through their first league season, asking visiting clubs to take IOUs instead of immediate payment, and on one occasion telling Liverpool that they would probably not be able to afford the trip to Merseyside, although eventually they did travel. Sunderland helped out in a comradely fashion, visiting St James's Park four times to play friendlies, as did Sheffield United, who sportingly travelled for a minimal fee.

But at the end of the 1893–94 season Newcastle owed other league clubs the colossal sum of £600. A foreclosure by any one of them would have been fatal. The largest sum, £50, was due to First Division Stoke, in return for a friendly. United's secretary James Neylon approached his opposite number at Stoke and explained the dire situation. Stoke not only agreed to sit quietly on their part of the debt, but also to approach the other clubs and persuade them to do likewise. This was accomplished, and Newcastle United's committee breathed again.

In the close season of 1894 the club changed its playing colours from red shirts and white shorts to 'black-and-white shirts (two-inch stripe) and dark knickers'. If they thought this might encourage a change of fortune they were sadly mistaken. The 1894–95 season proved to be the new club's lowest point.

On the field they were simply dreadful. Suddenly their defence leaked goals – during the first league season, 39 had been conceded in 28 games; in that second season 84 went past an inadequate back line. Newcastle finished the season in the bottom half of the Second Division, 11 points away from a play-off position. They had been knocked out of the cup 7-1 by league champions Aston Villa, and finished their league programme by being hammered 9-0 by Burton Wanderers. That remains Newcastle United's heaviest defeat ever, and it was suffered at the hands of a club which two years later would drop out of the Football League – and out of football history – for good.

Home gates were averaging less than 4,000, and the club was haemorrhaging both goals and money. In 1895 only a superman, it seemed, could save Newcastle United. Luckily, there was one waiting.

Frank Watt arrived in Newcastle from Dundee on 28 December 1895. A Scot, he had first played football for his Edinburgh cadet corps at the age of 18 back in 1872. He fell instantly in love with the young sport and became firstly a referee and then, in 1876, the first honorary secretary of the Edinburgh Football Association. In 1878 Watt helped to establish one of the oldest Scottish clubs, St Bernard's FC of Powderhall in Edinburgh. After a spell working as a joiner in England he was enticed back to his native Edinburgh when the local FA became the East of Scotland Football Association. Watt was offered £80 a year to be its actual, rather than honorary, secretary.

Early in 1895 Frank Watt moved north to become the first secretary of the two-year-old Dundee Football Club. Simultaneously, another Scot, J.S. Ferguson of the Lanarkshire FA, was appointed to replace James Neylon at St James's Park. But Ferguson resigned within a few months and Newcastle re-advertised. A notice in the *Scottish Referee* attracted more Scottish applicants, and Newcastle's directors – who were familiar with both Dundee FC (having poached a player from the club 12 months earlier) and Frank Watt – asked Watt for guidance.

Watt duly recommended Willie Waugh, the secretary of his old club St Bernard's FC, who had just won the Scottish Cup, and who a year before had celebrated their first season in the Scottish First Division by finishing third behind Celtic and Hearts. The Newcastle board responded to this considered advice with a note reading: 'Why not take the job yourself, Frank?'; followed that up by travelling to Edinburgh for meetings with him and Mrs Watt; offered them a house and £140 a year; persuaded Dundee to release him . . . and the deed was done.

It was certainly among the most inspired two or three managerial appointments ever made, before or since, by directors of Newcastle United. In those early decades the secretary of a football club was not merely a book-keeper: although the term did not yet exist, he was effectively the team manager. The secretary signed new players and released unwanted athletes. He recommended team selection to the directors, and frequently (as Watt was to do) came to monopolise that duty himself. The secretary appointed and instructed the trainer, whose job was not the implementation of tactics (what were tactics?) but the maintenance of fitness. The club secretary was the director of football.

Frank George Watt became to Newcastle United what Matt Busby would be to Manchester United, but with far less historical acclaim. He inherited a disconsolate club, a negligible support, and a hopelessly apathetic team. When he retired 34 years later, he left behind him one of the three best supported clubs in the land, and the most successful English soccer outfit of the early 20th century. Frank Watt worked steadily. It took him fully ten years to prepare Newcastle United for greatness. 'He never advocated any revolutionary measures,' judged a colleague in 1898, 'having to combine improvement with economy. His policy of gradually patching up the weak spots in the team has proved a great success.'

Perhaps time did move more slowly at the turn of the 19th century. There was certainly more patience to be found. Frank Watt had not finished 'gradually patching' until 1905. And then, in the 25 years between 1905 and his retirement in 1930, his Newcastle United won the league championship four times, a 20th-century achievement which was equalled only by Sheffield Wednesday and approached only by Huddersfield Town's three titles.

But Wednesday had won the FA Cup only once in that period, and Huddersfield not at all. Frank Watt's Newcastle United rounded off their four league titles with six FA Cup final appearances, two of which were successful. When he died in February 1932, the team which was still substantially his own were on their way to their seventh cup final appearance in less than 30 years, and their third cup final victory.

No football manager of his time was the equal of Frank George Watt. No manager of Newcastle United has since come close to matching his achievements; and only Busby at Manchester United, Herbert Chapman at Huddersfield Town and Arsenal between 1923 and 1934, Bob Paisley at Liverpool between 1975 and 1984, and Alex Ferguson at Manchester United at the ent of the 20th and the beginning of the 21st centuries would eventually achieve his stature elsewhere. And it is arguable whether any of those three started from so low and hopeless a base. Manchester United, Huddersfield, Arsenal and Liverpool at least had stadiums and money to spend. Frank Watt had a sloping field, a cabin, a terrifying accounts ledger, and a defence which was letting in three goals a game.

He was a striking figure, the 41-year-old Edinburgh man who walked into his new clubhouse by St James's Park in December 1895. His trademark handlebar moustachios, which he retained throughout his life, would have done credit to a water-buffalo, and his large dark eyes were unblinking and self-assured. There was humour in his face, and he had an easy laugh and a ready quip. He was a man at ease with himself and with his place in the world: the place of a man who helped to invent association football.

Frank Watt found some things to his liking at St James's Park. In the close season a public meeting had been called to address the emergency, and this had resulted both in a vote of confidence in Newcastle United as the town's sole representatives in the new world of professional football, and also (the two were not disconnected) in further financial contributions.

Armed with money and a modicum of confidence the directors had made several signings, mostly from north of the border. They had paid Edinburgh St Bernard's £100 for the Scottish international full-back Bob Foyers, and they bought a new goalkeeper, John Henderson, from Clyde. And they had taken on a skilled and highly popular 18-year-old inside-forward from Ayr known as Andy 'Daddler' Aitken.

When Watt arrived in December, the influence of Foyers and Henderson had helped to stem the flow of goals conceded. Newcastle had lost just two league games, had let in a respectable 25 goals in 16 matches, and were sitting comfortably in fifth place in the Second Division.

But the old frailties had not entirely gone. Just six days after Watt's arrival he was given a clear indication of this when United travelled to play promotion-chasing Manchester City (whose team included on the right wing the great Welsh international Billy Meredith), and returned home on the wrong end of a 5-2 thumping. Meredith had murdered the Newcastle defence, and young Aitken was conspicuous chiefly for missing a sitter late on, before City scored their last two conclusive goals.

Worse was to come. Seven days later Grimsby Town – like Newcastle, a middle-of-the-table Second Division side – visited St James's Park. The home support turned out in comparative force on a bright and crisp winter's day: 5,000 fans 'filled the stands, crowded the embankments round the barriers, and perched themselves in apparent contentment on the razor-edge of the park palisading, kicking their heels together for some minutes before the time set for the kick-off'.

They saw Grimsby inflict a 5-1 defeat on Newcastle United. An off-form Foyers had been dropped, and the midfield so reshuffled that they hardly knew one another, and the whole Newcastle performance, wrote one journalist, was 'sadly off-colour, owing largely no doubt to their unwonted arrangement'.

Slowly, however, Frank Watt's team took shape. The rush of blood which led to his hasty rearrangement of the side against Grimsby was not repeated. Foyers and the half-back Billy Miller, signed from Kilmarnock in the summer, were reinstated to the delight of the faithful, and Woolwich Arsenal were duly dismissed 3-1.

There was a typically minor flurry in the FA Cup, which began with a 4-0 first-round away win over non-league Chester-field, and ended a week later when First Division Bury – who had stormed out of the Second Division as champions in their first season just 12 months earlier – visited Newcastle for the second round. United's fans were allowed a moment of hope when centre-forward Billy Thompson (not just another Scot but also a former soldier in the Black Watch) pounced upon a fisted save from the Bury keeper and scored. Those fans could hang onto their hopes until the second half, when Newcastle collapsed under a spell of Bury pressure that yielded the visitors three goals in ten minutes. Bury sat out their 3-1 victory comfortably, in a slowly thickening north-eastern fog . . .

But the trauma of the early New Year had truly passed. Comprehensive home wins over Manchester City (an extremely satisfactory revenge scoreline of 4-1 – and Meredith was playing) and Burton Swifts (5-0) saw Newcastle regain fifth position by the end of the season. They were fully 12 points shy of the play-off zone, but they were proud once more.

Perhaps most significantly, they had won 14 of their 15 home league games, and scored 57 goals at St James's Park. This may offer some explanation for the remarkable series of fundraising friendlies with which they closed the season. Firstly Clyde FC, who had finished ninth in a ten-team Scottish Division One, arrived and drew 0-0.

They were followed by two English First Division sides.

Sheffield United, a lower-table outfit, were beaten 3-1. And on 25 April Derby County, who had finished as runners-up to league champions Aston Villa, arrived on a hot Saturday afternoon, to be dismissed 4-2. St James's Park was clearly no venue for the faint-hearted. It was not, as yet, so much the size or the passion of the crowd. In the 1890s professional soccer was quickly establishing itself as the recreational spectator sport of the British working man, but some areas were quicker to adopt the sport than others. As we have seen, London did not have a professional league side until 1893. In the north-east Sunderland had already established themselves as the premier club with three league championships in the seven seasons up to 1895. Newcastle, in this period, lagged behind. Their average Second Division attendance was 8,000, but it was too frequently lower. Their home gate against Manchester City was, for example, just 5,000, while the earlier match in Manchester had attracted 12,000. This difficulty with inferior attendances would correct itself in the most dramatic fashion over the next ten years, but in 1896 the question of whether or not the city of Newcastle was willing to support or capable of sustaining a professional football club was still troubling the directors. Still, they won an inordinate number of home fixtures . . . It must have been the travelling – or that infamous slope!

United also finished the 1896–97 season in fifth place in Division Two, although this time they were just four points off the play-off zone. And Frank Watt's excursions to Scotland were continuing to pay dividends. He went up there like a reiver, travelling light and returning always with fresh stock in tow.

The team which kicked off the 1897–98 season contained no fewer than seven Scots. There were the two full-backs, Tom Stewart from Motherwell and James Jackson from Rangers. There were half-backs Tommy Ghee from St Mirren, who was signed on while working part-time in a Paisley bar, and Jack Ostler from Motherwell. There was right-winger Malcolm Lennox from Glasgow Perthshire, there was the 21-year-old wonderboy Andy Aitken at inside-left, and the free-scoring Willie Wardrope of Wishaw out wide on the left. It is a curious indication of the strength of the game north of the border that out of this array of Scottish talent (and there were more waiting in the 'A' team) only one – Aitken – would win an international cap.

But they were more than good enough for the English Second Division. This auspicious season kicked off at home against the old sacrificial lambs, Woolwich Arsenal. Sensing the potential, 10,000 paid to get into St James's Park. They were well rewarded. After 23 minutes the former Sunderland stalwart, centre-forward Johnny Campbell, who had been picked up in the close season for £40, a tenner in his hand and £3 a week, took a ball from Ghee and whipped it past Ord in the Arsenal goal. It was the first of his 11 goals in 26 games, before Newcastle dismissed him for allegedly breaching his contract by running a hotel in his spare time.

The second came shortly afterwards, in a style which would have outraged the supporters of a century later. Campbell laid the ball off for Wardrope, who shot first time. Ord seemed to be in a position to save it, but Lennox, 'by means of a well-judged charge', knocked him clean out of the ball's path. Wardrope then headed home an Ostler free-kick to send the crowd into an exultant half-time break. Arsenal pulled one back when new goalkeeper Charlie Watts completely misjudged a clearance, but another Wardrope header completed the winger's hat-trick and the scoring at 4-1.

Not everybody was happy. The forward line, it was suggested, contained too many old, slow men (such as Campbell and his fellow former Wearsider John Harvey) who were no longer capable of taking chances, and who would certainly never make the grade in Division One. But Frank Watt was not thinking of Division One. Frank had his eye on the route out of Division Two. Division One could, in God's good time, take care of itself.

Another Scot, John White from Clyde, was instantly slotted into the left-back position. Jim Jackson moved into the half-back line, and the number of Scots in the 11 was thereby increased to eight.

And throughout that glorious, Indian-summer September of 1897, they went through their Second Division opponents like a knife. Walsall were beaten 3-2 in the Midlands (Ronnie Allan from Dundee making his début); 12,000 turned up at St James's to see Burton Swifts put to the sword by 3-1 (Stott, Allan, Wardrope) . . . although it was beginning to be noticed that upon winning the toss at home captain Tommy Ghee invariably chose to play down the slope, and that this tactic more often than not resulted in a handsome half-time lead for United . . .

They could also win away, however. The team which had previously won virtually all its home games and lost almost all away, now seemed capable, with that rugged Scottish half-back line, of scrapping out a result on foreign soil. Lincoln City were next, falling 3-2 in Lincoln to goals from Campbell and Wardrope (2).

After the first four matches of the season, Newcastle United were on maximum points. Unfortunately, so were Manchester City, Burnley and Small Heath, all of whom had either played more games or had a superior goal average – and so for all their efforts, United still languished in that familiar fourth position.

Worse was to follow. On 2 October they visited Burnley, in a first real test of their newfound fighting qualities against another promotion contender. Newcastle were thoroughly outplayed. By half-time they were 3-0 down, and Watts had saved a penalty. There was no further scoring in the second half.

But something was stirring on Tyneside. When Newton Heath (who would not become Manchester United until 1902) visited Newcastle seven days later, 14,000 people flocked to St James's Park. 'The crowd,' reported the *Evening Chronicle*, 'was a tremendous one a crowd that was more than suggestive of the gates that Sunderland used to draw in their palmiest days. Those present, too, seemed full of excitement. Hardly had the players got to business before there was evidence of it. Every movement of the men was followed with the closest attention, and breakaways and shots were either followed with a deathly silence [if they were the breakaways and shots of Newton Heath] or with a roar that was sufficient to break the clouds overhead.'

Frank Watt's gnarled Scottish professionals responded. Kicking uphill, Campbell put them ahead after just five minutes. Ten minutes later he, the experienced inside-forward John Harvey, Aitken and Wardrope moved forward in a phalanx, leaving Andy Aitken to smack home the second. Two-nil was enough. Newcastle were back in the hunt.

By early December United had clawed their way into second place in Division Two, five points behind Burnley but with two games in hand. Their most significant victory had arrived the previous week, when the (then) second-placed Small Heath arrived in Newcastle, and were destroyed 4-0 in front of 12,000 baying Geordies courtesy of two goals from Campbell, one from Wardrope, and a fourth headed home by new centre-forward Jock Peddie, whom Watt had picked up for £135 from Third Lanark.

It was the first of the 78 goals which this outstanding Victorian centre-forward – arguably the man who launched the cult of the Newcastle United number 9 shirt, although the versatile Jock was occasionally picked at outside-right – would score in 135 games in black and white. He may have scored that first goal with his head, but Peddie would become best known on Tyneside, and feared elsewhere, for the extraordinary power of his right-foot shot. On one occasion he hit the net so viciously that the pegs holding it to the ground were ripped out and sent flying. It was a minor miracle of the time that Jock Peddie was never selected for his country: he was surely denied a cap only by the Scottish selectors' stubborn refusal to give fair consideration to Scots who were based in England. The selectors' amateur pedigree led them for too long to regard men like Jock Peddie as carpet-bagging mercenaries. It was a problem faced by more than one of Newcastle's Scots.

It is possible to reconstruct, as through a glass darkly, the way that Newcastle may have played in such matches. It was very far from Total Football. Apart from one dramatic change in the mid-1920s (a change which was, as we shall see, forced upon the whole of the football world by United themselves), it would remain roughly the same for half a century.

They played matches in the afternoon, chiefly on Saturday but often in midweek. They would almost invariably travel away on Friday, staying close to their opponents' ground on the night before the game, and usually attempting to return to Newcastle on the Saturday evening, but frequently finding themselves delayed for another day. Matches early and late in the season – in the autumn and in the spring – would kick off at 3.30 p.m. to give the workers (who almost always still worked on Saturday mornings – it was only recently that they had won a five-and-a-half day rather than a six-day week) time to finish their lunches or visits to the pub before turning up at the ground. But in the winter months kick-off was brought forward to 3 p.m. or 2.30 p.m., and even so, in those days before floodlights, on a dull day half-time was often abbreviated by the referee to just two or three minutes, to avoid finishing the contest in darkness.

The players knew their places. There were full-backs marking wingers; and in front of them a three-man midfield half-back line which won the ball and fed the five-man forward row. The two wingers ploughed their lonely furrow up and down each flank, the inside-forwards were elusive, wily and slight, the centre-forward – often, in those days, quite unmarked – was there to beat the goalkeeper by any means possible, including shoulder charges. (The liberal use of elbows, knees, heads and even fists was frequently regarded tolerantly by late-Victorian referees. This game was not yet that far removed from the hacking, scrimmage and maul of rugby football.)

Most goalkeepers, and Charlie Watts was no exception, favoured punching or kicking the ball clear at least as often as they gathered it. A Newcastle attack might therefore, if it did not begin after the breakdown in midfield of an opposition move, begin by Watts finding his full-backs, or by Stewart and White themselves (they had a finely honed clannish understanding) stopping a winger in full flight.

White or Stewart would then perceive it as their task to feed the half-back line – and then retire promptly back into position. The half-backs – the calm and confident Ghee; the tough, balding, gimlet-eyed and uncompromising Jimmy Stott; the dependable, defensive Jackson; the rangy, vocal Ostler – would try then to set the forward line in motion, preferably by feeding Wardrope or Allan on the wings.

Once the forward line was on the move, they would set forth in a disciplined line strung across the field. They would move cautiously, because at that time the offside rule insisted that three opposition players (supposedly the two full-backs and the keeper) had to be between the forward on the ball and the goal-line. In the case of these Newcastle United players, their Scottish pedigree led them to favour short inter-passing movements rather than the mazy individual dribbles which had been the trademark of English forwards. Once within sight of goal, anything was possible. The wingers, as Willie Wardrope who scored 50 goals in 141 games liked to do, might cut inside and have a shot themselves. Or they might feed the tricky Aitken or the older, slower Harvey. Or they might, as right-winger Ronnie Allan preferred, swing the ball over towards the head or the fierce right boot of the cunning Campbell or the strong, quick and direct Peddie. The penalty area would be a busy place: full-backs rarely strayed, and half-backs accepted their defensive duties, and so a lot of goals were deflected into the net. When this happened, the arms of the scoring team might be almost involuntarily raised in the air – but they were just as quickly brought down again. It was regarded as unseemly to jump about and gloat. The scoring of a goal was properly celebrated on the pitch by gentlemanly handshakes as the players trotted back into position. The quality or the importance of the strike was marked by the number of handshakes offered.

The players were, by the standards of a hundred years later, not very fit. Even an ordinarily paced but busy match would see all 20 outfield players clearly struggling after 70 or 80 minutes' play. No substitutions were allowed under any circumstances, and so players were accustomed to remaining on the field throughout the game when fatigued, or when carrying an injury – even a serious injury. Poor training – it was frequently based on road-running – and medical facilities, combined with the aggravated injuries which resulted from footballers continuing to play with fractures, sprains, strains, torn muscles, and even broken bones, prematurely ended many a soccer career. The most feared injury was one of the most common: a torn cartilage. Broken bones could at least be set: there was at that time no cure for a damaged cartilage.

The year 1897 ended badly with a 3-1 defeat by Burton Swifts on the banks of a foggy River Trent, and a home defeat in front of 16,000 Tynesiders by Burnley on Boxing Day. Burnley, it was obvious, were likely to go into the test match play-offs. The question was, who would accompany them? Luckily, that 1-0 reversal at the hands of the Lancastrians – in a match which was billed locally as the 'game of the season' – would prove to be the only home league game which Newcastle did not win in that season of 1897–98.

But it dropped United back into third place, one point behind Manchester City, five behind Burnley, and level with Small Heath. They pulled themselves together and fought out a 1-1 draw with City in Manchester on 8 January, thanks to a Ronnie Allan header which struck a City defender and looped into the net.

When they had to, they scraped out results. Struggling Darwen arrived at St James's without, apparently, a hope in hell – until they discovered that Stott and Ostler were missing from United's midfield through illness. Aitken was put in the half-back line, and a new signing with a big reputation at Northern League Bishop Auckland, Jack Allen, was played up front. It was a gamble, and looked like it: Newcastle 'lacked system', Aitken failed immediately to adapt to the midfield role which would, in years to come, be his chosen position, and the new boy from Bishops missed an easy chance in the first five minutes before effectively disappearing from the contest. As half-time approached with no scoring, the crowd began derisively to cheer each successful Darwen clearance; then, in the 45th minute, Ronnie Allan curled a shot towards goal, a Darwen full-back mistimed his header, and put it into his own net. One-nil it stayed. Messy, unconvincing, unentertaining, low-scoring . . . but two points.

By March Newcastle had regained second place. Burnley were as far ahead as ever, but Manchester City were still breathing down United's neck. They completed the double over Darwen in more convincing fashion, Jock Peddie on brilliant form hitting all of United's goals in a 3-1 win.

And for once it was the opposition rather than Newcastle United who failed to last the pace. While Newcastle were pasting Grimsby Town 4-0 at St James's, Manchester City's nerve went. They dropped points and position, and on 2 April 1898 Newcastle faced mid-table Gainsborough Trinity at home knowing that a win would guarantee them second place if City failed to beat Leicester Fosse in Leicester.

City drew. And Newcastle . . .

Newcastle won the toss, and kicked off (downhill, with a following wind) with a large crowd still streaming through the turnstiles – a crowd which saw within minutes Jock Peddie race in from the left and hurl himself at a cross. The ball hit Peddie's head and then the net, where it was shortly joined by Peddie himself. The Scot then collected a pass from Harvey on the right, controlled it and drilled home a low left-foot drive. Inside-left Smith chipped the Trinity goalkeeper for United's third, and Peddie completed his hat-trick before half-time. The celebrations could begin. As so often happened at St James's, the visiting side discovered a bit of form themselves when kicking down the slope in the second half – Gainsborough got two back before Smith scored Newcastle's only second-half goal after Peddie had hit the bar – but it was too late. At 5-2 they had been mugged; the points had been hijacked in the first 45 minutes. Gainsborough Trinity were not the first and would not be the last to leave Newcastle suspecting grand larceny.

And Newcastle United were in the play-offs. The spectators, reported the evening pink, 'were delirious'. Their team would complete the 30-game season of 1897–98 with 45 points, three points behind champions Burnley but six ahead of Manchester City. They had scored 64 goals and conceded just 32. They had won 14 games at St James's Park but – in sharp contrast to earlier seasons – performed respectably away from home,

winning seven, drawing three and losing five on those long, one-
and two-night excursions from the North-east to Lancashire,
Nottingham, Lincoln and London.

Now all that Peddie, Stott, Aitken and the boys had to do was
get the better of Stoke FC and Blackburn Rovers, the bottom
two sides in that year's First Division. Burnley and Newcastle
would each play those clubs twice, at home and away. The four
teams would then, after those four matches apiece, be placed in
a mini-league, and the top two would play the following season
in Division One.

It started well. United beat Stoke 2-1 at St James's on the
afternoon of Wednesday, 20 April, in a game of such ferocity
that the recently signed full-back Billy Lindsay aggravated an
old injury, and Jock Peddie took a bad knock on the ankle.
Lindsay missed the next test match three days later, and Peddie,
to the horror of United's fans, missed the whole of the rest of the
series.

So it was no surprise when Stoke won the return 1-0 in a dour
encounter. No sooner had Newcastle returned from the Potteries than they had to set off for Blackburn, where they lost 4-3.

On the final day of the play-offs, then, on 30 April 1898,
Newcastle faced Blackburn at St James's while Stoke and
Burnley met in the other game. It was a situation open to
corruption. Blackburn and Newcastle had two points from their
three games, while Stoke and Burnley had four, with unimpressive goal averages. A draw, therefore, suited Stoke and
Burnley fine. If they drew, nobody could catch either of them,
whereas Newcastle's only hope was to win, and win well.

It was probably the performance of Newcastle United that
day which finally won them justice. Thirteen thousand fans paid
a total of £433 15s 6d to cheer them on. United pressed hard,
and after half an hour Tommy Ghee stepped up from the half-
back line to receive the ball from Aitken and hit a long, low shot
into the corner of the net.

They made it 2-0 shortly after the break with a sensational
goal. Full-back Jim Jackson had moved into the half-back line at
half-time. Once there he broke up an attack and, spotting the

Rovers keeper Carter off his line, lobbed him from distance. It would prove to be one of Jackson's two goals for Newcastle in 64 games. The packed crowd, in which a small boy had already suffered a fractured ankle, went delirious. Harvey made it three and John Campbell four . . . and then the news seeped through that Stoke and Burnley had drawn 0-0. 'SPLENDID VICTORY FOR UNITED,' headlined the *Evening Chronicle*, 'BUT THEY REMAIN IN THE SECOND LEAGUE'.

At first the position was accepted. The press and people of Tyneside congratulated their team on reaching the play-offs, and wished them better luck next time. 'The mere fact,' said the *Chronicle*, 'of taking part in the test games, without taking into consideration any chances of success, is a sufficient guarantee that throughout the season the team so fortunate must have proved themselves better than the rest. How this re-eminence has been attained is well enough known to northerners. A careful committee of management has fostered every resource, and strengthened every weakness . . .'

It was only later, when details of that 0-0 draw began to reach Tyneside, that this generous magnaminity in defeat dissolved and outrage took over. Needing a draw, the players of Stoke and Burnley had played so blatantly for a draw that the game of association football had been dragged into disrepute. The whole of England heard stories of that shameless fixture: of how the spectators had become so incensed by the spectacle that they had refused to return the ball three times (some said five times), requiring the use of three (or five) new balls. Getting hold of the ball was no problem to the angry fans, as Stoke and Burnley spent most of the 90 minutes booting the thing into touch.

The national press picked up on the incident, and the Football League was obliged to act. Fortunately, it was able to do so in a manner which satisfied all concerned. At its meeting in June, the league committee firstly discarded the test match play-off system, and introduced a fixed promotion and relegation procedure of two-up, two-down.

Secondly – and most crucially to Tyneside – four new clubs had applied to join Division Two. Barnsley St Peter's FC,

Burslem Port Vale, Glossop North End and New Brighton Tower were all admitted, bringing the Second Division up to 18 clubs. In order to raise the numbers in Division One also to 18, it was agreed that all four of the play-off teams would be put into the top level – Blackburn and Stoke would stay up, and two sides from Division Two would be promoted to join them. It was not automatically the top two, a vote was taken, but luckily Burnley and Newcastle attracted the largest ballot and were duly elevated. No action was taken against Burnley or Stoke for their part in quietly fixing an important competitive match, although two seasons later Burnley FC, to the satisfaction of many, was relegated to Division Two.

And so, after five seasons in the Football League, Newcastle United had become a First Division club. Frank Watt's men were no angels, on the field or off it. The goalie Charlie Watts was a famous gambler whom Watt suspected of getting small boys behind the goals to tell him the racing results during a match, and who actually became a professional tipster after his retirement in 1906 (and who tragically cut his own throat in 1924). Several of them enjoyed a drink too many at the Lord Hill public house on Saturday lunchtimes – one defender, having started a match in splendid form and made several beautifully judged clearances, supposedly turned to a team-mate and asked: 'Which way w' kickin'?' Jimmy Stott was so uncompromising in the tackle that – in a period when few half-backs were shrinking violets – the club (which had made him team captain) actually cautioned him about his ferocity on the field of play.

But they were Frank Watt's men, and they had accomplished the task that Frank had set them to do. Aware that survival in the First Division would prove a sterner test than success in the Second, he spent the summer of 1898 adding to their ranks. The 14-stone goalkeeper Matt Kingsley was bought from Second Division Darwen, despite the fact that Everton also wanted him, and the experienced defender Bill Higgins arrived from Bristol City. The Scottish winger Thomas Niblo had been tempted at the very end of the promotion season to join so many of his compatriots on Tyneside, and – from under the predatory nose of Manchester City – Joe Rogers was lured away from Grimsby Town to add to the forward line.

'Mr Watt,' pronouced the local press, as the 1898–99 season prepared to get under way, 'the energetic secretary, and a gentleman who in great measure has been responsible for United's present position in the football world, has now about got his preparations for the great campaign completed.'

And so had the directors. The stands at St James's Park were improved and extended in the close season, and the capacity of the ground increased to 35,000. It was now or never, do or die . . .

For a while it looked like death. Newcastle United's first match in Division One was played against Wolverhampton Wanderers at St James's Park on Saturday, 3 December 1898, before an expectant crowd of over 20,000 (a bank of faces relieved here and there, noted one observer, by the bright red colours of Tommy Atkins, for Britain was at war in the Sudan, Omdurman had fallen on the previous day, and soldiers home on leave were in the mood for celebrating).

Wolves were already a team with a pedigree – they had been FA Cup-winners in 1893 and had finished third in the previous season – and would not run scared either from a noisy crowd or a sloping pitch. Their confidence was boosted by the news that Newcastle would be missing Jim Jackson and new signing Joe Rogers, both injured two days earlier in an ill-judged pre-season friendly against Sunderland. Wolves won the toss and kicked downhill, and after 25 minutes they had gone 3-0 up. United, there was no denying, were being run off their feet.

The crowd, which at first had raised their voices when Newcastle launched the occasional attack, fell silent. Was this what First Division soccer would like – mercurial combination football denying United a touch of the ball, and defenders robbing Harvie, Campbell, Peddie and Wardrope as if they were children?

Only the quickly maturing Andy Aitken looked at home at the new level, but even he was edged out of the contest as the second half got under way. It took Bill Higgins to breathe some life back into the crowd: moving forward from his full-back's position he smacked a long-range shot against the crossbar, and Jock Peddie proved that he could poach goals as reliably in the First Division as he had in the second by pouncing on the rebound and driving it home.

United surged forward and applied several minutes of concentrated pressure. But Wolves absorbed it, and then broke upfield to make it 4-1 with the simplest of tap-ins. It was emblematic of United's afternoon that when they did grab another goal back just before full-time to make the final score 4-2, it came from a goalmouth scramble so scrappy that no one player could at first claim or be attributed the score (although Tommy Ghee finally put his name to it. He needed it: Tommy got only three goals from midfield in 140 games spread over five years with Newcastle United).

Welcome to the real world. United embarked on a demoralising series of fiascos against the big clubs that they had longed to join. They journeyed to Liverpool to face Everton, with Jackson back and Niblo making his début, and they lost 3-0. Fortress St James's was breached yet again in the third game of the season, when Notts County arrived and went home with a 2-1 win tucked under their belts: United's sole goal coming when an Aitken shot deflected off a defender.

After their first three First Division games Newcastle were bottom of the table with precisely no points, having conceded nine goals and scored just three.

Watt and trainer Tom Dodds refused to panic. They reverted to their old hard-bitten half-back line of Ghee, Ostler and Stott, and visited a Stoke team who had reason to be wary – 'Remember,' the Stoke trainer William Allen said before the game, 'they [Newcastle] will be getting more and more desperate through these reverses, and are bound to have some team as victim before long.'

Stoke were not the victims, but neither this time were United. Ghee, Ostler and Stott put up the barricades, Kingsley made several outstanding saves, and Newcastle won their first point in the Football League Division One with a dour 0-0 draw in the Potteries on 24 September 1898.

They got their first home point seven days later. Aston Villa arrived on Tyneside behind their formidable reputation which was born of an incredible three league titles and two cup wins in the previous five years. Peddie, no respecter of Englishmen's pride, collected the ball out wide on the left, made his way through the Midlanders' defence and – with the crowd roaring for him to shoot – squared it instead to Joe Rogers. There was a concerted sob of disappointment from the terraces, until Rogers banged his shot home. For the first time in Division One, United were ahead of the game. 'The scene that followed this point,' a local journalist recorded, 'will long live in the memories of all who had the fortune to be present.'

Villa equalised, but no matter. They were, as it turned out, on their way to yet another league title. For Newcastle it was another point, another small indication that the team were coming to terms with their new environment. And most crucially, the fans were not deserting the side.

It was not until 5 November that United got their first Division One win. Just as crucially, they received conclusive evidence that the support was there in Tyneside to sustain a top football club. Picture the scene: Newcastle had thus far played ten Division One matches, and not won any. They had drawn four and lost six, and were firmly at the bottom of the table. If ever relegation loomed, it loomed for Newcastle United in November 1898.

And yet as Liverpool ran out onto the St James's Park turf shortly before three o'clock on 5 November, there were already 20,000 people in the ground, and more were streaming through the gates. 'It would not be a difficult matter,' suggested the *Evening Chronicle*, 'to account for the vast crowd present. One reason we could give is the fact that, so far, the Newcastle men had been most unfortunate in their essays for points. Time after time had they been beaten, to use a slang phrase, only 'by a pip' . . .

'As disheartening to the players as anyone else was this, but the public are the great arbiters of many a destiny, and in football as in aught else they must have a voice.'

In other words, the Newcastle crowd had turned from spectators into fans. It was a transformation which was taking place all over Britain, and it would become the foundation and the life-blood of professional soccer throughout the next century. Where once the paying customer plainly preferred just to stand and watch two sides play football of a certain quality (which explained why, when they were in the Second Division, Newcastle's friendlies against First Division opponents attracted far higher gates than any of their competitive matches), suddenly he or she (although it was of course mainly he) was supporting a cause. The customers had begun to recognise, and enjoy, their own power to affect a match. They had begun to use their voice.

And they found, at last, plenty of opportunity to use it on the afternoon of 5 November 1898. Newcastle survived a first-half assault from Liverpool (who were kicking, naturally, downhill), and when the Dunstan Temperance Band left the field after half-time the United players bounded out – and scored. Three minutes into the second period a miskicked clearance found Peddie in front of goal in the inside-left channel, and he – as they did not say in 1898 – didn't miss those.

Fifteen minutes later the crowd grew ecstatic when a good United attack resulted in the ball being fed to centre-forward Sandy MacFarlane. MacFarlane had recently been signed for £30 from Airdrie to add penetration to the attack, and on this occasion he did not disappoint – although at an angle, he sent a scorching drive into the roof of the Liverpool net. Minutes later Jock Peddie collected a loose ball following a corner and, following MacFarlane's example, hit a shot which 'nearly broke down the net'.

That was the turning point. It was as though Newcastle needed to prove both to themselves and to their fans that they could not only beat First Division opposition, but beat them well. A fortnight later Bolton Wanderers arrived in Newcastle, and United repeated the exercise. The Lancastrians went one up but Rogers equalised before the interval, and three second-half strikes from Peddie (2) and MacFarlane wrapped it up.

So it was that by Christmas Eve Newcastle had crept off the

bottom of the table on goal average, just in time for their biggest test yet: their first competitive league match against Sunderland at Roker Park.

The trip to Wearside was then a big enough test for anybody. Along with Aston Villa, Sunderland had dominated the league in the 1890s, winning it with their 'team of all the talents' in 1892, 1893 and 1895, and finishing as runners-up in 1894 and 1898. Their great team had been largely dismantled after a flirtation with relegation in 1897 (they were saved by finishing second out of four in the test match play-offs), which is why Newcastle came to sign their former stars, the two Johns, Harvey and Campbell. But by December 1898 Sunderland looked comfortably back on track. They cast such an enormous shadow across the North-east of England that only the most optimistic Geordie can have considered that Newcastle United had a hope of ever matching Sunderland. Only the most optimistic Geordie and, perhaps, Frank Watt . . .

Newcastle had never before played them in earnest. As we have seen, Sunderland had been extremely generous in offering their services for attractive friendlies designed to ease United's shaky bank balance. By December 1898 the two neighbours had met no fewer than 19 times in six years. Sunderland had won ten of them, five had been drawn, and Newcastle had won four – although the latest of them, that pre-season friendly at St James's back in September, which had resulted in Jackson and Rogers getting crocked, had ended in a draw.

Nor were the Tynesiders particularly familiar with Roker Park. All but two of the friendlies had taken place in Newcastle, as United were then considered too inferior a team to attract a useful gate on Wearside. The 8,000 Geordies who set off on that crisp December day were off into uncharted territory, and the omens were not good . . .

But, despite the bookies' odds of 6-4 in favour of Sunderland, they travelled in hope. A record number of them – 4,659, according to the station-master at Newcastle Central – left on the 18 trains which departed for Sunderland from Newcastle every ten minutes between 11 a.m. and 2 p.m.

This unprecedented travelling support had one immediately notable effect. It meant that when Stott led his team out onto Roker Park, the noise made by 30,000 paying customers was at least one-quarter in favour of the visitors. Sunderland were just not used to that.

They *were* used to taking the lead at home, however, and did so shortly after kick-off, when inside-right Leslie tucked a half-chance beyond Kingsley. The home section of the crowd went delirious. The players showed their extraordinary delight by shaking hands with each other all around the field. One-nil to Sunderland. Everything was going according to the script.

But Willie Wardrope and Jock Peddie had not read that script. From Peddie's kick-off Newcastle surged forward, pinning Sunderland back in defence, playing like men inspired. Just when it seemed as if the Wearsiders might have seen out the storm, Rogers swung an elusive cross over from the right, the ball evaded Doig in the Sunderland goal, and Wardrope slipped in from the outside-left position to slide it home.

And before Sunderland could digest the fact, Newcastle were ahead. The game was held up while Wardrope took treatment for an eye which had been injured by the elbow of the Sunderland right-back, and immediately after the restart Peddie took possession outside the box, controlled the ball and sent a thunderous shot past Doig.

Two-one to Newcastle at half-time. The Sunderland support fell silent, while those 8,000 Geordies whooped, and the small handful of amateur clarinettists in their midst blew gaily upon their instruments.

Into the second period, and Newcastle were playing like the old masters. They were performing like the home side; it was as though Newcastle United were already the North-east's champions, and Sunderland the stuttering newcomers. Newcastle's brisk, quick-moving forward line, with the subtle skills of Aitken offsetting the dynamism of Peddie, was asking questions that the Sunderland defence could not answer. Just minutes after the restart Wardrope had slung a cross over from the left, Peddie shook off his marker, stuck to the ball 'like a burr', and having created a foot or two of space, banged it remorselessly past Doig.

Sunderland were beaten. Leslie pulled back a face-saver late in the game to make the final score 3-2, but it flattered the Wearsiders and they knew it. They also must have known, with a shock that we can only imagine, that their days as the unchallenged rulers of North-eastern football were numbered.

If the home win against Liverpool seven weeks earlier had been the turning point in Newcastle's First Division fortunes, this was the clincher. This was confirmation that they had found their place in the world. No club that was capable of taking 8,000 fans to the mighty Sunderland, no team which could come away from there with such a comprehensive win, was a Second Division club. Relegation, from that day onwards, was not only unlikely, it was unthinkable. Newcastle United and their supporters had breathed the air on the mountain top, and they were not going back down to the foothills.

That away game against Sunderland was Newcastle's 18th of the league season. It was therefore the first game of the second half of their programme of 34 matches. In the first half of the season they had won two matches, drawn seven, and lost eight. In the second half of the season they would win nine, draw one and lose seven – form which, if they had spread it out over the entire eight months, would have seen them finish in fourth place, seven points behind champions Aston Villa.

As it was, Newcastle United finished their first season in Division One in 13th position, four places and five comforting points clear of the relegation zone. Perhaps most hopefully, despite averaging less than a point per game (they took 30 points from 34 games) Newcastle scored more goals (49) than they conceded (48). Jock Peddie was still repaying his £135 transfer fee.

The next five years were seasons of consolidation. Only once between 1899–1900 and 1903–04 did Newcastle finish outside the top five in the Football League. But neither, in that period, did they look like winning anything. The closest that they got to the league championship, third in 1902, was still seven points adrift of the winners, Sunderland. And only once, again in 1901–02, did they get as far as the last eight of the FA Cup.

But in the steady, methodical manner of Frank Watt, a team was being built. Andy Aitken – the only player to survive from the promotion squad of 1898 to the championship side of 1905 – was moved back into the midfield area which he would come to dominate. Aitken was first capped for Scotland in a 2-2 draw with England in 1901, when he was 24 years old, and he would represent his country for a further ten years.

The locally born Colin Veitch, who had been captain of Newcastle Boys when Frank Watt arrived in 1895 and an 'A' team player since then, had signed as an amateur in 1899 and turned professional in 1903. Along with 'Daddler' Aitken, the intellectual college graduate Veitch was one of the heroes of the 1900s. Aitken and Veitch became emblems of the club which had become known as the Magpies. Both men were soccer sophisticates, both could and would fill virtually any outfield position on the pitch. Both became captains of the club. Both played over 300 games for Newcastle. And both, for what it's worth, scored 40-odd goals . . .

As for the rest, Frank Watt just kept them coming in. In 1899 the Scottish international full-back Dave Gardner arrived from Third Lanark and the cultured winger Alec Gardner came from Leith Athletic. Watt promptly turned Alec Gardner into a right-half, and the two Scots were joined in the summer of 1899 by a superb full-back from Seaton Burn, Jack Carr, who would go on to win two England caps. Newcastle had got it right: over the ensuing years the figure in the Goals Against column steadily decreased from 48 to 43, to 37, 34 in 1901–02 (the best in the division) . . . and 33 in the championship season.

Bob McColl arrived from the Scottish amateur side Queen's Park in 1901, having drifted south out of a desire to play for Newcastle for absolutely no payment. The club did not turn him away. McColl headed north again, to Rangers in 1904, thereby becoming possibly the most celebrated footballer ever to play for Newcastle and never win a trophy. McColl was already a Scottish legend with 11 caps and ten international goals (including a hattrick against England) when he arrived at St James's Park. The fact that Newcastle were handed his signature on a plate when any other club in Britain would have fought for Bob McColl, was as significant as his contribution of 20 goals in 67 matches.

Ronnie Orr arrived from St Mirren at about the same time – May 1901 – but lasted a little longer. Orr was a miniature inside-forward of the old school: five foot five in his stockinged feet, and deadly in front of goal. Within weeks of his début he scored four times as United beat Notts County 8-0 at St James's in October 1901. This and other goalscoring feats (he totalled 69 in 180 appearances) won him two Scottish caps and stored up a good deal of credit for Ronnie Orr with the home support: credit which would be drawn upon in later years, when he took to arguing back with the critical terraces during the course of a game.

The right-winger from Percy Main, Jack Rutherford, signed up in 1902. Frank Watt took the 17-year-old from Willington Athletic, and later claimed that Rutherford was the club's greatest outside-right. He may still have had claim to that title a century later. Rutherford was a magnificent footballer: he had magnetic control, electrifying pace and a sure touch near goal, as his career total of 92 strikes in 334 games indicates. He was also the only Newcastle right-winger ever to be capped by England, making eight appearances and scoring three times for his country between 1904 and 1908. When the inside-right 'Gentleman Jim' Howie arrived from Bristol Rovers in the close season of 1903, he and Rutherford quickly developed a telepathic understanding which would serve them as a United attacking partnership for seven years and more than 200 games. Howie was as inelegant as Rutherford was fluent; but 'Gentleman Jim' would deploy his stumbling, stuttering run to take players away from Rutherford and leave the winger free to scorch in on goal. Jim Howie also netted 83 goals in 235 games, which justified a good deal of supposed clumsiness.

Although Howie also won caps for his country, the two men only played in one international together, the Scotland v

England game at Hampden Park in April 1908. It was a 1-1 draw, which may or may not have pleased both Rutherford and Howie, as the deadly duo were playing on opposing sides. Jim Howie was, of course, Scottish.

In August 1902 a 19-year-old footballer from the Highland League side Inverness Thistle was journeying south to visit a friend and former team-mate. Peter McWilliam was on his way to Sunderland to see his fellow Highlander Andy McCombie. McWilliam may have had hopes of ending up, like McCombie, on Sunderland's books. But what happened that August has become the stuff of legend. We can be certain that McWilliam changed trains in Newcastle, possibly in order to visit his sister, who had a café in the Groat Market. He seems after that to have called upon his fellow Scot Frank Watt at St James's Park, perhaps with nothing more in mind than a guided tour of an English First Division ground. Watt himself said later that McWilliam was 'cunningly intercepted and signed on while actually on his way to Sunderland'. Whether or not – as the story has it – the 19-year-old put his name to paper in the middle of Newcastle Central Station, is another matter.

So by the end of August Peter McWilliam, who would be capped eight times for Scotland between 1905 and 1911, and play 240 times in United's midfield, was a Newcastle player. And ironically, 18 months later, in February 1904, he was joined by his old friend Andy McCombie. Newcastle paid Sunderland a record £700 for the former Highland League full-back, who had already won the first of his two Scottish caps. It was money well spent: McCombie would serve the club in one capacity or another for the rest of his active life.

Like pieces of a jigsaw, the team which would dominate England was almost complete. Almost, but not quite.

Bobby Templeton was an Aston Villa left-winger who had already been capped for Scotland when he intimated to Newcastle in February 1903 that he would like to join the club. United snapped him up, but he injured himself later the following year. A signing from Southern League club Chatham, Albert Gosnall, took Templeton's place – and proceeded to play so well that he kept it. Templeton, an idiosyncratic character who once for a bet placed his handsome head in a lion's mouth, picked a dressing-room fight with Gosnall. But it was to no avail. Gosnall won the fight and won the team place too, and Bobby Templeton moved on to Arsenal, Celtic and finally Kilmarnock, winning a good haul of further Scottish caps.

The great Jock Peddie had gone, and John Campbell had long retired, and Newcastle had no acknowledged goalscoring centre-forward. At the end of the 1902-3 season a big, burly, 14-stone striker from Grimsby Town was brought to the club. 'Clever of foot and fearless of heart', as the local press would describe him, Bill Appleyard turned out to be an inspired buy. He would serve Newcastle United for five successful years, in the course of which his goalscoring record was a superb 87 goals in 145 games.

On 18 March 1901 England beat Wales 6-0 at St James's Park. It was the first international to be played in Newcastle, and it was also the occasion of the first Newcastle United footballer to be capped by England (as opposed to Scotland, of course) while on the club's books. The honoured man was the goalkeeper, Matt Kingsley.

But shortly into the 1904-5 season Kingsley was injured, and the reserve goalkeeper Jimmy Lawrence took over between the posts. As we have seen, Lawrence proved impossible to dislodge. The longest run of matches by any Newcastle footballer ever was under way. Not until 1922 would the Glaswegian Lawrence leave St James's Park, having chalked up no fewer than 496 appearances.

In 1904 Frank Watt also made the signing which would ultimately have the greatest effect, not just on Newcastle United, but on the world of football. There was much talk in England of a young Irish defender named Bill McCracken. The boy had already been picked for his country twice, the first time in 1902 at the age of 19. He was compact, fit and highly intelligent.

He also did not wish to leave the Emerald Isle. Arsenal and Rangers were actively on the trail of the young full-back, but McCracken was happy playing for Belfast Distillery and completing his building trade apprenticeship in his home city. During Newcastle's close-season tour of Scotland in 1904, United official James Telford took an optimistic ferry journey over to Ireland (the island had not yet been partitioned, and Belfast was not yet in the province of Northern Ireland – all of Bill McCracken's caps, therefore, were won not in the colours of Ulster, but in those of Ireland).

To everybody's astonishment, and to Arsenal's and Rangers' chagrin, he signed instantly. There would be talk of illegal approaches and illicit payments – Colin Veitch's name was mentioned – but an FA inquiry cleared all parties. McCracken immediately joined Newcastle on a tour of Denmark, and made his début at the start of the 1904–05 season. Unfortunately he suffered a bad injury in October at Preston, and complicated the matter by starting again too early three months later.

United had consequently to put Jack Carr in at left-back, and the McCrombie-Carr full-back partnership proved so effective that the management stuck with it. So Bill McCracken missed out on that first cup final, and played just 13 games in United's first championship season. He would make up for it in later years. Nobody could have guessed it at the time, but one of the results of Bill McCracken's 432 appearances for Newcastle United was a change in the football laws so stunning and so influential that it altered the face of the game, and remained in place for a further 70 years. But that is a later story . . .

Give or take a footballer or two, Frank Watt had his team. It would be, at its core, a long-lasting squad of players. Many of them were set to serve Newcastle United until the eve of the First World War, and some for years after that. As that 1904–05 season began, people from the south were looking expectantly, nervously, at the sleeping giant in the north. They admired its 'scientific' approach, and its Scottish flair. They feared its roar. They had good reason to.

CHAPTER THREE

KINGS OF ENGLAND: 1905–14

'We are in the happy position,' declared the Newcastle *Evening Chronicle* on 26 August 1905, 'of being able to write in the most hopeful vein of the prospects of Newcastle United – League Champions 1904–05 – in the forthcoming season. They never had such a rosy outlook before them, as a matter of fact, for they will have this season the consciousness within them that they are blessed with the capacity to excel themselves in the two great Association tourneys of the country, the Football League and the English Cup.'

Additional ground had been secured on the Leazes, and St James's Park was in the throes of a massive improvement and extension, which would lead to a capacity of 60,000. Season tickets would cost two guineas (£2.10) for the best seats, down to 15 shillings (75p) for uncovered areas. Afternoon standing admission to the Leazes Terrace would cost 6d (2p).

They got off to a poor defence of the title, from which they never sufficiently recovered. They lost their opening game against Sunderland 3-2 at Roker Park, and by the end of September were firmly in the bottom half of the table. After seven matches they had just five points and only one win – an away victory at Everton thanks to goals from Howie and Orr.

The team rallied in October, and seemed set to crown an excellent month when Middlesbrough arrived at St James's Park. Twenty-five thousand fans were not disappointed. Bill Appleyard netted twice in the first half – one a brilliant turn and powerhouse shot. Hewitt pulled one back for 'Boro straight after the restart, but Appleyard completed his hat-trick in the 55th minute after collecting a neat pass from Orr, and McWilliam made it 4-1 with five minutes remaining.

It had been, by all accounts, United's best performance of the season, and it helped lift them up to seventh position. But they were troublingly inconsistent. Scrappy performances followed . . . and then, on 11 November, Wolves arrived in Newcastle.

Nobody anticipated the slaughter. There was bad weather, sand was laid on the pitch, and the attendance was poor. Howie, Orr and Appleyard hardly seemed to notice, however. After six minutes Appleyard released the ball to Howie, who let rip from 20 yards and gave Wolves' keeper Baddeley no chance. With Veitch and the cocky McCracken dominating the midfield and defence it was 25 minutes before Wolves had a shot (McCracken in particular amused the home support by sarcastically shouting out, every time a Wolves player bore down on him on yet another hopeless errand, 'Look here! Look here!').

With the Wolves goal under constant seige, it was astonishing that United took 30 minutes to increase their lead. But once they did so, the goals came in droves: Howie hit another long-range effort to make it 2-0; Orr got one five minutes later, and another two minutes after that. Baddeley carried a high shot from Appleyard over the line to make it 5-0 before half-time; and the big centre-forward collected another two in the second half before Colin Veitch rounded things off at 8-0 from the penalty spot in the last minute after Gosnell was brought down in the box.

It was Newcastle's biggest win by far in league football, and it signalled more than anything their astonishing potential. On song, on their day, this team were capable of taking anybody.

A week later they rammed home the point by travelling to play second-placed Aston Villa. This game had particular resonance because, of course, it had been Villa who had taken advantage of United's nervous, flat performance to steal the cup final at Crystal Palace seven months earlier.

Revenge was sweet. Veitch and Orr gave United a half-time

lead, and after 20 minutes of the second period the little Scottish-inside forward nipped in to make it 3-0 from close range, and crown what most observers applauded as an even better performance than the demolition of Wolves.

Suddenly Newcastle were third in the First Division, a point behind Villa and two behind Sheffield Wednesday, with a game in hand over both and more than half of the season left to play. Suddenly, anything was possible.

The last Saturday of the old year, 30 December 1905, saw the traditional holiday-period fixture with Sunderland. More than 50,000 paying customers crammed into St James's hoping to see revenge taken for that opening day's defeat. They were disappointed: an Orr equaliser just managed to salvage a point out of a poor game.

The FA Cup came round again in January. One lesson that the Newcastle board had learned from the previous year's experiences was that the league gates might buy the club's bread and butter, but a good cup run provided the jam. Of the £16,000 profit made in season 1904–05, precisely half of it had come from the FA Cup. That was the money which paid for the extensions to St James's; that was the money, in short, which made sure that the 60,000 people who wanted to watch an occasional league match could be accommodated.

United started as though they meant business. Second Division Grimsby Town arrived for a first-round game in the city to which so many of their players had emigrated, and they received poor hospitality. Orr made it 1-0 before the inevitable happened and Bill Appleyard scored against his old side. Gosnell made it three, Appleyard picked up his second, and Rutherford and Orr rounded off a 6-0 trouncing. 'The Fishermen' went home despondent. United's fans thought, bring on the next.

Derby County were dismissed with difficulty in the second round, 2-1 in Newcastle after a 0-0 draw in the Midlands. Second Division Blackpool had reached the third round for the first time in their history after a shock 2-1 defeat of Sheffield United at Bramall Lane. By four o'clock on the afternoon of 24 February 1906, they were wishing they had never bothered. In front of 27,000 fans Gardner, Jack Carr, Appleyard and Orr (2) ensured a 5-0 Newcastle victory, and passage to round four. (Carr's goal was, as it was scored by an Edwardian full-back, exceptional – in fact he had been up for a corner, and was jogging dutifully home when he was fouled. He quickly took the free-kick himself, and it struck the surprised Blackpool keeper on the leg and wound up in the net. In 276 other games for Newcastle, he would score four more goals.)

Exciting as all this was, the cup run was masking a disastrous slip in league form. Since that 3-0 win at Villa Park which had put Newcastle into a challenging third position back in November, they had lost seven and drawn one out of 13 league matches. It was not championship form. Liverpool in the same period had won ten and lost just two, to leap over United to a clear lead in the table. Not for the first time or the last, Anfield was witnessing true championship form.

So by the time Newcastle visited Birmigham City in the fourth round of the FA Cup on 10 March, it was pretty clear that, barring miracles, the 1905–06 season would see cup glory or no glory at all.

For the moment it was cup glory, but only just. After 14 minutes Birmingham's inside-right Green got his head to the ball in the goalmouth; Lawrence slapped it clear, but Green's head popped up again to put his side in front. Jones made it 2-0 before the break, and United looked on their way out of the cup. But Colin Veitch, who was replacing Appleyard at centre-forward, got one back 18 minutes into the second half and scored a penalty in the dying seconds to take Birmingham back to St James's for a replay . . . where, inevitably, Newcastle won 3-0.

Veitch kept his centre-forward role at Appleyard's expense for the semi-final against Woolwich Arsenal, which took place at Stoke on 31 March. While Everton were simultaneously playing league leaders Liverpool in the other semi-final at Birmingham, it was Veitch who cottoned on to a cross from the right to fire a shot beyond the Arsenal keeper and put United ahead. With 14 minutes to go, after some superb combination play from Newcastle which had seen Howie hit the post and

Arsenal's goal survive severe pressure, Arsenal were forced into some suicidal attacking which left their defence so empty that Rutherford and Howie could advance unopposed upon the Arsenal goal. Ashcroft came off his line to meet them, and Howie looped the ball over his head for a 2-0 win and a second consecutive FA Cup final.

They met Everton, who had disposed of their neighbours 1-0. Liverpool wrapped up their consolation prize, the league title, shortly afterwards.

In retrospect, it was all too similar to the 1905 final. Even the team was virtually the same: McCracken was once again edged out by the Carr-McCombie partnership; and only Orr – fit this time – played in his first final, poor Appleyard being the unlucky man who lost his place despite being United's top scorer in the campaign with six goals.

The idea was, no doubt, that practice makes perfect. Those footballers would surely not make the same mistake twice on neutral ground against a team below them in the league – and one over whom they had done the double in the season just ending.

Once again the crowds gathered outside the newspaper offices in Newcastle to receive the bulletins as they were telephoned home. Once again the thousands of excursionists left Central Station on the Friday night, to swig beer, wave their colours out of the window, fall asleep and wake up to see dawn rising over Peterborough, and blossom in the orchards and hedgerows of the south of England. Once again Geordies roamed up and down Gray's Inn Road after eight on cup final morning in search of breakfast, or Everton fans with whom to exchange banter or a bet, or all of the above. Once again they made their way to Sydenham and the Crystal Palace ground to join a crowd which was, this time, merely 75,609.

And once again they were all let down.

'Newcastle were confidently expected to carry off this year's trophy,' reported an FA anniversary annual, 'although much was expected in the way of good football from two teams of such proved pace and ability.

49

'These great expectations were never realised; the play was commonplace, if not uninteresting, and the only satisfaction about the match was that on the day's play the worse side lost.'

This scathing judgement was justified. The Newcastle midfield in particular was appalling. Aitken, Gardner and McWilliam were accustomed to dominating the middle of the park: in the 1906 cup final Aitken was on typical form but the others were nowhere to be found.

Veitch kicked off at half three with just about his only accurate touch of the game. (When the news of his having started the game was broadcast to the 1,500 people assembled outside the *Chronicle* offices in St John's St, it was scrambled in the transmission, so that a rumour quickly swept town to the effect that Colin had scored. If only . . .) Everton had the ball in Lawrence's net ten minutes later, but it was disallowed for offside. In a game which was regularly interrupted by offside calls and scrappy fouls, Everton had the better of the exchanges, but it was the better of a thoroughly bad deal.

'The football was a mere lottery from beginning to end,' recorded the FA booklet. 'The chances went mostly to Everton, but even Everton relied only on its one bit of real football to win.'

That one bit of real football came in the 75th minute. Everton's inside-right Bolton drew Carr towards him, and slipped the ball to right-winger Jack Sharp. Sharp, an England international at both football and cricket, took off into open space and crossed low and hard for centre-forward Sandy Young to knock the ball home from close range past a helpless Jimmy Lawrence.

Newcastle had not much of a sting to be pulled on that day, but the goal pulled it. They counter-attacked half-heartedly for the remaining quarter-hour, failing to get a good shot on target – trying too hard, it was commented, to walk the ball into the net – and then watched as the opposition were presented with the FA Cup.

The criticism hurt so much that Newcastle United, whose cup run had left them with four league matches still to play after the final, won two and drew two of those games, and thereby catapulted themselves from mid-table into fourth position in the league.

But it was not enough. Newcastle United had fielded no fewer than nine internationals. (Veitch and Gosnell had won their first England caps a month or two earlier. Lawrence, one of the two uncapped players, would get his sole international selection for Scotland five years later. Out of those 11 men, only Alec Gardner would remain uncapped.) Ten internationals, and they had been beaten by a single inspirational stroke from the England right-winger.

But Frank Watt and his directors kept faith with their men. The inside-left Harry Brown was signed from Southampton in July for £380, and only one other notable purchase was made early in the 1906–07 season, when the utility player Finlay Speedie – another Scottish cap – was bought from Rangers for £600. Speedie was so adaptable that he made those all-rounders Veitch and Aitken appear stuck in their ways – unlike them, he actually went on to play in goal for United on one necessary occasion.

Watt and his board could not be blamed for sitting tight. Newcastle United had still won just the one trophy: that league title two seasons earlier. But overall their record could not be bettered in England. First and fourth in Division One, and cup finalists in two consecutive years: Newcastle had risen from middle-of-the-road semi-anonymity to become the most accomplished squad in the land. Their style of play, that quick, accurate, short-passing game which frustrated so many of their supporters when they seemed to want to walk the ball into the net, that style of play was applauded the length of Britain as being not only new and 'scientific', but also, on its day, absolutely unstoppable. It was the perfect fusion of Scottish science and English flair. Why change it? If nerves could be held, surely trophies would inevitably follow.

There was a single note of discord in all of this apparent continuity. Andy 'Daddler' Aitken, the Scottish international who had been with United since 1895 and was 29 years old by

1906, was reluctant to re-sign at the start of the season. Aitken had played only 19 matches that season, and he was, in fact, the only member of the cup final squad who had not agreed new terms by the morning of the final itself. The invaluable forward-turned-half-back, and club skipper, was clearly looking for pastures new.

Aitken was in position as captain and right-half, however, when United kicked off the season at St James's against Sunderland. September 1st 1906 was a baking hot day: the Tyneside barometers registered 90 degrees fahrenheit in the shade; in the stands most of the men were hatless, 'whilst many went so far as to remove coats, collars and ties'; and several of the Newcastle players wore skull-caps as protection against sunstroke. A 60,000 capacity crowd jammed into the ground to watch this most desirable of North-eastern football matches – 60,000 people who wondered aloud whether it was not too hot to permit the players to take part.

For once, the Geordie fans need not have worried. Aitken won the toss and elected to play uphill with a following southerly breeze and the sun on Newcastle backs. From the beginning, it was United's day. In defence McCombie and Carr were unassailable: Jack Carr in particular established complete dominance over the dangerous Sunderland winger Hogg. Aitken and Veitch were majestic in midfield, and when the first goal came after 27 minutes it was a beauty: Appleyard collecting the ball outside the box, squeezing between two attentive Sunderland defenders and hitting a low shot past Naisby.

Sunderland came out in the second half looking like a changed outfit, and within 25 minutes they had scored twice to take a 2-1 lead. Then Jack Rutherford struck. The little right-winger, whose already thinning hair and serious expression belied his youth (he was still only 21), bore down on the Sunderland defence with the ball at his feet. He released it, and Howie, Appleyard and Veitch all had shots blocked before it ran loose to Rutherford, who slammed home the equaliser.

The huge crowd roared its approval, and six minutes later Gosnell repeated the feat out on the left wing: tricking and fooling the Sunderland defence before releasing a cross which was met by the onrushing Rutherford to put United ahead again, 3-2. Howie and Appleyard combined neatly to set up the fourth for Howie, and the final whistle blew. Game, set and match to Newcastle. For the first time since 1903, they had beaten the Wearsiders in a First Division game – and beaten them so thoroughly that there could no longer be any doubt about who were the new champions of North-eastern football. The only question remaining was could Newcastle United equal Sunderland's historic feats on the national scale?

They could. An astonishing revival at Birmingham seven days later saw Newcastle come back from being two goals down to win 4-2, thanks to a hat-trick from Harry Brown on his first-team début, and a penalty from the dependable Veitch.

So Everton came to town on 15 September. As well as being the side which had robbed United of the cup back in the spring, Everton had got off to an equally good start in the league: they were above Newcastle at the top of Division One only on superior goal average. (Back then, and for a further 80 years, teams level on points were separated by dividing the goals for by the goals scored against, rather than subtracting goals against from goals for.)

Forty thousand people flocked to St James's. A ding-dong first half finished goalless, but after 25 minutes of the second period Gosnell slung over a cross from the left. Left-half Peter McWilliam, the boy from Inverness whom Frank Watt had kidnapped on his way to Sunderland, trapped it, pushed it on to his good left foot, lined up his shot, and thumped the winning goal into the net.

Newcastle were top of the league. An Appleyard hat-trick took the points from Middlesbrough in a 3-0 win at Ayresome Park, in a match which had further significance. It was Andy Aitken's last 90 minutes in a black-and-white shirt. After 349 matches this magnificent footballer – who more than anybody else was symbolic of Newcastle's meteoric rise – was sold at the end of October 1906 to Middlesbrough for £500. One week he was running rings around them, and the next he was showing them how it was done. As player-manager he worked wonders at Ayresome Park, lifting the Tessiders from bottom place to a comfortable 11th in his first few months, and consolidating them as a First Division force before leaving for Leicester in 1909.

There would be other setbacks. The promising Harry Brown developed a serious eye infection and had to retire from the game before the end of that season. But thanks in large part to the astonishing support which had mushroomed on Tyneside over the past ten years, Newcastle United had over 40 professional footballers on their books, and fully 20 of them were competing for first-team places. They had what a later age would call strength in depth.

That other new signing, Finlay Speedie, began to repay his £600 fee towards the end of the year: picked at inside-right, his two goals helped clinch a 4-0 win over Bolton which consolidated United at the top of the table, and he netted again as Newcastle once more came from behind to beat Manchester United 3-1.

There was one mixed blessing. On 12 January 1907 Crystal Palace, the team which played on that cursed Sydenham cup final venue, visited Tyneside in the first-round of the FA Cup. It was one of the cup's all-time bankers: Newcastle were stretching ahead at the top of the league; had been in the last two finals; were generally regarded as undefeatable at home; and Palace had only been founded two years earlier – they were not even a Football League team, but played in the Southern League which would remain their home until 1920.

Naturally, Crystal Palace knocked United out of the cup by 1-0. They had many northerners in their line-up, including some who had previously been released by Newcastle, and they held on to their first-half goal despite being reduced to ten men.

There was only one thing for it: the league title must be regained. By early March the lead over Everton was five points and holding. It never slipped. A couple of shaky draws and a bad away defeat at Bolton only dented Newcastle's position. A late run by Bristol City saw them jump over Everton into second place, but the destination of the Division One title was settled by the first week in April – St James's Park. United celebrated the return of the championship shield with a dour 0-0 draw against Sheffield United, but that no longer mattered. By three clear points they were kings of England once more. They had scored more goals (74) and conceded fewer (46) than any other side in their 38 games. Their record over three short years was second to none. If only they could capture that elusive cup . . .

United had actually won another trophy in 1907. It was a tradition of the day that the top amateur side in England would play the top professional team for the Sheriff of London Charity Shield. In March Newcastle, as league leaders, were invited by the Sheriff of London to play the famous leading amateur team Corinthians at Craven Cottage in the metropolis.

It was truly a meeting between the old world and the new. Corinthians were a relic of the Victorian public-school game. Only public-school old boys and graduates of Oxford or Cambridge universities were allowed as members. Until 1922 they never entered any competition other than the Charity Shield, on the principle that competition in sport corrupted the gentlemanly amateur ethic. On the same principle, they would have absolutely nothing to do with penalty kicks. This led to some strange sights on a football field when Corinthians AFC were playing. They believed that no gentleman player would concede a penalty. So if a penalty was awarded against them, their goalkeeper walked away and left the opposing spot-kick taker with an open goal. And if a penalty was awarded for them, they deliberately kicked it high or wide of the goal.

In the past Corinthians had won famous victories against professional teams, and had actually provided the whole of the England international team which beat Wales in 1894. But by 1907 their day was gone. Jackie Rutherford, Bill Appleyard, a brace from Harry Brown and an own-goal saw United coast to a 5-2 win over the public schoolboys, and win the forerunner of today's Charity Shield. Oddly, the two teams would meet again almost exactly 20 years later, when Newcastle were once again

champions, and Corinthians had relaxed their rule about playing competitive games . . .

By Christmas 1907 it was clear that United would have
difficulty in retaining their league title. It was not that they
were playing badly, but that Manchester United, who had only
been promoted two years earlier, were running away with it.
The team from Old Trafford made their intentions clear when
they visited St James's Park and inflicted the heaviest home
defeat thus far upon Newcastle, winning 6-1 with the help of the
inspired Welsh winger Billy Meredith. More than one Geordie
fan must have shaken his head in knowing despair, recalling
Meredith wreaking similar havoc in the colours of Manchester
City. And, sadly, that home defeat record would last for only 12
months . . .

Having disposed of Nottingham Forest in the first round of
the FA Cup by 2-0 at St James's Park, by the time non-league
West Ham United visited Tyneside for the second round on 1
February 1908, Newcastle were seven points behind league
leaders Manchester United, and had played two games more
than the Mancunians. The league was virtually out of reach.

For 45 minutes the West Ham cup-tie reminded the home
support of that fatal defeat by another Southern League team,
Crystal Palace, a year earlier. United had all the play. Billy
McCracken – by now established at right-back – spent much of
the first half camped outside the West Ham penalty area,
lobbing shots and crosses into the danger zone, but all to no
avail. Newcastle just could not score.

Luckily, neither could the Londoners. But, with the minutes
ticking away, a dangerous replay down in the East End looked
ominously likely. A few minutes into the second half Howie
charged the Hammers' goalkeeper Kitchen, and the ball wound
up in the back of the net. The goal was disallowed for offside,
but Kitchen was carried off to the changing-rooms and didn't
reappear. The centre-half Piercey took his place, and West Ham,
in those days before substitutions, were down to ten men.

And still Newcastle could not score. Finally, with 15 minutes
left, Rutherford sent over a fine cross for Appleyard to head

home. It suddenly looked easy – so easy that 60 seconds later Rutherford and Appleyard repeated the trick. Newcastle were into the third round by 2-0, after a thoroughly worrying 90 minutes.

They were rewarded with another home draw, against Liverpool. Once again United put their large and faithful support through the mill. Forty-six thousand Geordies watched aghast as a period of fruitless Newcastle pressure led only to Liverpool taking the lead when a header came back off the post and their centre-half Raisbeck followed up to score. With the strong wind behind them in the second half, however, United put the visitors to the sword. It was their first truly convincing 45 minutes of the 1908 cup campaign. After four minutes Bill Appleyard scored a trademark equaliser: he received the ball with his back to goal out on the by-line, turned sharply and, all in the one movement, thumped a fierce shot between the keeper and the near post. Fifteen minutes later, after the Liverpool goal had led a charmed life and Newcastle had forced corner after corner, McWilliam wriggled past four men on the left flank and laid the ball inside for Speedie to score. Sixty seconds later Rutherford swept in from the right, survived a foul in the box which the referee waved on, and made it 3-1 from close range.

The crowd, sensing another afternoon out at Sydenham, went delirious, improvising flags to wave from handkerchiefs tied on to the end of walking-sticks. On the following Monday, safely back in their homes or places of work, they were more quietly satisfied by the news that Newcastle had drawn their fourth consecutive home tie – against struggling Grimsby Town, who were languishing at the foot of Division Two.

No favours were given. Once again Bill Appleyard punished his old club, scoring a hat-trick as United romped to a 5-1 win. It was a memorable campaign for the centre-forward. When he finished off yet another Rutherford cross in front of an open goal late in the game, he was netting his seventh cup goal in four matches.

Their opponents in the semi-final at Liverpool were Fulham. It was all looking just too easy to be true. Fulham were yet another Second Division side. They had knocked out Norwich City, Manchester City and – unbelievably – league leaders Manchester United. Even more gratifyingly, the other semi-final was between Second Division Wolverhampton Wanderers and non-league Southampton, who had somehow seen off West Bromwich Albion, Bristol Rovers and Everton. In short, Newcastle United, the reigning league champions and two-time cup finalists in recent years, were the only First Division side left in the FA Cup. It should have been a stroll.

And, initially, it was. On paper Fulham were the most difficult of the lowly threesome. They at least were challenging for promotion: Wolves were sunk in the bottom half of Division Two, and Southampton were exactly midway in the Southern League table.

United dismissed Fulham like chaff. A good 8,000 Geordies had travelled to Liverpool to join the 35,000 crowd, and they enjoyed a massacre. Newcastle overran the Second Division defence; Appleyard giving them the lead with a 30-yard shot on the half-hour, and Howie increasing it with yet another neat chip over the keeper. Following a free-kick Alec Gardner made it three in the second half, and a brace from Rutherford and another one from Howie completed the rout at 6-0.

Their cup final opponents would be Wolves, who had dismissed Southampton by a mere 2-0. If Newcastle United had been favourites to win the FA Cup in each of their two earlier finals, you could hardly get money against them for this one. In Aston Villa and Everton, they had at least been facing First Division opposition with good recent records. Wolves were, in 1908, simply nowhere. In their five cup ties they had luckily faced so far just one First Division team (Bury, whom they beat 2-0). Two of their other opponents had been non-league, and of the two Second Division sides which they had dismissed, one of them (Stoke FC) was about to drop out of the league.

En route to the final Newcastle had scored 18 goals, and Wolves only nine. None of the Wolverhampton Wanderers players (all of whom were English) had any cup final experience. Six of the Newcastle United team (which was made up of six

Scots, four Englishmen and one Irishman – McCracken finally got his place) had been at the Crystal Palace final two years earlier, and a seventh – Appleyard – had played the year before. Add to all of that the fact that when Wolves had last visited St James's Park two seasons earlier they had lost 8-0, and surely a slaughter was on the cards. 'Looking at the different positions of the teams in the First and Second Leagues,' said the *Evening Chronicle*, 'Newcastle's prospects of winning the cup at the third try looked rosy.'

'Judgement inclined to the United,' added the FA's later report, 'whose skill, science and artistry were considered to be in an entirely different class to the Wanderers.'

The defeat, as a result, was the most bitter so far. After half an hour one of Edwardian football's most colourful characters, the amateur international right-half (and clergyman and teacher) the Reverend Kenneth R.G. 'Parson' Hunt, gave Wolves the lead with a drive which flew over the diving Lawrence. Three minutes later, with Newcastle desperately pressing for an equaliser, Wolves centre-forward Hedley took possession, tore through the two isolated full-backs, and made it 2-0.

In Newcastle the news of the half-time score 'seemed to fall like a wet blanket' on the crowds gathered in the streets . . . 'It had not the effect of thinning the crowd all the same; and on the principle of "where there's life there's hope", the people kept on gathering.'

They gathered in vain. Down south, United could make no headway against the determined, hard-tackling Second Division defence, and there were just 17 minutes left before Veitch shot and Howie turned the ball into the net.

It was Newcastle's first goal in more than four hours of FA Cup finals, but it would not be enough. With five minutes left Wolves made it 3-1, again on the break, right-winger Harrison shaking free of his marker and racing in on goal where McCracken tackled him. Both men fell to the ground but Harrison was first to his feet, and with Veitch coming in for a challenge, he quickly stuck the ball past Lawrence.

The indignity, the shame of it was such that some Geordie

fans accused their players of taking bribes. This was not un-known in football, but those men were almost certainly inno-cent. No money could have compensated for such humiliation.

(One good thing did come out of the 1908 cup final. A man named Gladstone Adams from South Shields had decided to drive his new-fangled motor car from Tyneside to Sydenham for the game. On the way back he encountered hail. Unable to see through his windscreen, Adams improvised a mechanical device to scrape it clean. He would later refine and perfect that device, and in doing so the Newcastle United supporter Gladstone Adams invented the windscreen wiper.)

It was partly a measure of Newcastle United's prestige, that there should have been such widespread shock at their losing the 1908 cup final. Rather like one of the club super-squads of the 21st century, this team, with its preponderance of interna-tionals, was reckoned to be at least as good as any national select.

They had pride, those players, and they entered the 1908–09 league season determined to prove it. Appleyard and Speedie moved on after the final. Appleyard was replaced by another Grimsby Town player, Bob Blanthorne, who could be the most unfortunate man ever to don a black-and-white shirt. Bought in the close season for £350, Blanthorne broke his leg ten minutes into the opening game against Bradford City. He was carried off and never won back his place.

Andrew 'Sandy' Higgins, who had been signed from Kilmar-nock three years earlier but had hardly been given a chance to prove the quality which would eventually win him two Scottish caps, stepped in at centre-forward. The England international Jimmy 'Tadger' Stewart was signed from Sheffield Wednesday to consolidate the forward line – and United got off to a brisk start in their attempt to win back the league title.

The crowds were, by 1908, sensational. No fewer than 30,000 turned up at St James's in early October to see a goal apiece from Stewart and Higgins see off Preston North End. By the end of November Newcastle were second in the league. And then disaster struck.

It is still difficult, almost a century later, to judge exactly what went wrong when Sunderland visited Newcastle for a league game on 5 December 1908. But we can try. Two weeks earlier Aston Villa had inflicted a rare 2-0 defeat on Newcastle at St James's. For the next game, away at Nottingham Forest, Albert Shepherd was signed from Bolton for £800. A proven goalscorer who had netted 90 times in 123 games for Bolton, Shepherd would deliver a similar strike rate in the same number of games for Newcastle – 92 in 123.

Shepherd was put into the starting line-up at Forest, along with five relatively unknown reserves – Whitson, Liddell, Willis, Duncan and Wilson – who replaced the established international stars McCracken, McWilliam, Rutherford, Howie and Stewart. This untested side covered themselves with glory at lowly Nottingham. Shepherd scored on his début, and Newcastle won 4-0. So Frank Watt and the directors rewarded them by maintaining much the same side for the visit of Sunderland a week later.

There were few signs of the disaster in the first 45 minutes. Sunderland took the lead before a record 56,000 crowd, but Shepherd equalised from the penalty spot. After the break, the deluge began. Sunderland just could not miss. They scored five goals in eight minutes; eight goals in 30 minutes, before easing off at 9-1 during the last quarter-hour. Over at Roker Park, where Sunderland reserves were playing, the Wearsiders cheered as the progressive score was put up on the board, but stopped responding after the fifth, under the impression that somebody was playing tricks.

Nobody was playing tricks. Sunderland won 9-1. It is still a record away win for the First Division. And it was achieved against the champions-elect. Watt and company hastily rearranged the United side, brought back the big boys, and got back on their winning ways.

They won the league with a record 53 points from 38 games. Ironically, Newcastle's defence was clearly their strongest point – they scored far fewer goals than second- and third-placed Everton and Sunderland, but conceded massively fewer – only

41 to their rivals' 57 and 63. And nine of those 41 came in one unforgettable match . . .

Newcastle extracted some kind of revenge by knocking Sunderland out of the FA Cup quarter-finals by 3-0 in a replay at Roker Park. (Sunderland, however, did go on to complete the league double over their rivals, winning the home fixture 3-1 after the dependable Shepherd had given United a first-half lead.)

Following this cup win, there was some excited talk on Tyneside of another shot at the double, but Manchester United intervened. The Old Trafford team, who would go on to win the cup, knocked Newcastle out of the semi-final by 1-0.

By any standards, Newcastle's record since 1905 was amazing. Three times league champions and three times losing cup finalists – nobody else in the land could match that achievement. But it was the prefix 'losing' before the words 'cup finalists' which haunted them.

It was, in 1910, almost as though Newcastle sacrificed a fourth league title in order to win that elusive cup. They were still, on paper, the best side in England – stuffed with internationals, and with an overflow of capped players in the reserves. They were certainly in a challenging league position into the New Year, when the cup contests began, and were in fact in second place in the league on the morning of the semi-final in late March. But they would finish fourth, eight points behind champions Aston Villa, and they would be fined a whopping £100 by the Football League for deliberately fielding weak teams in the league late in the season.

But the club swallowed that fine painlessly. They could, quite literally, afford to. After a worrying hiccup against non-league Stoke in the first round, which was only settled with a 2-1 win in a home replay, Second Division Fulham arrived on Tyneside for the second round. This was more like it. After three minutes McCracken sent Higgins on his way, and the centre-forward made it 1-0. Nine minutes into the second half Sandy Higgins was elbowed off the ball in the penalty area. With no Shepherd on the field, there was a buzz around the ground as to who would take the spot-kick – a buzz which turned to excited comment as full-back McCracken walked up to the ball, patted down the ground around the penalty spot, and then comfortably scored. Rutherford laid on the third for Higgins with 15 minutes left, and Higgins returned the compliment for Rutherford in the dying minutes to make it 4-0.

Blackburn arrived for the third round on 19 February 1910, contributing 1,500 supporters to a 45,000 gate. Shepherd was back, but it was Higgins – moved to inside-left – who proved his worth in the first minute, pursuing a rebound almost to the touchline before swivelling and scoring from what had seemed an impossible angle, the ball finding the net just inside the far post. Rutherford made it two after 25 minutes, and, although Blackburn pulled one back, Howie made sure with a beauty in the second half.

It was beginning to be noticed, in this season and in many of the previous years, that full-back Billy McCracken was applying unusual methods in the back line. With the offside rule insisting that three players (notionally both full-backs and the goal-keeper) must be between a forward and the goal-line when the ball was played to him, there was room for some intelligent use of space. As there was, as yet, no such thing as a deep-lying centre-half, all that an alert full-back needed to do was step forward in the instant before a through ball was played. His companion could stay put: it would not matter. If one full-back was forward, that would inevitably leave just two men back – and the opposition forwards invariably were offside.

Billy McCracken was both intelligent and alert, and he did not mind breaking up the flow of a football match if that meant winning games for Newcastle United. The amateur, Corinthian legacy was still immensely strong in English soccer before the First World War, and such tactics were not usually considered gentlemanly. They may have been within the letter of the law, but they were not in its spirit (the offside rule had been instituted, after all, to protect full-backs from goal-hanging forwards). But much as some sexual legislation could not be brought before Queen Victoria because the monarch would simply not understand the transgression, so the football authorities were reluctant to believe that a soccer player could be capable of so exploiting their laws, and nothing was done about it.

But McCracken was doing it, with impunity, and referees had no choice but to scowl at him and whistle once more for offside. Even the partisan local press was in two minds about the tactic – it was routinely referred to as 'McCracken getting up to his tricks again'. The crowd, so far as we can gather, did not much care.

One of Billy McCracken's most distinguished contemporaries, the Welsh international Don Davies, talked affectionately and at length about him and his Newcastle tricks many years later, and in the process gave some idea of what it was like to watch and play against the Newcastle defence which dominated English football.

'McCracken,' said Davies, 'though widely respected as an individual and always feared as a player, was not exactly a universal favourite . . . Who but a snake-charmer would fall in love with a serpent? It was his province as a setter of offside traps of unwonted slickness and cunning to jolt his contemporaries out of their conventional ruts and make them substitute adaptability and resource to rule of thumb; to force them to realise that the only antidote to subtlety and deceit was even more subtlety and deceit.

'In short, he made them think, and that has never been a popular mission. Crowds flocked to watch him, composed mainly of angry and prejudiced men, and few there were who had the patience to acknowledge the beauty of McCracken's technique in the abstract. All they saw was a player whose phenomenal mastery over a defensive mood could repeatedly disrupt and arrest a game, the smooth rhythmic ebb and flow of which was its greatest charm; matches in which McCracken appeared usually degenerated into dull repetitions of tiresome infringements and stoppages. Tempers frayed and angry scenes developed. On one occasion at Hyde Road [Manchester City's ground until 1923] McCracken teased and tormented the

Manchester City forward line to such purpose that the crowd felt obliged to intervene.

'Where McCracken outstripped all his rivals was in his ability to judge his opponent's intentions correctly, and to time his counter-strokes effectively. Until he retired no one arose who could match his superiority in that.'

McCracken's matchless defensive timing was most classically employed early in the second half of that third-round cup game against Blackburn in February 1910. Immediately after half-time, with United leading by just 2-1, Rovers came out fighting. McCracken was up against the Scottish flyer (and eventual international) Billy Aitkenhead. Aitkenhead was giving the entire Newcastle defence serious trouble until 'McCracken was now trying his offside tactics, and they worked against Aitkenhead, who was pulled up . . . play on the whole [was] confined to the centre of the field.'

And Blackburn were thus contained and the slender lead held without much difficulty, until Howie pounced to make it 3-1 . . . and all because Billy McCracken had the wit and the timing to take a step forward at the appropriate moment. He would do it for the remainder of his career.

Newcastle's luck with home draws held for the fourth round, when Second Division Leicester Fosse arrived and were duly despatched by 3-0 thanks to goals from the record signing left-winger George Wilson (£1,600 from Everton), Shepherd and Howie. Shepherd hit the post with a penalty in the last minute – and rather curiously ran in to attempt to net the rebound, but put it wide. Curiously because since 1892 a penalty kicker could only play the ball once without it striking another player. Football was in its infancy, however – Shepherd had been a boy in Lancashire in 1892, and perhaps his childhood habits died hard.

The semi-final opponents were even more lowly. Swindon Town were yet another Southern League team, who had never before reached this stage in the FA Cup. But they had done so in 1910 at the expense of stiffer opposition than had Newcastle – Swindon had seen off Burnley, Spurs and Manchester City.

Forty-five thousand fans packed into White Hart Lane for this game, and the Geordies in their midst had an anxious time of it. The game was goalless until the 65th minute, when a pivotal incident took place. Two Swindon players advanced unmarked on Lawrence's goal. The keeper came out to meet them – and the ball was sharply played to a third, Wheatcroft, in front of an open goal. Wheatcroft steadied himself to slide it home, but McCracken, hurtling across, shoulder-charged him just in time to upset his aim, and the ball went wide. Immediately it was played up to the other end, where Rutherford made it 1-0 . . . and 60 seconds later, Stewart sealed the win with a second.

So it was once more to Sydenham, once more to the Crystal Palace for the fourth time in six years, once more the crowds flooding south from Newcastle Central on the Friday evening before the game, once more the gathering outside the newspaper offices in the middle of town.

Once more the opponents were a middle-of-the-table Second Division side (the FA Cup was a democratic institution in those days) . . . and once more, things looked bad. After 37 minutes the Barnsley inside-left Tufnell gave them the lead with a swerving shot low into the corner of the net.

With fingernails being bitten to the quick, Newcastle pressed on the hard, bumpy, unsuitable surface for an equaliser. It came nine minutes from the end. A well-flighted free-kick from Higgins was met by Rutherford's head – and in Sydenham and the middle of Newcastle, scarves were waved and relieved roars split the sky.

The replay took place before 69,000 fans at Goodison Park, Liverpool, on the following Thursday. Away at last from the cursed Crystal Palace, Newcastle hit form. The surface was wet and slippery, but their control was masterly. Rutherford and Howie wreaked havoc, and six minutes into the second half Albert Shepherd ran through to score with a great shot. The same player sealed it at 2-0 shortly afterwards when he was brought down in the box, and scored the resultant penalty himself.

It was almost an anticlimax. Almost, but not quite. At last the

FA Cup returned to Tyneside, where eight horse-drawn landaus carried the team and officials through the streets behind a pipe band. It would surely not be the last time.

A certain mythology would spring up around this Newcastle United cup-winning side. Writing in 1944, the former amateur player and director of Bringhton and Hove Albion, Alec Whitcher, would say: 'In 1910, the season they won the cup, the Magpies' team was composed entirely of internationals . . . This must be unique in the history of soccer.'

In 1944 it would have been, were it strictly true. In fact Jimmy Lawrence and Wilf Low – the magnificent centre-half who had been signed in 1909 for just £800, and who would play for United for 15 years in 367 games – would not gain their first Scottish caps until the game against England a year later. The very comment, however, and its widespread acceptance, was as indicative as anything else of the awe in which the Edwardian Newcastle squad was held – to play for them, it was often repeated, was as great an honour as winning an international cap.

But this great team was coming to an end. It had time for one last fling. The 1910–11 season was clearly not going to be a good one in the league: United got off to a bad start and rarely got close to the top three. But having once won the cup, Newcastle were prepared to hold it.

Sadly, their great half-back and inside-forward lines were the first to disintegrate. Emblematic of this was the departure, early in December 1910, of the magnificent inside-forward Jim Howie. Signed at the start of the 1903–04 season from Bristol Rovers, Howie had been through all of the great days, putting in 235 appearances and netting 83 goals. He left for Huddersfield Town in the week that Newcastle – only just in the top half of the table – received the news that they would begin their defence of the FA Cup at home to Bury.

The following Saturday, while Howie was making his début in Yorkshire, Newcastle were well beaten in the league at Ewood Park by Blackburn Rovers, and the *Evening Mail* wondered 'when last a Newcastle United downfall could be attributed to the failure of the middle division.

'The great achievements of the Tynesiders in the past have been accomplished largely as a result of their stability here, and no part of the team has earned greater praise in both the club's successes and its failures. For many seasons past United have been wonderfully well endowed with half-back ability; they have so many good men that it has often been a source of difficulty to choose a line without giving offence to some of their players, and the slowing up of the older brigade never caused misgivings to the directors, so many good half-backs had they at call.'

Replacements were made. Wilf Low had already been bought, and another wonderful Newcastle career was underway. Equally notably, a full-back named Frank Hudspeth had been signed from North Shields Athletic, and made the first of his remarkable 472 appearances early in December 1910.

And they were good enough to hammer struggling First Division Bury in the first round of the cup 6-1 at St James's – and, by the end of January, to have joined the tail end of five teams chasing league leaders and reigning champions Aston Villa at the top of the table.

The second round of the cup went to a replay on Tyneside after a 1-1 draw against non-league Northampton Town. It was nerve-wracking stuff; only a first-half penalty from Shepherd after Town's right-back Brittain had handled saw United go through to face Second Division Hull City: a club composed mainly of amateurs.

Once again they were at home: Newcastle's extraordinary luck with the cup draw continued. Hull carried a large and vociferous support with them to St James's Park, and began their third-round game in determined form: centre-forward Tom Browell opening the scoring, but only after a handling offence which the referee had fortunately spotted.

It was virtually Browell's last gasp. McCracken took care of him after that. As the *Evening Mail* delicately put it: 'Like most visiting centre-forwards against Newcastle, Browell was freely piped offside. But Veitch opened the scoring for United with a soft long shot which crept in past Roughley; Joe Smith equalised but Shepherd regained the lead, and in the end United finished as 3-2 winners.

After that, it seemed easy. Derby County were dismissed 4-0 in the quarter-finals at St James's Park before a crowd of 63,000, an attendance record which would stand for 16 years, and Chelsea were knocked out of the semi-final at St Andrews, Birmingham, by 3-0. Almost unbelievably, Newcastle United were in their fifth FA Cup final in seven years. They would meet at Sydenham the footballers of Bradford City, who had never previously reached that ground, but who were, on 22 April 1911, three places above Newcastle in Division One.

Newcastle had the worst possible build-up to that final. At Ninian Park, Cardiff, on 7 March, Peter McWilliam was winning his eighth Scotland cap in a 2-2 draw with Wales, when the 29-year-old half-back from Inverness, who had been 'kidnapped' by Frank Watt back in 1902, and who was yet another essential member of the first great Newcastle team, suffered a serious ligament injury which not only put him out of the final but finished his playing career. Luckily, McWilliam was to be able to build a marvellous managerial reputation firstly at Tottenham and then at Middlesbrough.

And a week before the final, in a no-account end-of-season league game against Blackburn Rovers, Albert Shepherd was racing for a 50-50 ball with the Blackburn keeper Ashcroft, when Ashcroft grabbed Shepherd's leg and the free-scoring centre-forward wrenched the ligaments and tore the muscles behind his right knee. Shepherd was out of the final (he would not return for a year and a half, and never entirely regained his phenomenal form). Newcastle fielded against Bradford City their most inexperienced cup final team. Of the old boys, only Lawrence, Veitch, McCracken and Rutherford were left – Lawrence, Veitch and Rutherford having played in every one of the club's cup finals since 1905.

Collared by a member of the press shortly before the game, one of those survivors, Jack Rutherford, gave an insight into cup final preparations before the First World War. 'We had a fine run down from Saltburn on Friday,' said Rutherford (Saltburn being the team's favourite place of rest before important matches). 'We left about eleven o'clock, and picked up the officials at Darlington. We came on right along to London, and about seven o'clock sighted the Endsleigh Palace Hotel, where we put up. Then we had a nice time at the Lyceum with *The Prisoner of Zenda*, after which we all turned in for the night. We are all well – fit as fiddles, and spoiling for the game.'

For once, the fans' hopes were not ecstatically high before a cup final. It was ironic, not only because United were for the first time going to the Crystal Palace as holders, but also because Bradford City had muddled through to the final with three 1-0 wins and one 2-1 win against mediocre opposition, whereas United had scored 15 goals in their passage. But eight of those goals had come from the absent Shepherd (and another one from McWilliam). And everybody was aware of United's phobia of the pitch at Sydenham – 'Palaceitis', as it was dubbed. And the pessimists were proved right . . . 'FINAL TRAVESTY', headlined the *Evening Mail* the following Monday, after a dismal 0-0 draw at Crystal Palace in the 1911 final. 'Cup Game Unworthy of Two Great Elevens . . . Never have the Tynesiders failed so painfully to crown their midfield endeavours as in this instance. We have previously had the mortification of watching them fritter away opportunities to ultimately come with a goal; even the semblance of a repetition of such a desirable climax was missing in this Palace final, and it may with truth be repeated that had the team played for 90 hours they would never have got the ball ultimately into the netted haven with the clueless endeavour shown in this particular game.

'In the worst final for nigh-hand a decade Bradford's appearances in the limelight were scarce as green leaves in winter. The mission of the representatives of the House of York was apparently to defy the endeavours of the Tynesiders in the first half, and then go in and win in the second.'

This they almost did: only some desperate defending, particularly by McCracken, and judicious use of the offside trap by the same player, prevented Bradford from snatching a win.

As it was, they had to wait for the replay at Old Trafford on the following Wednesday. Fifty-eight thousand fans were crammed into the Manchester ground, with thousands more still queueing outside, when with 15 minutes gone there was a collision in the Newcastle penalty area. Bradford City's left-winger Thompson was apparently badly injured – there was blood spilt – but play continued. A high ball was lofted into the Newcastle penalty area; Jimmy Lawrence appeared to have it covered, but the City inside-right Jimmy Speirs followed it through. Lawrence, distracted either by the injured Thompson, or by Speirs, or by the swirling wind and unpredictable bounce, moved off his line – and missed it completely. Speirs seems to have given the ball a helpful nudge with his forehead; certainly the big centre-forward Frank O'Rourke was racing in; and the ball wound up in the back of the net. After some dispute, it was officially credited to Speirs, the City captain.

So the seventh cup final (including replays) in which Newcastle United had been involved in seven years between 1905 and 1911 ended in yet another defeat: 1-0 to Bradford City. 'In winning this match,' stated an FA report, 'Bradford must be regarded as particularly fortunate. The strong wind blowing was a spoiling factor in many promising movements, and the resolute, if unpolished, tactics of Bradford quite upset the plans of Newcastle, admittedly the most scientific team of the day. Scarcely ever did their forwards show a glimpse of the sound combined play for which they were famous.'

Five of those cup finals had taken place at the Crystal Palace ground at Sydenham, where Newcastle United, the club side packed with internationals, the greatest league side of the era, never won a cup final. The reasons were manifold. Newcastle's patient pressing game was certainly better suited to a long league campaign than the hurly-burly of the cup, although that rarely stopped them from reaching the final. Equally surely, the pitch at Sydenham was uneven and frequently hard, which did not suit United's 'scientific' passing moves.

But most of all, the club's players developed a phobia about Crystal Palace. They came to dread playing there. They cited all of those explanations at the time – making their excuses, as it were, in advance of losing. And there is no better way of guaranteeing defeat in football than to anticipate it. When the Football Association moved the cup final to another ground things would improve. But that, to the disappointed fans of 1905 to 1911, was in the unforseeable future.

The great Edwardian days were gone. United finished third in the league in 1912, but slipped down to 14th place the following year (when, humiliatingly, Sunderland won back the championship), and 11th in 1914. Andy McCombie became coach, with the assistance of Jack Carr. In January 1914 the extraordinary sum of £1250 was paid to Norwich City for a 32-year-old full-back named Willie Hampson. Those who carped about paying such a price for a pensioner were not to know that Willie Hampson would, ten years later, be picking up a cupwinner's medal at the age of 41!

A lad from South Shields called Tom Curry made his midfield début, and thereby started a career that was to end tragically on 6 February 1958 when a chartered BEA Elizabethan aircraft carrying the Manchester United team of which 'Tosher' Curry was by then trainer, crashed at Munich airport. Curry was among the 23 who died.

In the intervening years, many more had met a violent death. The 1914–15 season was just about to kick off when, on 4 August 1914, Great Britain declared war on Germany.

CHAPTER FOUR

A Cup, a League . . . and Hughie: 1915–30

❖

The 1914–1915 season was allowed to run its course, and Newcastle finished in 15th place in Division One. But when the war that was supposed to be over by Christmas 1914 dragged on into the summer of 1915, there was clearly to be no place for the peacetime recreation of professional soccer.

In August 1914 there were no fewer than 7,000 professional footballers in Britain, and jingoistic calls were made to enlist those fit, trained young men into the armed forces as a matter of priority. A Mr F.N. Charrington of Mile End in London tried to set up a 'Footballers' Battalion'. His idea was rejected by the Football Association, and so Mr Charrington went to the Fulham versus Clapton Orient match in September 1914 and attempted to address the crowd at half-time, before being forcibly ejected by the Craven Cottage officials.

Footballers were no more immune than anybody else, however, to the mobilising war fever of the day, and a good number joined up voluntarily. And by December 1914 the War Office bowed to Charrington's demands and formed its Footballer's Battalion. It was officially named the 17th Service Battalion of the Middlesex Regiment, its members while based in England were to be allowed Saturdays off to rejoin their clubs, and although it contained such soccer luminaries as Major Frank Buckley, the future manager of a great Wolverhampton

Wanderers team, no Newcastle United player joined this southern outfit.

They were more likely to be found in the Northumberland Fusiliers, with whom the young half-back Tommy Goodwill, who had scored seven goals in 60 games since his début in 1913, was killed in action in 1916. Five others died on the battlefield, a handful lost their lives in the post-war influenza epidemic, and several were maimed. And many more served their country, as they would do in the second conflict three decades later, in the essential industries of the North-east: the munitions factories, steelworks and coal pits.

The club itself was effectively suspended throughout the conflict. While almost every other major professional English club was able to put out makeshift sides in wartime leagues in London, the Midlands, the North-west, Yorkshire, and even the South-west (where Portsmouth, Bristol and Swindon tussled for supremacy, if not for trophies or money – the authorities insisted that no cups or medals should be given for wartime football, and no sportsmen's wages were paid throughout the conflict), there was no such competition in the North-east. St James's Park was commandeered as a military base, and there was effectively no senior football played in a Newcastle United shirt – nor in those of Sunderland and Middlesbrough – between the spring of 1915 and the autumn of 1919, when the Football League started up again.

(Although the pitch at St James's suffered some damage from the occupying military, this was nothing compared with the experience of neighbours Hartlepool United. Their Victoria Ground was hit by two bombs from a German Zeppelin on 27 November 1916. The wooden grandstand was destroyed, and after the war the club at first corresponded with, and then tried legal action against, the German authorities in an attempt to gain compensation. The only reply came with the outbreak of the Second World War in 1939, when Hartlepool was bombed once more. After that the club seemed to get the message, and wrote off its losses.)

Even allowing for the fact that most other clubs had suffered similar depredations, Newcastle picked themselves up well in 1919. Colin Veitch retired from playing and became coach, but a gratifying number of other old boys trickled back unharmed and ready to play again. There was the redoubtable Jimmy Lawrence, fit for another three seasons. There was Frank Hudspeth, Wilf Low and Bill Hibbert. And there, shaking hands with the Arsenal skipper before the first league game of the 1919–20 season – the first league game in four and a half years – with a knowing smile and a twinkle in his Irish eyes, was the 35-year-old offside king, Bill McCracken.

It was undoubtedly the presence of that wise and experienced back three, Lawrence, McCracken and Hudspeth, that kept United in the top half of the First Division in that first season back. McCracken had not forgotten his offside game, and there before him, like lambs to the cooking pot, was a whole generation of opposing forwards who had hardly heard of him or of his stonewalling tactic.

Although finishing eighth in season 1919–20, United scored only 44 goals. That was not only fewer than anybody else in the top half of the table (the champions, West Bromwich Albion, netted 104); it was also fewer than all but relegated Sheffield Wednesday in the bottom half of Division One – the other relegated team, Notts County, scored 56.

But Lawrence, McCracken and Hudspeth only conceded 39 goals in 42 games. It was an astonishingly small number for the time. Champions West Brom let in 47, second-placed Burnley 59, third-placed Chelsea 51 . . . Newcastle's defence had let in an average of 0.928 of a goal per game. This would not seem quite so extraordinary at the start of the 21st century, but in 1920 it was simply startling. United's defensive record had only been beaten once in the history of Division One, back in 1904, when Sheffield Wednesday let in an average of 0.823 of a goal per game. And Wednesday had won the title that year: no middle-ranking side had ever got close to such a shut-out rate. Unsurprisingly, the other clubs sat up and began to give the tactics of Newcastle United's full-back pairing careful attention. Equally unsurprisingly, so did the Football Association.

Newcastle's obvious immediate problem, however, was at the other end of the field. It was in an attempt to find a solution to their painful goalscoring difficulties that they made a signing which would influence the club for much of the rest of the century.

Stan Seymour was born in Kelloe, County Durham, in 1893. He worked as a joiner down the local pit, and in 1911 at the age of 18 he achieved every fan's dream – a trial at St James's Park. There then followed a story which would be repeated painfully many times over the decades to come. Only the names of the promising young North-eastern players change. It could be Bobby Charlton, or Bryan Robson, or Alan Shearer. Back in 1911 it had been Stan Seymour who was told he wasn't good enough: 'Sorry, son, come back when you've grown a few inches.'

Seymour, with a compensatory half-sovereign in his hand, promptly went to Bradford City (who had, we recall, just beaten Newcastle in the final of the FA Cup). In February 1913 he became that rare phenomenon: a Geordie who moved to play in Scotland; the traffic was more usually in the other direction. His seven years with Greenock Morton were impressive. Unlike England, a fairly normal league season was played throughout the First World War in Scotland, and for all of Seymour's time in Greenock, Morton never finished outside the top four of what was a highly competitive league (the moment he had gone they slipped dramatically down the table).

A goalscoring left-winger, Newcastle signed him in May 1920 for £2,000. He was then 27 years old, and few commented that they could have had him as a teenager for nothing. As the years wore on and Seymour's contribution compounded in a dozen different ways, it seemed increasingly irrelevant.

To assist Seymour United signed another Highland League player. Tommy 'Dirler' MacDonald actually came originally from the same club, Inverness Thistle, as had McCrombie and McWilliam, although United signed him from Glasgow Rangers. Initially a left-winger, Newcastle played him to great profit inside Seymour at inside-left. And yet another free-scoring centre-forward, Neil Harris, joined the club.

In 1920–21 the Goals For column showed a healthy increase to 66, and Newcastle finished fifth. The Football Association's eyes, however, were more firmly fixed upon the champions, Burnley, who were deploying a ruthless offside system and had conceded just 36 goals in their 42 games – thereby beating Newcastle's defensive record of the previosu year by letting in an average of 0.857 of a goal per game. In Division Two, meanwhile, almost-promoted Bristol City were boring everybody rigid and letting in just 29 goals – an awesome 0.690 of a goal per game. Clearly, McCracken's lesson was sinking in. Equally clearly, something would have to be done.

Back at St James's Park, by 1923, more signings had been made. The inside-forward Willie Cowan was bought from Dundee for £2,250; a local boy from Washington, Charlie Spencer, was brought in at centre-half; half-back Willie Gibson arrived from Ayr United, Bill Bradley came from Jarrow and the 38-year-old Sandy Mutch competed to replace Jimmy Lawrence between the posts. But the fans were getting restless. War or no war, it was 13 years since the club – once the greatest in England – had won a trophy. The league, that season, looked a possibility throughout the first four months – by January Newcastle were fifth in the table, just five points behind leaders Cardiff City, and were thrashing the likes of Nottingham Forest 4-0 (Harris 2, Cowan 2). But come the New Year of 1924, the FA Cup competition began once more.

It was a truly extraordinary campaign, even by United's standards. Drawn in the first round away at non-league Portsmouth, they were 2-0 down at half-time but fought back to win 4-2 thanks to goals from Harris, Gibson, Seymour and Jimmy Low. This team was firing on several cylinders.

Then came an astonishing second-round duel with Second Division Derby County. The first game was at the Baseball Ground before a record 27,873 crowd, and United seemed to have it sewn up by half-time. Tommy MacDonald had scored twice (the second a gentle header which somehow trickled through the keeper's legs), and Derby had missed a penalty after reserve full-back Russell handled on the goal-line. But

Derby stormed back in the second period to draw level, and with United's half-back Ted Mooney injured and hobbling about uselessly on the wing, County were in the end unlucky not to win. As it was, the tie went to a replay at St James's – where it also finished 2-2.

In those days long before penalty shoot-outs, the tie went to a third game at neutral Bolton, where it looked as if United were finished with Derby leading 2-1 into the dying minutes, when Stan Seymour smashed home an equaliser from 20 yards in the last seconds of extra time.

On the toss of a coin, it was decided that the fourth game should be at St James's Park. Here Neil Harris at last reigned supreme, collecting a hat-trick in United's 5-3 win: after 420 minutes, Newcastle were through to face Watford in the third round.

All this cup action played havoc with the club's league programme. By the time they travelled to Huddersfield Town seven first-team players were missing from United's line-up: they were beaten 1-0 and slipped back into eighth position – while Huddersfield moved ominously closer to the top.

On 23 February a ninth-minute volley from Seymour into the roof of the net saw Newcastle scrape past Watford of the Third Division (South), to progress to the fourth round of the FA Cup. There they faced First Division Liverpool at St James's, and a Dirler McDonald header put them through.

By now the league cause was virtually lost. On 15 March lowly West Bromwich Albion, themselves fighting to avoid relegation, visited Newcastle, went behind to a headed Harris goal, but equalised and snatched a valuable point thanks to a boy from Scotswood, 'Morepeth' Reed. Reed's goal lifted West Brom out of the danger zone – but it also established Newcastle, with just six league games to play, in ninth position, 12 points behind leaders Sunderland.

It was the cup or nothing. Manchester City waited in Birmingham in the semi-final. United approached this game with some confidence. Their mood improved further when the lawn at their Droitwich hotel was visited every morning before the semifinal by a black-and-white blackbird. When on the Saturday morning the blackbird failed to appear, consternation flew through the camp – and then all was well; the feathered mascot fluttered down on to the grass. Trainer MacPherson breathed again.

City were fielding the same brilliant Billy Meredith who had played against Newcastle 30 years earlier, in 1894. But his time was gone. Neil Harris crowned an excellent first half for the Geordies by scoring with an admittedly soft shot a minute before the break. And seven minutes into the second period United clinched the game with a strange goal. The City amateur goalkeeper J.R. Mitchell held a shot from Cowan, and was then tackled fiercely by McDonald. There was an undignified scramble, during which the referee penalised Mitchell for 'carrying' the ball, or retaining unfair possession.

(Goalkeepers did not have an easy life in the 1920s. United's keeper Sandy Mutch, who ended his working life as a groundsman at St James's Park, would in later life sit in the bar of the Strawberry Inn and reflect that 'Goalkeepers today seem to be scared of going after the ball – and they don't have to face forward lines full of big fellows like we used to. When I shouted "mine" to my backs everybody on the ground knew I wanted the ball. And this charging of goalkeepers! When I jumped I made sure I had my knees up – that stopped a lot of them from trying to bowl me over! The games was dirtier then . . .')

As a result of Mitchell's offence United were awarded an indirect free-kick inside the City box; Seymour chipped it across goal, and Harris headed it neatly home: 2-0. And an enormous roar went up from the United support in the 50,000 crowd when a scoreboard announced that their cup-final opponents would be Aston Villa, who had beaten Burnley 3-0 at Sheffield.

So an eighth cup final beckoned – with one crucial difference. The previous season the Football Association had unveiled their brand new showpiece ground: the Empire Stadium in Wembley. Newcastle no longer had to travel to Sydenham. The curse of Crystal Palace had been lifted.

If ever there was a game to exorcise ghosts, this 1924 cup final was it. Newcastle faced Aston Villa, their conquerors back in that first final of 1905. This time their respective league positions were reversed: Villa had finished three places above United in sixth position, and were strong favourites.

But this new generation was not in a mood to be denied. Significantly or not, centre-forward Neil Harris pocketed a 1901 good luck penny before the match. That penny was to see Wembley again. As if to make doubly sure, Newcastle resorted to their old trick of fielding weak sides in the league fixtures between the semi-final and the final. Although they actually won four of those seven games (while losing some of the others outrageously, such as 4-1 to Birmingham, and 1-0 to relegated Chelsea, which led even the local press to complain about 'reserve sides', 'poor form guides', and 'not the United we know') matters came to a head when they played their cup-final opponents in the league on the Monday afternoon before the final. Villa fielded their full squad, but United – who had already lost full-back Wilf Low, injured on the previous Saturday in that 1-0 defeat by Chelsea – put out just goalkeeper Mutch and left-half Willie Gibson of their intended cup-final team. The Football League took umbrage and Newcastle were fined a colossal £750. Ironically, Mutch managed to collide with Gibson in that Villa game, as if in illustration of the catastrophe that United were so anxious to avoid. The keeper was carried off on a stretcher, and five days later at Wembley Bill Bradley took his place.

Of all the players, it would be a particularly happy day for full-back Bill Hampson. No spring chicken when he was first signed back in 1914, Hampson knew that, if Newcastle were successful, he would become the oldest footballer ever to win an FA Cup medal. He was 41 years and eight months old.

By 1924 the Geordie cup final ritual was well established. There were those who travelled in their thousands. Among them many took the opportunity of this first Newcastle United cup final since the end of the First World War to visit the Cenotaph, and to lay upon that newly erected memorial to the war dead a posy, a nosegay, or a small wreath carefully picked from a

North-eastern garden and carried reverently to the capital. And there were those, also numbering thousands, who gathered outside the offices of the *Evening Chronicle* in Westgate Road, on the wet afternoon of 26 April. This time, they would not be disappointed.

'All through the first half and the early portion of the second,' the FA would report, 'Newcastle played second fiddle to the Villa, but in a thrilling last eight minutes, when extra time seemed certain to be played, they twice pierced the Aston defence.'

Villa were indeed the better team throughout the early stages, their 'fast-moving, every-man-in-his-place forward line' causing United endless difficulties. But the Newcastle defence held firm, and then, late in the second half, 'the Aston half-backs lost their grip of the Newcastle attack.'

There were just eight minutes to go – eight minutes of a game in which Newcastle, and particularly Bradley (who pulled off a series of double reaction saves with the slippery ball, and who was so badly hurt in a collision just before half-time that an ambulance was driven up behind his goal, only to be waved away as the keeper limped back into action) and Gibson, had had to perform miracles in defence – when centre-half Spencer set Seymour free down the left: Seymour's cross was met by McDonald; his first-time shot was palmed out by the Villa keeper Jackson, and Harris came crashing in to fire the ball low into the corner of the net. The centre-forward 'was almost pulled to pieces by his excited comrades'.

The roar of the 15,000 Geordies in the 91,000 Wembley crowd had hardly subsided when a long diagonal pass once more found Seymour. The winger met it at the corner of the penalty area, and released a thunderous half-volley which beat Jackson comfortably and hit the roof of the net just behind the crossbar.

Newcastle United had won their first Wembley cup final by 2-0. 'Newcastle,' it was reported, 'took very good care to give [Villa] no opportunity of recovering.'

The result was greeted in central Newcastle with loud cheers and waving of hats; the newsboys on Grainger Street were beseiged; and out in the suburbs, in the distant western and eastern outskirts of the city, where no telegraph or newspaper had yet penetrated, small crowds of men and boys gathered around the tramcar stops, asking outward bound passengers for the result and details of the game.

It was a brilliant victory, won in some kind of adversity against a side with an outstanding cup record and, on the day, a decided psychological advantage over Newcastle. It had also, unlike too many of its predecessors, been a marvellous game of football. 'Congratulations,' offered 'Hereward' in the *Sunday Sun*, 'to the players of both teams for serving up an exhibition of football the like of which has not been seen in a cup final so long as I can remember, and my recollection goes back many years, to those Crystal Palace days when Newcastle was the team of all the talents.' Plainly, by 1924, the great days of the 1900s were history.

The celebrations were long and deserved, as the FA Cup returned to Tyneside for only the second occasion in eight attempts. It was also United's first cup-final victory at the first time of trying.

At this point in history, Newcastle United's effect upon the course of the game becomes briefly more interesting than their own achievements. They finished seventh in 1922, and fourth in 1923 despite scoring only 45 goals in 42 games (they conceded just 37). But the whole of the rest of the league had picked up on the offside trap which Bill McCracken had introduced and used to such deadly effect for almost 20 years. Champions Liverpool conceded just 36 and 31 goals respectively in their two title-winning seasons of 1922 and 1923. In 1924 Herbert Chapman's Huddersfield (who pipped Cardiff City and Sunderland to the league post in Newcastle's cup-winning year) let in 33 – and then, in 1924–25, the same manager put out a side playing tactics which won the title and smashed all records by conceding just 28 goals, or 0.666 of a goal a game.

That was the straw which broke the FA's back. They had watched the number of goals scored in league matches diminish steadily since McCracken's heyday. Back in the pre-First World War days, when 38 games were played in a league season, fans could ordinarily expect to see between 1,100 and 1,200 goals a season, or roughly 3.00 goals a game.

In the first season after the war, the 42-game First Division saw 1,332 goals – or 2.88 goals a game. By 1921–22 that was down to 2.69 goals a game. And in the season of 1923–24, when Herbert Chapman won his first title with Huddersfield, an average of 2.47 goals were scored in each fixture. Games involving Chapman's champions Huddersfield featured an average of 2.21 goals.

The FA acted in the close season of 1925. And they acted drastically upon the offside rule, which had stood since 1866, intact except for its limitation to the attacking half of the field in 1907. With one stroke of a pen, on 15 June 1925, they reduced the number of opposition players required to be between an attacking footballer and the goal-line (within the defending half) from three to two – effectively, one goalkeeper and one defender. No longer could just one full-back step forward and put an opposition forward offside. And given the standing of the English FA within the fledgling world of international soccer, this adapted rule – which would remain with only minor modifications until the 21st century – soon became the rule followed across the entire world.

Nobody was in any doubt as to who was responsible for this measure. 'I believe,' the grand old man Alec Whitcher would write in 1944, 'McCracken of Newcastle was the leading artist in the exploitation of this offside game.' The former secretary of the Football Association and president of FIFA, Stanley Rous, wrote in 1979 of the 'intelligent interceptor and tactician' Billy McCracken that he 'became so adept at playing forwards offside that the law had eventually to be changed'.

Billy McCracken never had to play a professional match under the new rule. With his last act of typically wonderful timing, he had left Newcastle in February 1923 to become the manager of Hull City.

The effect upon football of this attempt to stop McCracken's tactics in their tracks was sensational. As that old Welsh international Don Davies put it: 'It appeared as though the earthly paradise had indeed arrived, for all, that is, except the poor goalkeepers'.

There were 2,260 goals scored in Divisions One and Two in season 1924–25, the last season before the change – an average of 2.44 goals a game. In the first season after the change, 3,190 goals were scored in the same number of games – an average of 3.45 goals a game. The fifth-placed team in Division One, Sheffield United, scored 102 league goals. Next season two Second Division sides broke the 100 barrier, including Middlesbrough who scored 122 in their 42 games. The number of draws was reduced by a fifth in Division One (from 254 to 208) and by more than a quarter in Division Two (260 to 192).

Seven league matches alone produced 64 goals in one afternoon! There was just one strange exception to this glut of goals at the start of the 1925–26 season. Down on Humberside, Second Division Hull City did not concede a single goal, even under the new offside law, in their first five matches. Hull City's manager was one William McCracken.

Other defences just could not cope, until Herbert Chapman, who had moved from Huddersfield to Arsenal on the very day the off-side rule was amended, developed a brand new concept. He simply moved the centre half-back from the centre of the midfield line to sit in between the two full-backs, creating a defensive line of three. The centre-half, who for the first 60 years of organised soccer had been a midfield player, became a defender – a 'stopper'.

Chapman is credited with bringing this revolutionary new defensive idea to perfection, but his contemporary Don Davies reckoned that others had attempted it at the same time. 'Actually,' said Davies 40 years later, 'the idea was tried out by Newcastle United at Villa Park as early as September 1925, and there is reason to believe that Andrew Cunningham of Glasgow Rangers was advocating its adoption even before that.' Andy Cunningham of Rangers would, as we shall see, soon be commencing an eventful career at St James's Park.

As a result of the new defensive centre-half, the 'third full-back', more forwards were played onside, of course – but at least there was an adequate stopper at the back to contain them. After this, throughout the 1930s, the haul of goals gradually diminished.

If Bill McCracken was not on the field any more to deal with the havoc that he had created, Newcastle United were soon to sign another footballer who would make merry hay with the new system.

Everybody wanted Hughie Gallacher. Born in 1903 in the Lanarkshire coalfield, a day's hike or less from the breeding-grounds of such as Alex James, Matt Busby, Bill Shankly and Jock Stein, Gallacher was a footballing prodigy. Standing just five foot three inches tall at the start of his career, he would never top five foot five. But he was quick, strong, brave, and aggressive, and had a shot and ball control to dream of.

Hughie Gallacher signed for Scottish First Division Airdrieonians from non-league Queen of the South in May 1921, at the age of 18. His effect on his new club was electric. Airdrie went from languishing in the bottom third of the division to Scottish League runners-up for four consecutive years, and cup-winners in 1924. In 137 games for them, Gallacher scored 116 goals. 'He was a fast, elusive, jinky player,' wrote the historian of Scottish football, John Rafferty, 'very difficult to dispossess as he shielded the ball and worked towards goal. Close to goal he was sharp in taking a chance with foot or head, and slick in the short, cool pass to make the chance for others. He scored in threes and fours for Airdrie and in one spell scored 30 goals in five matches.'

By December 1925, when the interest of southern clubs in this phenomenon was reaching fever pitch, little Hughie had been capped five times for Scotland, scoring five goals for his country in the process, and had twice represented the Scottish League, scoring six goals in those two games – five of them in one match.

Yes, everybody wanted Hughie. Newcastle United got him because he was seriously unhappy in Scotland (one of his sons had died before reaching 12 months of age, and Gallacher had

separated from his first wife), because of United's long relationship and reputation with their Caledonian cousins, because their
directors were willing and able to trek to and from the lowlands
of Scotland, cheefully taking rebuffs and braving demonstra-
tions from the outraged Airdrie fans (the directors made four
unrewarded visits before Gallacher himself stepped in and said
he wished to join Newcastle), and because they were prepared to
pay, on the spot, at least the officially reported club record
transfer fee of £6,500 (it could well have been more; it could
well have been a British record of more than £6,550, but £6,500
is the sum for which the cheque was made payable).

So, at the end of November 1925, the Gallacher era began, and
the true birth of the cult of the Newcastle United number 9 shirt.
There had, as we have seen, been great centre-forwards in the first
30 years of the club's history. There had been Jock Peddie with 78
goals in 135 appearances, Albert Shepherd with 92 in 123, and
Bill Appleyard with 87 in 145. Neil Harris, whose career was
coming to an end in 1925 and whom Gallacher was bought to
replace, was no slouch with 101 goals in 194 games.

Gallacher would outstrip them all, and not only statistically.
Wor Hughie was, in the Scottish vocabulary, thrawn; he had
attitude. He was also one of the most magnificent footballers of
all time. Frank Watt thought that Hughie Gallacher was not
only the greatest international player that he had seen, and the
greatest football individualist, but simply that – in Watt's words
shortly before he died – 'Gallacher is the greatest player the
game has ever known'. Watt, it should be recalled, was the
Newcastle secretary responsible for signing Peddie, Shepherd,
Appleyard and Harris, as well as Aitken and Veitch.

His legacy was an aura which hung around that number 9
shirt for the best part of a century, and seemed likely to stay
there for as long as Newcastle United existed. Very few clubs
have such a tradition, and none have it in such depth and quality
– the short history of the Queen's Park Rangers number 10, for
instance, which passed from Rodney Marsh to Stanley Bowles
to one or two fading talents in the 1980s and 1990s, is negligible
by comparison.

In truth, Newcastle United themselves would only rarely find somebody capable of filling Hughie's shirt. Jackie Milburn was a fine example of a suitable successor (and, as we shall see, Gallacher knew it). But all of the rest, from Stubbins to Macdonald, Keegan, Ferdinand and Shearer, however varied in real ability, were nonetheless uplifted and inspired by an awareness of the tradition, and of the great responsibility which it laid upon their shoulders. Those who could not carry that weight would quickly be found out.

There was no television in 1925, and very little Pathé News, and when Hughie Gallacher first ran out at St James's Park to play Everton on 12 December 1925 it was, for the vast majority of the crowd, their first view of the new star. They may have been told he was small, but they had no idea he was *that* small. 'The home fans cheered the first few players tremendously,' Gallacher remembered. 'As I ran out the deafening cheers turned to a . . . *oh!* Never had I been more aware of my size.'

The crowd soon forgot his lack of inches. The season had not started well – United were thumped 7-1 at home by Blackburn early in September – but Hughie turned things around. The Everton game finished as a 3-3 draw, with the legendary Dixie Dean grabbing all three of the Merseysiders' goals, but Hughie got two of Newcastle's and laid on the other.

The next four and a half seasons were Hughie Gallacher's. United were not short of other fine footballers. As well as Seymour, Hampson, Hudspeth, Gibson and MacDonald, they had signed the English international winger Tommy Urwin and the full-back Alf Maitland from recently relegated Middlesbrough. They had yet another Highlander, Roddy McKenzie from Inverness, at right-half, and in 1926, a few months after Gallacher's arrival, they paid Glasgow Rangers £3,000 for the genial and skilful inside-right Roddy McKay.

They were the stars in Hughie's firmament. Gallacher was the sun. Everybody else reflected his light. He shone off the park as much as on it – 'He strode regally round the Newcastle pubs,' recorded his compatriot John Rafferty, 'and accepted, as of right, the favours of the ladies of the town. He set out to be the best-dressed young man in the north with well-cut suits and he affected white spats and sometimes a white hat and often a rolled umbrella. He was a dandy, living hard but training hard. He surprised many with the seriousness with which he treated the game and the tools of his trade, his feet and legs.'

It is hardly Hughie Gallacher's fault that the fashions of his day mean that a later age, viewing photographs of him in fedora and double-breasted suit and ready to paint Gateshead red, is irresistibly reminded of some Chicago gangster chief at his casino. Gallacher was no gangster; he was a young professional footballer, possibly the best that Tyneside has seen. On a number of levels it is difficult not to see Hughie as the first of the great modern centre-forwards: stylish, determined to milk his celebrity for all that it could deliver, and capable of scoring a variety of goals from any position against any defence.

He arrived too late in the 1925–26 season to do much other than score an astonishing 25 goals in 22 games (including 23 goals in the 19 league matches remaining to him).

He made an instant impression. Just a month after that brilliant début against Everton, Newcastle played two home league games in two days, on 1 and 2 January. They lost the first 3-1 to Burnley. The second, against Bolton Wanderers, was Hughie's revenge on Lancashire. A 35,000 crowd peered, along with the mesmerised men of the press, through a thick fog as Gallacher performed like 'a phantom in the mist'. After three minutes he took a pass from McDonald, swivelled inside the box, and hit on the half-turn a left-foot drive high into the opposite corner of the net. Six minutes later he drifted onto a low through-ball and passed it carefully into goal. In the 25th minute he completed his hat-trick by seizing on a forward pass from inside-right Robert Clark, 'which Hughie took first time to volley the ball into the roof of the net at incredible speed before Pym could move a muscle,' commented the *Sunday Sun*. 'Goal-keepers deserve sympathy when they are beaten with shots like these.'

Gallacher's fourth came with 25 minutes to go (he got his foot first to a low cross from Urwin). Newcastle won 5-1. Urwin got the other: a brilliant effort which left Pym standing, but all of the talk was of the phenomenal Hughie. 'In six matches since he joined Newcastle,' the *Sunday Sun* reminded its readers, 'he has now found the net 11 times, but quite apart from his wonderful opportunism he is playing remarkably fine football. Full of little whimsicalities, which tickle the crowd no end, he yet knits the attack well together.'

He got two more the following week, in a 4-1 third-round cup defeat of the Welshmen from Aberdare. Gallacher scored the first in the fifth minute, bundling both the keeper and the ball over the line. Aberdare then recovered, and equalised shortly after half-time. Gallacher promptly restored United's lead by getting the deftest touch of his forehead to a 40-yard free-kick from Hudspeth. Gibson and Cowan wrapped the matter up.

He could do nothing, for once, at Homerton on 21 February 1926 when Newcastle were humiliatingly knocked out of the fifth round of the cup 2-0 by Second Division Clapton Orient. His lowly opponents put three huge defenders on Gallacher, with the result that he was allowed not one shot on goal, 'and on the few occasions that he did get the ball at his feet the merciless marking of the Orientals never gave him a chance to use it'. More worryingly, Gallacher's fellow forwards – Urwin, Cowan, McDonald and Seymour – failed to exploit the additional space they were given (although Tommy Urwin came closest from the right wing), and Newcastle were bombed out of the cup 2-0.

With his new team 14 points shy of the league leaders, Hughie Gallacher used the rest of his first season as a warm-up session. The goals continued to flow: two in a 4-0 hammering of Bury, the second one being a sensational run through the defence, pushing the ball to one side of the last defender and going the other, collecting it and placing it carefully to the diving goalkeeper's right.

In between league games, Gallacher's international career rolled on. He was the only Newcastle United player on the Old Trafford field on 17 April 1926 when Scotland beat England 1-0 (a far cry from 15 or 20 years earlier, when United had been the team of all the internationals). The result meant that England had not beaten Scotland since 1920, and nobody was in any doubt about the star of the occasion. Gallacher hit the bar with a header, and then laid on the winning goal with a devastating break down the wing followed by a low, fierce and accurate cross.

And in the last league game of the 1925–26 season he laid out his stall. With Newcastle comfortably but ingloriously marooned in mid-table, Manchester City – that year's beaten cup finalists – arrived at St James's needing just a point to escape relegation.

Almost everybody believed they would get that point. Most people considered that such a venerable club deserved the point. But they reckoned without the unsentimental Hughie Gallacher. Within 60 seconds he dashed into the box to meet a Seymour cross, and while the Manchester City defenders were wondering whether the ball was theirs to deal with or their goalkeeper's, Hughie settled the issue by burying it in the back of the net. City equalised before half-time, but immediately after the break Gallacher hauled his short frame above the visiting defence to head Newcastle once more into the lead. Fourteen minutes later another header completed the centre-forward's hat-trick and, despite a late consolation goal which made the final score 3-2, Manchester City were headed for the Second Division.

All of that prodigious, astonishing football had, however, won Hughie Gallacher and Newcastle not one trophy. Gallacher had still just one medal to show for all his seasons of brilliance: the Scottish Cup-winners award picked up with Airdrie in 1924.

But 1926–27 would be another story. With a whole season laid out in front of him, Gallacher took the English Division One by storm. Made captain of Newcastle United at the start of the season, replacing the veteran Frank Hudspeth, Wor Hughie started as he intended to continue – by bagging all of United's goals in a 4-0 home thrashing of Aston Villa. The fourth and last goal in particular was a typical piece of inspired Gallacher cheek. The Villa centre-half Mort was waiting on the by-line for a soft cross to land and be cleared. Before any of this could happen, Hughie nipped in and removed the ball. The angle being too tight for a shot, Gallacher then dribbled back into the middle of the penalty area, looked up, saw both full-backs and the keeper covering the goal, and placed it calmly past all of them into the net. The only thing he did wrong, that afternoon of 28 August 1926, was to lose the toss – and he sent a message to Newcastle's fans saying that he 'intends not only to take classes in that art, but to put in intensive practice in all his spare time'.

They loved him, of course. Who would not? And while it lasted, the players loved the fans and the grand old club. It was a fine life for Hughie and his comrades in that blessed season between the wars. On Monday mornings they reported for a hot salt-water bath and the treatment of knocks and injuries. And that, on Mondays, was that.

Tuesdays and Thursdays saw them report at about ten o'clock, put on two or three sweaters, and walk and jog for five road miles. Repairing to the gymnasium, they would take some athletic exercise of their choice – punch-balls were popular – and then eat dinner ('lunch' was a word unused on Tyneside in the 1920s). In the afternoon it would be two or three sprints on the cinder track, and perhaps a circuit of the pitch, before a final spell of physical jerks, punch-balls and skipping in the gym.

Wednesday mornings only (for Wednesday was early-closing day back then, and footballers as well as most of the other professional classes enjoyed the afternoon off) saw some ball practice. Wingers would practice corners; centre-forwards would take endless shots; goalkeepers would attempt to collect or save their efforts. Friday was an easy day. If the team were playing away nothing was done, as they might have to start travelling in the afternoon. If they were playing at home, there might be some light jogging in the morning, followed by massages.

On this training diet – a routine which, it might be noted, left plenty of time for enjoying the delights of Gateshead pub life, particularly if there was no weekday match – Gallacher and his colleagues assaulted the English league in 1926.

Following their sensational start, Newcastle slumped to two consecutive home defeats to Burnley and (with Gallacher absent injured) Bolton Wanderers. After three games they had just two points, and were fifth from bottom of the First Division.

The turnaround came on 11 September when Manchester United visited Tyneside. After 14 minutes Seymour sent in a cross from the left, and Gallacher stepped over it, letting it run to the better-placed Tom McDonald, who thumped it home. Manchester equalised from the penalty spot, but two minutes after the interval Gallacher raced through and drove for goal; Steward saved the shot but could only push it out as far as Seymour, who scored comfortably. Five minutes later Gallacher did precisely the same thing, only this time it was McDonald who profited from the rebound. Eleven minutes after that Hughie sealed the points and finally got his own name on the scoresheet when Urwin set Seymour free on the left; Seymour knocked the ball into the middle; and the little centre-forward side-footed it past Steward. Manchester got one back to make it 4-2, but Newcastle and Hughie Gallacher were on their way . . .

Sheffield United went down 2-0 thanks to a brace from Gallacher. Let the newspapers of the time describe what it felt like to watch this man, and this team, in their prime: 'Fourteen minutes after the resumption,' reported the *Sunday Sun* of 26 September 1926, 'Gallacher shot a gem of a goal. [Right-half Roddy] McKenzie made the chance for him with a sinuous run through, but when the half-back tapped the ball forward Gallacher still had an obstacle to overcome. A deft flick of the foot baffled [centre-half] King, and with [goalkeeper] Alderson racing out and both backs closing in, the Newcastle centre drove the ball hard and true into the net, a fraction of a second before he was clashed to the grass.'

No wonder the Gallowgate loved him.

Slowly, painstakingly, they crept up the table. Liverpool arrived, and a single, typical side-footed effort from Gallacher took the points. But, astonishingly, it was not until the 11th game of the season, in mid-October, that United gained their first away win, a 3-1 victory at Everton thanks to Robert Clark,

McDonald and Gallacher. Suddenly, Newcastle were sixth in the First Division, just three points behind the leaders Burnley, and with a game in hand.

Their run up to the end of the year was little short of brilliant. Blackburn Rovers were dismissed 6-1 in a match which took Newcastle into second position late in October, and in which, astonishingly, Gallacher failed to score. But Stan Seymour got three in succession: his first, the best, was a trademark volley from an Urwin cross which flashed inside Cope's post before the goalkeeper could move.

By 20 November St James's Park had recovered most of its old image as an impregnable fortress. In three home games United had scored 16 goals, taking maximum points. The latest was a 5-1 thrashing of Birmingham City. Gallacher scored, but once more his colleagues proved that they too were capable of finding the net. McKay and Urwin on the right flank were particularly impressive, and as the *Sunday Sun* commented: '[McKay's] dainty footwork often had an attendance of 31,000 roaring appreciation, and he found a ready acceptance every time he called upon his wing partner, Urwin, who maintains a consistent level of excellence which is unsurpassed. Welding together these two fine wings was a mercurial Gallacher, shooting from what appeared to be impossible positions with stinging force and accuracy and always weaving insidious passages goalwards, such as to reduce his opponents to the verge of despair.'

Newcastle were still only in third place – but they had two games in hand over Sunderland, who sat just two points ahead of them at the top of the league.

A week later, the difference was still the same. Sunderland beat Sheffield United 3-0, while another hat-trick from Gallacher helped Newcastle to a 3-1 win over Spurs. Meantime, second-placed Burnley were defeated at West Ham, so United leapfrogged them into second place.

And a week after that, on 4 December, United made it. While Sunderland crashed 4-2 at Derby County, Newcastle entertained West Ham United. A flick of Gallacher's head in the

21st minute despatched Seymour's cross to give them the lead, and ten minutes into the second half the roles were reversed: Gallacher beat three men before screwing the ball back to Seymour, who swept it home.

For the first time since 1909, Newcastle United were on top of Division One. It was only by virtue of goal average, but thanks largely to Hughie Gallacher the club's goal average was substantially better than that of Sunderland or of anybody else in the First Division, and they still had games in hand.

It was nonetheless a precariously early date to go top of the league. Could they sustain it?

No, in the short term, they could not.

They were promptly beaten 3-2 by The Wednesday in Sheffield – and the tightly fought skirmish at the top of the division meant that this single narrow defeat immediately dropped United into fourth position. Sunderland, Huddersfield and Burnley all won on the same day, and skipped gleefully over Newcastle. Gallacher was marked out of the Wednesday match, although in the dying seconds, while sandwiched between two defenders, he wriggled free and managed to slap an unsaveable shot against the crossbar.

With just five points separating the top seven sides it was clearly going to be hard work regaining the lead. United applied themselves to the job, hammering Cardiff City 5-0 in an exuberant display on Tyneside on Christmas Day, with a hattrick from inside-left McDonald and two goals from Gallacher.

On New Year's Day Leeds United came to town. In a first half which saw Newcastle dominate, Hudspeth had a penalty saved after Gallacher was felled in the box. But three minutes into the second half Hughie grabbed the winner with a typical strike. Right-half Roddy McKenzie swung the ball over to his fellow Highlander Tom McDonald, who pushed it forward for the tiny team captain to take possession and rattle his shot in off the underside of the bar before the goalkeeper could move. With Burnley losing at Everton and Sunderland going down 5-2 at Blackburn, United were at last on top of the table on points.

The FA Cup, that fickle mistress to Newcastle United, arrived again to taunt the club with a third-round tie at home to Second Division Notts County. This time, though, there were no hiccups. United won 8-1, thanks to a hat-trick apiece from Gallacher and McDonald.

On 29 January one of the oddest games in football took place. Newcastle were drawn in the fourth round of the cup against their old amateur opponents of 1907, Corinthians AFC. These high-minded representatives of pure, unsullied soccer had only deigned to enter the FA Cup four years earlier (they had previously scorned competitive tournaments for the same reasons that they had eschewed the penalty kick: they considered them corrupting and unworthy). For the rest of their existence they would look back upon that 1926–27 season, and particularly the game with Newcastle, as being a pinnacle in their history.

Corinthians were drawn at home, and chose to play the game at Crystal Palace in Sydenham. This choice of venue was surely simply convenient: it is impossible that such gentlemen as the Corinthians committee could have chosen Sydenham because Newcastle had lost five FA Cup finals there, and famously regarded it as a bogey ground.

For 76 minutes of the game, a bogey ground it was, though. In the first 15 minutes Corinthians ran their illustrious opponents ragged, and could have sewn up the tie if only their finishing had been better. As it was, in the 38th minute they did go 1-0 ahead when inside-left C.T. Ashton cracked the ball past United keeper Willie Wilson (who had been bought from Peebles).

The neutral spectators rubbed their eyes and wondered if they were really watching the leaders of the Football League against a bunch of public-school amateurs. Nothing that United tried could pierce the Corinthians defence, until 14 minutes from time, when McDonald hit a desperate free-kick from outside the box. It cannoned off the wall and spun past the wrong-footed Corinthians keeper to draw United level. Immediately afterwards Corinthians were reduced to ten men when their centre-forward Jenkins limped off, and suddenly all of their brave resistance collapsed. McDonald headed in a Seymour cross six minutes later, and McKay put the issue beyond doubt in the final minutes. The 3-1 scoreline did not, in the end, flatter Newcastle, but the hour and more of anxiety experienced in achieving it did nothing to ease their fear of that terrible Crystal Palace arena.

Back in the league, Newcastle were discovering that the leaders could expect treatment from their opponents which the Corinthians would have rejected with alarm. Derby arrived at St James's and proceeded to kick Gallacher almost senseless – twice he had to receive treatment, and twice he limped back into action. He was able nonetheless to give United a lead which McDonald and Urwin made into a 3-0 victory.

The day of 19 February was doubly black. Newcastle were drawn away in the fifth round of the cup at the Dell in Southampton. It was traditionally almost as unlucky a ground for them as Sydenham. On three previous occasions they had made the long haul south to the home of this middling Second Division side, and on each of the three they had hauled themselves back north disillusioned and defeated. They did not like the place – it was 'cramped, cabined and confined, where the wingmen almost tread on the toes of the spectators'. In other words, the Dell felt to the players of Newcastle United much as St James's Park felt to the footballers of virtually every other English side: it was foreign, hostile, and a long way from home.

And, once more, they were beaten there. Against the run of play, Southampton took the lead to the delight of their baying crowd. Tom McDonald, who had taken over the penalty kicks from Frank Hudspeth (it is a minor wonder that Hughie Gallacher never fancied penalties – one can only imagine what his goal tally might have been had he taken them) equalised from the penalty spot, but Rowley headed a late winner.

For good or for bad, United were once more out of the cup. That Saturday afternoon brought more discouraging news. Huddersfield, who had been shockingly knocked out of the third round of the cup by lowly Millwall, had taken advantage of Newcastle's absence from league duties to beat Leicester 4-2 and go to the top of Division One.

There was only one thing to do. A fortnight later Huddersfield had a Saturday off because their scheduled opponents were in the quarter-finals of the cup. Newcastle faced Everton at home. The score was just 2-1 in United's favour at half-time, but after the break they ran riot. Gallacher completed yet another hat-trick, and his three compatriots McKay, McDonald and McKenzie got one apiece, with Seymour adding the last to complete a 7-3 victory and put Newcastle back on top. They had, in 30 games, scored 74 league goals. So had fourth-placed Sunderland, but they had conceded 56 to United's 42.

After that they were never again knocked off the top. They went to Blackburn and won 2-1 thanks to a brace from Gallacher: the first of which involved dancing past a defender to the by-line and then beating the keeper at his near post from a seemingly impossible angle.

On 19 March Sunderland, who were still in with a chance of the title, visited St James's. A record crowd at the time of 67,211 crammed into the ground, breaking the previous official total of 63,000 for that cup quarter-final against Derby in 1911. The directors of Newcastle United had long since forgotten their concerns of just 30 years ago that the Tyneside public might not be willing to support a professional football club.

The game was won 1-0 by a single stroke of genius. In the 32nd minute Gallacher – who else? – received a ball from Jimmy Low on the right wing. Hughie deceived the defence with a quick wheel-and-turn, and shot instantly and accurately into the bottom left-hand corner of the net. The ball flicked the inside of the post and nestled there, and the crowd roared their love.

At Easter they played Huddersfield twice, and each game finished 1-0 for the home side, Gallacher providing Newcastle's winners.

There were hiccups. A visit to the Hawthorns resulted in a 4-2 defeat by West Bromwich Albion on the same day that Huddersfield beat Liverpool 1-0 to crawl once more to within a point of United. But with Gallacher absent on international duty on 2 April they beat Bury 3-1 – and it was as well they did, for Huddersfield also won that day.

They slipped up away at Birmingham, losing 2-0, but Huddersfield also lost – and although Sunderland took advantage by beating Arsenal 5-1 to slip into second place (and top Newcastle in the Goals For column), Sunderland had played two matches more and were not really in contention. This was proved on 16 April when Spurs visited Newcastle. United won a close encounter 3-2 thanks to Seymour (2) and Urwin, and on the same day Sunderland crashed 2-0 at Sheffield United and Huddersfield had an astonishing 4-4 draw with Derby. By the close of the day United were six points clear of Huddersfield with just four games to play, and Sunderland were back in third place.

'NEWCASTLE ALMOST CHAMPIONS' headlined the local press. A hard-won 1-1 draw at West Ham while Huddersfield were drawing 0-0 at home to Manchester United meant that Newcastle could not, with two games left, be overtaken on points – and their goal average was immensely superior.

They finally wrapped it up with a game in hand when The Wednesday from Sheffield arrived at St James's on 30 April. After half an hour Seymour crossed for Gallacher to score. Wednesday, whose England international keeper Brown was on brilliant form, held out and equalised immediately after half-time. But 15 minutes from the end Urwin flung in a cross from the right wing which Gallacher leapt to meet and bullet with his head past Brown. It finished 2-1. The players trooped off to the strains of 'The Conquering Heroes' from a brass band, and the Lord Mayor shook each hand as the players departed.

It was Newcastle United's fourth league title. Nobody could possibly have predicted, as that squad of star professionals accepted the applause of the biggest and most effective support in England, that it would also be the club's last league title for eight decades and counting.

They finished five points clear of Huddersfield, scoring 96 goals and conceding (in those post-McCracken days) 58. Third-placed Sunderland, blast 'em, scored 98 goals.

Above all, it had been Hughie Gallacher's season. He collected a breathtaking haul of 36 goals in 38 league matches. Others scored as well – Seymour picked up 18, McDonald 17, and McKay ten. But Gallacher's total of 36 (plus another three in as many cup games) set a Newcastle record which would stand for a further 67 years. (Although astonishingly it did not make him the division's out-and-out top scorer that season – Sunderland's Halliday and Wednesday's Trotter also netted 36. The 1920s, after the change in the offside rule, were truly a golden era for centre-forwards.)

Hughie was a hard man. He had to be to survive. His legs were a tapestry of scar tissue. 'He was a selfish wee fellow,' said another Scotland international, Bob McPhail, 'he thought of no one but himself . . . he had a vicious tongue and he used it on opponents. I learned swear words from Hughie I had never heard before.'

On the pitch it was no more than could be expected of a footballing genius struggling to raise the beautiful game to heights which defenders could not be expected to appreciate. (The famous old amateur international centre-forward Viv Woodward, who scored 29 goals in 25 appearances for England between 1903 and 1910, felt obliged to write to Gallacher in 1931 regretting that 'you are most unfair [sic] treated than any other man in the game, because you are clever and nobody knows what you are doing next, not even your own men . . . take my advice and don't take any notice of these so-called footballers who can't play the game under any conditions. Let them all go to——.')

Off the pitch, it was a different story. Virtually everybody sympathised with Gallacher when he swore at defenders, or fouled them back, or nursed resentments against insubstantial referees. But when he was arrested for fighting with his future brother-in-law under Newcastle's High Level Bridge, that was a different matter. The quasi-amateur traditionalists of British sport did not expect that kind of embarrassing behaviour from its supernovas.

And occasionally his feelings against referees could hardly be dismissed as mere resentment. The season 1927–28 did not begin well for the title-holders (through no fault of Gallacher's: he would still score 21 league goals in 32 games). On New

Year's Eve 1927 Huddersfield Town, the dominant side of the mid-1920s whom Newcastle had pipped to the post in 1926–27, entertained the Tynesiders in Yorkshire. Huddersfield were above United in the league, and it was clearly a grudge match, played on a hard, frosty ground.

Gallacher saw rather too much of that ground during the game and was sucked into a running acrimonious debate with the referee, Bert Fogg. After Fogg rejected a penalty claim, Hughie made an unfortunate – and obvious – pun upon his name, and was booked.

Perhaps we should listen here to Hughie's version of events, as recorded by him five years later. Before the match had started, he said: 'The referee, Mr A.E. Fogg, came out and chatted to us. He remarked on the hard, slippery ground and warned us that he would not allow heavy charging because of the treacherous surface.

' "That suits me," I said, and went on to play quite well and get two goals – Alex Jackson scoring the winning goal from a penalty given against us. [Huddersfield won the match 3-2.]

'But before Alex got his goal I had my little drama. Huddersfield had just equalised and a ball was sent through to me. Goodall and myself raced for the ball. I was dead set for position inches ahead, but certain of getting in my shot when the centre-half, who came into range, then came to assist Goodall.

'They sandwiched me, and I went down with a thud. I shouted for a penalty. No penalty was given. Almost within a minute of this incident I went down again, and in the same fashion.

'My claim for a penalty was again refused. Apart from the fact that I was captain of the team I thought my claim strong enough to justify protest.

' "Look here, referee," I said, "didn't you see that?"

'The referee turned away from me, and said curtly, "No penalty."

' "Everyone but you saw it," I said in disgust.

' "I'm reporting you," he said.

'. . . [After the game] I felt that I wanted to say something to the referee. Inside the pavilion I saw Mr Fogg. A crowd of people were discussing the match. "Fogg," I said furiously, "is your name, and you've been in a fog all day." '

Shortly afterwards Hughie decided – or was persuaded – to apologise. He ambled into the referee's changing-room to find Fogg bending over the steaming bath. It would have been a temptation to anybody; to Gallacher it was irresistible. He pushed the official in.

On 20 January the Football Association announced the suspension of Hughie Gallacher for two months. That accounted for most of the ten league matches which the Newcastle captain missed in the 1927–28 season. They could not afford to lose him. The club finished ninth.

At the close of the season he was stripped of the captaincy. It was given to Joe Harris, a left-half signed from Middlesbrough in 1925 who had only turned out nine times in the championship season. Gallacher was reprimanded by the board and told to concentrate on his football.

The remainder of the 1920s were not happy years for Newcastle United Football Club. A team was clearly dying on its feet. After United, still marooned in mid-table, had lost 7-2 at home to Burnley early in the 1928–29 season, an attempt was made to shore up the defence by buying Burnley's six-foot-two-inch centre-half Jack 'Ginger' Hill for a British record £8,100. Hill, a County Durham man by birth, was instantly made captain. Frank Hudspeth went off to Stockport County late in 1929 after 472 matches, taking with him Tom Curry.

The clearout had no immediate effect. United finished tenth in 1929. Gallacher scored 24 goals in 33 games, but his absence from those other nine league matches was not, this time, attributable to lengthy suspension. His drinking feats were notorious, and on many occasions it was reported that he would turn out on a Saturday afternoon only after a few pints, or not at all. Drinking before matches was not altogether unusual in the 1920s – even drinking at half-time was not unknown back then – but Hughie was not a man for half-measures of any kind. Not only the directors but most of Tyneside suspected that he was not the athlete that he might have been.

In the close season of 1929 Newcastle embarked on an ill-advised European tour to Italy, Czechoslovakia, Hungary and Austria. In Milan they faced the Ambrosiana club. Little Tommy Lang, the quick-tempered left-winger, quickly shaped up to the Italian right-half, who bit him on the neck. The Austrian referee promptly ordered Tommy off. Newcastle won, however, and left the field to – in Hughie Gallacher's words – 'the accompaniment of screams and threats of violence. Going back to our hotel we had to run the gauntlet through a teeming crowd of enraged Italians. Worse than that, after we got aboard our coach the crowd smashed the windows and bombarded us with stones and any kind of missile available. Jack Hill and another member of the party were hit. Even when we got to the airport the crowd beseiged the plane. We left Milan that night under escort, glad to get a rest from the Fascisti idea of football enthusiasm.'

Reading between the lines it is apparent that the Italian fury was provoked as much by an early – and unexpected – exhibition of robust British tackling of the gentle artisans of Ambrosiana, as by their native excitability and fondness for fascism. But things did not improve.

In Budapest United went down 4-1 to a Hungarian XI. Both Gallacher and full-back Alf Maitland were sent off, and after the match the Hungarian officials accused the Newcastle players of being drunk when they took the field. Their match fee was withheld, and the club flew quickly home.

An FA inquiry into the incident heard evidence from Maitland and Gallacher that their breath had smelt of alcohol during the Hungary match because it had been a 'boiling hot day', they had been thirsty, and had 'rinsed our mouths out with a drop of Scotch and water'. The FA accepted their explanation, exonerated the players, and United received their match fee.

Immediately after the tour, before the start of the 1929–30 season, Stan Seymour left the club in bitter circumstances. Seymour was 36 years old and had represented Newcastle – the club which had spurned him as a boy – for nine seasons, during which time he had done arguably more than any other player to help them win both the cup and league trophies which were their only successes of the decade.

He thought that he was due a testimonial. The rules of the game were that after five years' loyal service to one club a footballer was entitled to a £750 bonus payment (which Seymour had already received), and after ten years he was due a testimonial match.

Seymour considered that he was good enough for – and entitled to – the extra, tenth consecutive season which would bring him that valuable testimonial. The directors disagreed, and offered him only a free transfer. Seymour resigned in disgust and retired to his Newcastle sports outfitters and to local journalism. Shortly afterwards the sports outfitters ceased supplying Newcastle United FC. 'After that,' pledged Stan, 'I swore I'd never kick a ball again.' Nobody in 1929 could possibly have predicted the winger's long and eventful future at St James's Park.

And shortly before the 1929–30 season kicked off, Seymour's old henchman Hughie Gallacher requested a transfer. It was turned down, but the great days of Wor Hughie were plainly numbered.

That season was almost a disaster. Gallacher, as ever, did more than his fair share, getting 29 league goals in 39 games, and five cup goals in a run which saw United reach the quarter-finals by beating three Second Division teams, all of whom were drawn at St James's (although in the third round Newcastle had to take York City back to Bootham Crescent in a replay to finish them off). In that quarter-final they faced Hull City, who were not only in the Second Division, but were about to be relegated to the Third. Hull, who were still managed by Bill McCracken, drew 1-1 on Tyneside before 63,486 fans, and then defeated Newcastle 1-0 on Humberside.

In the league Newcastle's fortunes had gone from bad to worse until the very last game of the season, which saw them needing to beat West Ham to survive. Joe Devine, a desperate recent purchase from Burnley for the immense sum of £5,575, scored in the second half to ensure a 1-0 scoreline. Devine's goal proved priceless. On the same Saturday afternoon of 3 May 1930 Sheffield United and Burnley, who sat in the two places immediately below Newcastle, both won handsomely. Had United drawn their match against West Ham, they would have dropped two places and been relegated on goal average. As it was, they finished in 19th place, a single point clear of the bottom two. Devine played a total of 22 matches and scored 11 goals, which works out at roughly £250 a match and £500 a goal in 1930. But one of those goals alone was worth uncountable tens of thousands of pounds to Newcastle United.

That West Ham game was also Hughie Gallacher's last at St James's Park. Early in 1929 the club had signed the legendary Andy Cunningham from Glasgow Rangers. Cunningham, with 450 games for the Scottish champions under his belt and 12 Scottish caps, arrived at Newcastle at the grand old age of 38 years. A year later, after just 15 games, he considered himself too old for the inside-right position.

Luckily for Andy, the specialist post of football club manager, which had been created in its modern sense by Herbert Chapman at Huddersfield Town in the 1920s, was coming into vogue. In January 1930 the directors decided to swing along with the fashion. Andy Cunningham was made player-manager of Newcastle United, and then in May simply manager. He was the first man to hold that title.

And he did not get on with his old Scotland team-mate Hughie Gallacher. Hughie was, in his own interpretation, messed about. 'Once Cunningham arrived as boss,' the centre-forward would say, 'I knew my days were numbered at Newcastle United.' He signed a contract for the 1930–31 season, and then heard that he was being sold to Sunderland. The club denied this, and Hughie went to France with the Scotland squad. When he returned he learned that Newcastle had sold him to Chelsea for between £10,000 (which was just short of the British record) and a rumoured £12,000 (which would have broken the record).

The Hughie Gallacher era on Tyneside was over. It had been a privilege to watch him and, said most of his team-mates, a privilege to play with this tormented genius. 'We missed his goals,' said the reserve half-back George Mathison in one of the understatements of the decade, 'for quite a while.' In 174 games for Newcastle, he had scored 143 times. Statistically or in any other way, there would never be another Hughie.

A young schoolboy in Ashington would remember for the rest of his life the song that he and his six-year-old friends sang in that last winter and spring of 1929 and 1930. It went, recalled Jackie Milburn, something like:

Do you ken Hughie Gallacher the wee Scots lad,
The best centre-forward Newcastle ever had . . .

CHAPTER FIVE

ALMOST THE DEPRESSION YEARS: 1930–45

❖

There was an instant reprise of the Gallacher years, a timely and necessary and utterly remarkable farewell.

In the second game of the 1930–31 season Chelsea were due to play Newcastle at St James's Park. It was a Wednesday evening, 3 September 1930. As none of the fans had known for certain that that crucial West Ham game back in May was going to be Hughie's last game in a black-and-white shirt, the proper honours had not been done to the man.

The gate against Chelsea for that midweek, early season league match broke all records. It was 68,386, the biggest for a midweek game anywhere in England, and the standing Newcastle United home record. Thousands were locked out, and hundreds gathered on the grandstand roof. Gallacher failed to score, but the reception afforded to him was unique even in the astonishing history of Tyneside farewells. Fully 17 years later he would tell the journalist Arthur Appleton that the evening of 3 September 1930 was 'the most touching and memorable occasion of my football life'. It was a demonstration, said Appleton, 'which the little man could hardly believe had happened because of him.'

There was even a satisfactory scoreline: Newcastle won 1-0 thanks to a second-half header from winger Jackie Cape.

United won only another 14 league games that season, and

scored another 77 goals to finish in 17th place. The top three clubs, Arsenal, Aston Villa and Sheffield Wednesday, scored respectively 127, 128, and 102 in their 42 matches. (Chelsea only netted 64, of which Gallacher got 14.)

There had, of course, been further changes. Jackie Cape had been bought from Carlisle for £1,500 (enabling the Cumbrian club to complete a whole new grandstand). The newly capped England goalkeeper Albert McInroy was bought from Sunderland. Tommy Lang from Scotland settled in on the left wing, while that great old goal-maker Tommy Urwin moved to Sunderland, thus completing his personal hat-trick of North-eastern clubs, as he had arrived from Middlesbrough six years earlier.

With both Urwin and Seymour gone, Jimmy Boyd, who had arrived from Frank Watt's old club Edinburgh St Bernard's in 1925, was able to stake a claim on the right wing, which he did to such effect that he was finally capped for Scotland against Ireland in 1933. Dave Fairhurst, who came from Blyth but was signed from Walsall, began a career at left-back which would not finally end until 1946.

It was almost a complete clearout. The 30-year-old Jimmy Nelson from Cardiff City arrived to fill the right-back slot, at the astonishing cost – for an ageing full-back – of £7,000, just a third less than Gallacher's official asking price. Nelson would, however, quickly prove his worth in the biggest stadium of them all. Roddy McKenzie stuck in there at right-half, assisted by new arrivals David Davidson, who was signed from Liverpool as a full-back but quickly slotted into the new defensive centre-half role, and Sammy Weaver. Weaver was a particular bargain at £2,500 from Hull City. Tenacious and useful with the ball, this left-half would win three England caps, and be remembered especially on Tyneside for his prodigious throw-ins. Weaver could easily reach the penalty spot from a throw-in, and once, against Huddersfield, he sent a throw 48 yards – two-thirds the breadth of the pitch – over the heads of all the players and out into touch on the far side.

Then there were Joe and James Richardson. The first was a

defender, bought from Blyth Spartans. The second, Jimmy, was an inside-forward from the Ashington nursery. Initially Hughie Gallacher's sacred number 9 shirt was worn by his reserve Jonathon Wilkinson, but Wilkinson was quickly replaced by a bargain £3,500 purchase from Sheffield Wednesday, Jack Allen. Typically, Allen, who came from Newburn, had been spotted by Newcastle in the early 1920s playing for Prudhoe Castle Juniors. Equally typically, Leeds United were allowed to sign him, and he proceeded to make his name in Yorkshire as a swashbuckling centre-forward before eventually being persuaded back to the North-east. Another prodigal son who could once have been had for free, thereby returned at a price. Still, better late than never – although Allen, as we shall see, had to run a gauntlet of suspicion from the supporters, particularly after he missed a penalty in his first game and then struggled to find consistent form.

Add inside-forward Harry McMenemy from Strathclyde Juniors, and it becomes clear that Andy Cunningham was taking his managerial task extremely seriously. In creating his own team, he had by 1931 retained just one of the great old Gallacher squad. Perhaps he was just a little afraid of the fearsome Roddy McKenzie. Many others were.

Little good it did him. Cunningham's new side took an age to settle in. Middlesbrough inflicted a cruel 5-0 hammering at St James's, and Portsmouth, once that lowly whipping-boy, came all the way from the south coast to win 7-4.

The season 1931–32 did not begin on a happier note. On 31 October United travelled to Everton, and were crushed 8-1 by the champions-in-waiting. After that low point things looked up a little. Newcastle were steadily dragging themselves towards the middle of the table when, early in January 1932, they were drawn away at First Division Blackpool in the third round of the FA Cup.

Former player Colin Veitch, for one, did not give his old side much of a chance. United, he wrote a week before the match, 'will have no easy task at Blackpool, where, in league games last season and this, they have not struck a good game. I believe that part of the reason for this lies in an attempt to play the wrong type of game, pretty but not effective, on a ground which does its best to defeat ball control.'

Veitch may have been still haunted by his own cup disappointments at Crystal Palace, which were frequently attributed – not least by Veitch himself – to the bumpy surface. In the event, Newcastle ran out at Blackpool in determined fashion. Allen hit the post in the first minute. The home side came back into things, but after the break Tommy Lang gave the Magpies a one-goal lead by sidestepping two defenders, finding space on the edge of the box, and despatching a fine shot. Allen missed a good chance to settle the issue before Blackpool's Hampson equalised. Both sides were happy enough with the 1-1 draw – United in particular, as the replay at St James's was won 1-0 by a single goal from Jimmy Boyd in the second half.

In a league match at home to Grimsby later in the month, the Newcastle squad was tragically weakened when reserve centre-forward Joe Ford, who was being given his first chance to claim the striker's spot from Allen (who was attracting a good deal of stick from the fans and the press, and was generally agreed to be suffering from a crisis of confidence), was carried off with a double break of his left leg after just a few minutes of his début. Ford would never again play for Newcastle. When his injury had healed he was transferred to Partick Thistle, where his début match in January 1934 was assisted by a telegram from the Newcastle squad reading, simply, 'Good luck'.

In the short term, it seemed, the club was stuck with Jack Allen. He was no Hughie Gallacher but he would not, in the ultimate arena, let the club down.

The fourth-round ties with Southport were among the most curious in FA Cup history. Once more Newcastle were lucky enough to draw a lower-division side at home (Southport were in the Third Division (North)). And once more they almost blew it. It was a week after Ford's injury, and Allen returned for the home tie – and proceeded to squander a number of chances after Boyd had given United the lead after just 30 seconds. Those misses from the centre-forward – as well as his dubious lay-offs and frustrating tendency to rush with the ball into an unbeatable ruck of defenders – almost proved extremely costly, as Southport equalised to force a replay on the following Tuesday.

That also ended a 1-1 draw, and so the tie went to a third game at Hillsborough. Jack Allen was dropped, and this time no mistakes were made. Although the score stayed at 0-0 for the first 30 minutes, Newcastle crashed in four goals in the quarter-of-an-hour before half-time, and another five after the break to complete the rout at an astonishing 9-0. Jackie Cape, in at centre-forward, got two, while inside-forward Jimmy Richardson picked up a hat-trick. It is still Newcastle United's record score in the FA Cup, and was at the time the biggest winning margin in the competition's history.

By the middle of February the club's league chances were virtually written off, and all eyes were on the FA Cup draw. The fifth round took Leicester City to St James's. Forty-three thousand turned out to see United win 3-1 over their struggling First Division opponents. With the wind at their backs United dominated the early stages, but Leicester took the lead before Sammy Weaver, who was generally agreed to be the man of the match, equalised with a low drive through a crowd of players from outside the box, and Lang put Newcastle ahead just before the break.

The beleaguered Allen, who had been reinstated, did his cause some good with a third goal in the second period, albeit a messy, scrambled effort which the critical watching eyes of Colin Veitch saw as 'fortunate'.

Fortunate or not, United were through to the quarter-finals of the FA Cup once more. And, once more, they were drawn at home, this time to Watford of the Third Division (South).

In the week before that match, on 27 February 1932, Frank Watt died. He was 77 years old, and had as long ago as 1921 been presented by the Lord Mayor of Newcastle with a watch and a cheque subscribed by friends all over Britain to mark 25 years of service to the club. By 1932 he had slipped into the sidelines, leaving his son – also Frank – to take over the secretaryship. (His old trainer, James McPherson, had also been replaced by James McPherson Junior.) He was recognised throughout the footballing world as being the rock upon which Newcastle United's three generations of top teams had been built. 'Our first duty this week,' wrote two of his former players, Stan Seymour and Colin Veitch, in the *Sunday Sun*, 'is to pay homage and tribute to the late Frank Watt, Newcastle United's respected secretary for more than 36 years, revered by all and without an enemy anywhere. The football world and his many personal friends are considerably poorer by the loss of one of nature's gentlemen. It is no exaggeration to state that the great edifice known as Newcastle United was built around Frank Watt – and, largely, by him.'

The crowd of 57,879 (who, Frank Watt would have been gratified to learn, paid a season's record of £3,846 10s 3d to enter the ground) stood for two minutes' silence at the start of the game. The players of both sides wore black armbands, and the managers of each team, Andy Cunningham and Neil McBain, lined up with the officials in the centre circle to observe the memorial tribute.

Then the game kicked off, and Newcastle honoured Frank Watt in the best way possible by winning 5-0. Jack Allen, who used the occasion to silence his critics, got the first by following up on a Boyd header. The centre-forward then hit the bar, and shortly afterwards made it two with a strong drive. Jimmy Richardson got the third before half-time; and Allen completed his hat-trick after the break with a wonderful goal: beating the Watford defenders to a McMenemy through ball, and strolling round the keeper to walk it into the net.

Boyd got the fifth, but it had been undeniably Jack Allen's match. Even Colin Veitch was moved to agree that 'Allen has suffered so many disappointments this season, despite incessantly trying to recover confidence, that he must have been a particularly happy individual after the match, as he was during the game. United's centre substituted "Have a go!" for his former "Have a care!" with the result that he came into greater confidence.'

The draw for the semi-final was poignant indeed. Newcastle

United were scheduled to travel to the neutral ground of Huddersfield Town to play Chelsea . . . whose forward line was still led by one Hughie Gallacher.

The augurs were not good. The Saturday before the Chelsea tie United travelled to Maine Road to play in the league another of the semi-finalists, Manchester City. The result was a 5-1 massacre: City tore United apart on a slippery surface, and only McInroy saved the score from being even worse.

As it turned out, seven days later it was City who went out and Newcastle who went on to Wembley. While fancied City crashed to an 89th-minute goal from Arsenal's Cliff Bastin, Newcastle scored twice in the first 26 minutes of their match. Gallacher was constantly threatening, but it was his much-criticised replacement in a black-and-white shirt, Jack Allen, who broke the deadlock when a corner was headed straight out to his feet, and he drove it back into the net. Boyd laid on the second with a far-post cross for Lang to head home. Ten minutes later Gallacher did pull one back for Chelsea – his sixth in five cup games for the club that year – with a typical burst past centre-half Davidson to intercept a poor backpass from McKenzie and flick the ball over the onrushing McInroy. But after that Davidson rarely let Gallacher off his leash; Sammy Weaver was inspired and Newcastle delivered their performance of the season to take them into their second Wembley cup final, and their seventh in all (ninth, including replays). Allen was even allowed the luxury of missing another good chance towards the end as Chelsea faltered, and McMenemy headed a cross against the bar in the last minute.

'Well,' said Gallacher after the final whistle, 'Newcastle are through and good luck to them. I thought we were going to pull through in the middle of the second half, after Newcastle had had the best of the first half. But it was not to be, and that is the long and the short of it.' The little striker had never been before, and would never be again, so close to an FA Cup final. He took his revenge on his old club by getting a hat-trick in a 4-1 hammering of Newcastle in a league match at Stamford Bridge towards the end of the season.

Not that Tyneside cared by then. Ten thousand Geordies turned up at Wembley on 23 April 1932, and it was not just to celebrate goalkeeper Albert McInroy's birthday. The tube stations were observed to be full of boisterous North-easterners buying penny tickets for journeys that they never made – they amused themselves by riding up and down the unfamiliar escalators. Then, buoyed up by the news that the great Alex James would be missing from the Arsenal line-up due to injury, they made tracks for Wembley Way.

Jack Allen pocketed the old 1901 penny which had brought centre-forward Neil Harris such luck in 1924. It turned out to have magical properties – one of the most entertaining and controversial FA Cup finals was duly won 2-1 by Newcastle United, and Allen himself, who was carrying a knee injury, would never again experience such a blissful afternoon in the Newcastle number 9 shirt.

After the players had shaken hands with King George V (who had been briefed that Jimmy Nelson had suffered injury in the previous season, 'and expressed the hope that the Newcastle captain's leg would be equal to the task') they kicked off. With Queen Mary peering fiercely through a lorgnette from the Royal Box, and with those Newcastle supporters making, it was generally agreed, more good-humoured noise than any previous cup-final support, it was nonetheless Arsenal who made the better start and took the lead after 15 minutes when Hulme looped a cross in from the right wing. McInroy came out for it, but mistimed his approach and flapped vainly at the ball before it reached the head of John, who nodded it down into an open goal at the far post.

As it bounced home the Arsenal left-winger raised his arms as much in surprise as joy. No team, it was constantly repeated, had ever lost the FA Cup at Wembley after taking the lead. No team had ever won it after going behind.

But Newcastle did. After 38 minutes they drew level with one of the most controversial goals in cup history. Jimmy Richardson chased an apparently lost cause to the right-hand by-line. He slid in to rescue the ball and scoop it back from the edge of the penalty area to the edge of the six-yard box. Newsreel and newspaper photographs later proved that the ball had gone out of play – but that bothered neither Richardson nor Jack Allen, who was racing in surrounded by three desperate Arsenal defenders. The defenders hit the ground in vain attempts to block the ball or slide-tackle Allen, but the centre-forward got there first and smacked a shot into the roof of the net.

Referee W.P. 'Percy' Harper instantly blew for a goal and pointed to the centre spot. The Arsenal goalkeeper Moss was on his feet and charging towards the official almost before Allen could claim his goal, but Harper stood firm. 'I gave my decision,' said Harper in his changing-room after the match, 'according to the rules and regulations.'

'You felt no doubt at the time,' asked a journalist, 'that it was a goal?'

'No,' he replied succinctly, 'otherwise I should not have given it.'

Newcastle were suddenly on the ascendency. Immediately before and immediately after half-time, Moss had to save brilliantly from two Boyd headers; Allen hit a left-foot drive just wide; and then in the 71st minute Jimmy Boyd turned the ball inside to Allen.

The striker received the ball ten yards outside the penalty box, and with the fans and the Arsenal defence alike expecting a trademark headlong dash for goal, he wrong-footed two defenders, turned inside, entered the box through the inside-left channel and, from 15 yards out, placed a low shot to the left of Moss's despairing dive.

After the cheering, which 'lasted for several minutes', had died down, 'Blaydon Races' rang out from the sea of black and white on the Wembley terraces for all of the remaining 19 minutes. 'Black-and-white megaphones and rattles danced for joy,' reported the *Sunday Sun* . . . 'An ageing supporter turned his back on the players and led the singing of an impromptu Tyneside choir. What they sang no one knows – and no one cared.'

Ten minutes before time Jack Allen's bad knee required attention and he limped off the field. With Weaver and Davidson holding the defence together magnificently, Nelson battling on heroically despite his own dodgy knee, and Dave Fairhurst, who played with a swollen throat thanks to a debilitating virus, solid as a rock in front of the confident McInroy, Newcastle never looked likely to allow Arsenal a way back in – indeed, Jimmy Boyd found time to hit the post.

Nonetheless, when Allen hobbled back on for the last five minutes the cheer 'was as terrific as if he had done the hat-trick'. The centre-forward from Newburn, so dubious a choice just three months earlier, was suddenly a local hero. There already is a monument to (captain) Nelson here, the Geordie support which gathered later in Trafalgar Square would jokingly insist – what about one now for Jack Allen?

The final whistle blew with Newcastle still 2-1 ahead. As it sounded a hush descended upon the ground, as if the fans could hardly believe it, and then the roar of success rent the air. Everything about that sunny afternoon pointed to one thing: after all of the cup disappointments of the Edwardian period, Newcastle United and its fans had discovered a new destiny. It was to win the FA Cup at Wembley. The Sydenham jinx was finally dead and buried.

Jimmy Nelson collected the cup from Queen Mary, and, chaired back by his team-mates onto the field, clutching the trophy like a lover, told a newsreel camera in his strong Scots accent: 'We're very happy to have won the cup. Every man in Newcastle has done his duty.'

Nelson, with another uncanny subconscious allusion to his seafaring namesake's message that 'England Expects That Every Man Will Do His Duty', was referring specifically to the players, to the stirring team performance. He could just as fittingly have intended the statement as it reads – as a tribute to the community which swept those players to success. Those of that community who had made it to Wembley wandered off to paint Piccadilly black and white, and buy opportunistically printed postcards depicting the grave of Arsenal Football Club. The cards pre-printed with the grave of Newcastle United would never be put on sale in the streets of London. By the late 1990s they were thankfully out of fashion.

Newcastle United FC made £8,229 from the receipts of the final alone. Over the season they ran up a profit of more than £20,000. The 11 cup-winning footballers were given a bonus of £8. The Arsenal manager Herbert Chapman presented each of his losing finalists with a copy of the match programme.

A famous father expressed his joy. 'The best side won,' said former trainer James Q. McPherson, 'and if Jack Allen had stood up the result would have been more decisive. It was my seventh final altogether, and the team won twice in my time. Now it is my son's turn.'

Secretary Frank G. Watt, whose own father was surely smiling down from above, remarked that he was 'proud indeed' to be connected with United 'in another year of victory for the old club'.

And manager Andy Cunningham was almost speechless with delight. 'This is the greatest night of my life,' he said before sitting down with 400 others at a dinner for both teams generously hosted by Arsenal Football Club at the Café Royal. 'We have the most wonderful set of boys in the world – both on the field and off it. I am proud of them. Even when there was a goal against us I never had the slightest qualms about the result.'

Cunningham did well to bask in his hours of glory, on that Saturday evening and on the following Monday when the team paraded triumphantly through the streets of Newcastle to the Empire Theatre. He would not have any more like them.

The depression which had already descended upon industrial Britain in the 1930s, and which was to blight the North-east of England more than any other region, was strangely reflected in the fortunes of Newcastle United. The 1932 cup victory proved to be the giddy high before a long and bitter low.

It did not fall immediately upon the club. The holders were summarily dismissed from the FA Cup in the third round in January 1933, losing 3-0 at home to Leeds United. But their league form, riding on the back of the Wembley euphoria, was vastly improved. They finished in fifth place, nine points behind the champions – Herbert Chapman's Arsenal, in the first of their three successive titles.

But in the following season disaster struck. It crept up on them slowly. A start to the season which was nothing worse than mediocre saw United sitting calmly in the middle of the table at New Year, with half the fixtures played. They beat Everton 7-3 on Boxing Day, and on New Year's Day they murdered Liverpool 9-2 in Newcastle.

On 6 January 1934 Leeds United visited St James's Park. The interest in this fixture was partly connected with the two Leeds full-backs, Jack and George Milburn, both of whom were from Ashington, and one of whose cousins, the young Jackie, was still playing schoolboy soccer back in Northumberland. 'The Milburn lads,' reported the *Sunday Sun*, 'can hit hard – man and (or) ball. And they do. They played a strong game in defence. They usually do so.'

But not strongly enough to prevent Sammy Weaver and new centre-forward Ronnie Williams from delivering a 2-0 win which sent Leeds further down the table into a dangerous 15th place, and lifted Newcastle into the apparently harmless 12th spot, seven points clear of the relegation zone and seemingly secure.

Appearances are deceptive. It would not be Everton, Liverpool or Leeds United, Milburn brothers and all, who would finish in the bottom two of the First Division table.

By March, with ten games to go, Newcastle's position still did not look perilous. Even when they crashed to a 4-0 defeat at lowly Sheffield United in an 'inglorious performance' where the Tynesiders looked laborious – 'so laborious, in fact, that there were periods when one wondered if they were moving at all' – they were still five places clear of danger.

But the omens were there. Sheffield United were in desperate trouble themselves, and would in fact finish the season relegated in bottom place, but with just nine games to go they made Newcastle look like amateurs, if that was not a slur on such courageous, fighting amateurs as Corinthians AFC. Newcastle were a team on the slide.

Andy Cunningham bought urgently, which is no way to buy. A six-foot-two-inch, 14-stone Scotland international half-back called Bill Imrie was bought for £6,500 from Blackburn Rovers. A week after the Sheffield débâcle they were thrashed 3-1 at home by Spurs, and only Imrie's penalty kick gave the scoreline an element of respectability.

Long-term reserves such as Bob Dennison were called up and given a rare outing in the first team – and Dennison's headed goal did deliver a badly needed point at home to Villa early in April. But by then United were only one point clear of relegation, with just three games to play.

Seven days after that, they travelled to Huddersfield. It was the repeat of an old rivalry, but one in which, traditionally, both sides were battling at the top of the league. On 14 April 1934 Huddersfield were still chasing the title, but United were at the other end of the table. Nobody gave them much hope, and they were right. In desperation, Cunningham blooded several youngsters, and they could not cope – the young keeper McPhillips lost his confidence before a Huddersfield onslaught, Alec Betton at centre-half was reduced to covering for his goalkeeper's inadequacies, and United were routed 4-1. Only the experienced Jimmy Boyd in the forward line caused Huddersfield any anxiety, and the single consolation goal was netted by Ronnie Williams when Huddersfield were 4-0 ahead.

For Andy Cunningham, the manager who as a player at Rangers had been credited with such far-seeing defensive innovations as the 'stopper' centre-half, it was truly humiliating. His mood cannot have been helped by the fact that on the same day, Chelsea's Hughie Gallacher – the genius whom Cunningham had edged out of St James's Park – was inspiring the Scottish attack against England at Wembley . . .

And then came a ray of hope. In the penultimate match Wolverhampton Wanderers visited St James's Park. Wolves had nothing to play for; they were anchored in mid-table. United had, by 21 April, gone 12 consecutive matches without a win.

The thirteenth proved lucky. Big Bill Imrie, red hair ablaze, ran riot. After Ronnie Williams had given United the lead in the 20th minute, Imrie smacked home a direct free-kick five minutes later. Jimmy Richardson made it three before the 26,000 crowd had time to settle, and then Imrie charged upfield once more, played a wall pass with Boyd, and ran on to make it 4-0. David Davidson, playing at centre-half, unfortunately put through his own-goal to make it 4-1 before half-time, but Imrie converted a penalty in the 59th minute to complete a 5-1 victory.

Suddenly, the talk was of goal-average saving United from the drop. On the evening of 21 April 1934 the bottom of the Division One table looked like this:

	P	W	D	L	F	A	Pts
Birmingham	40	11	12	17	46	50	34
Newcastle Utd	41	10	14	17	67	75	34
Chelsea	39	13	7	19	62	64	33
Sheffield Utd	40	11	7	22	56	99	29

With Sheffield United already doomed, and Chelsea with three games still to play – two of them at home – it was commonly agreed that Birmingham were most at risk if Newcastle won their remaining fixture away at Stoke City. Birmingham had to face Huddersfield, who were still in with a distant chance of the title, and Leicester City. If the two (or three) clubs finished level on points, goal average would be totalled. Goal average was the sum of the goals scored divided by the goals conceded. Chelsea had the best of the three, with a goal average of 0.96. But Birmingham's of 0.92 was only 0.03 better than Newcastle's 0.89. Two goals either way would tip the balance in United's favour . . .

So did football fans, then as now, feverishly calculate their chances. It was all to no avail. On Saturday, 28 April 1934, while Manchester City were winning a rousing cup final at Wembley, Chelsea – who had defeated Leicester at Stamford Bridge on the previous Monday – drew 2-2 with Arsenal to pull themselves to safety. Birmingham went to Leicester and slaughtered the opposition 7-3, thus settling the issue both on points and goal average.

Neither of them needed to worry. Newcastle United concluded their season with a pathetic performance at Stoke. After nine minutes they gifted Stoke a goal when a Boyd backpass was intercepted by Stoke's left-winger Johnson, who lobbed the ball towards goal. Poor McPhillips attempted to turn it over; it hit the bar and bounced back for centre-forward Sale to score. Sale then hit the post, and it was against the run of play that United equalised in the 39th minute when left-half Jimmy Murray, whom Cunningham had signed from Glasgow Rangers, thumped home a 20-yard drive.

But this Newcastle forward line was poor. Despite sterling efforts from the defence, which held out until 12 minutes from time, the United forwards could make no impression on the game: they were unable even to hold the ball up, let alone find the net. It was almost a relief, like putting down a panicked animal, when McPhillips could only deflect a shot to the feet of the Stoke City right-winger, a 19-year-old called Stanley Matthews, who made it 2-1 from close range.

So the young Stanley Matthews sent Newcastle United into Division Two for the first time since 1898? Not quite – as we have seen, Birmingham and Chelsea had already taken care of themselves. 'That they were not beaten,' wrote Colin Veitch of the Stoke City match, 'by an even greater margin was cause for gratification under the circumstances. Nothing in their second half at Stoke was more indicative of the fact that they deserved to go down than that last 45 minutes of inept forward work.'

The road to Division Two had been taken since February. In their last 14 league games Newcastle won once, drew five times and lost eight. For the first time in 36 years of glory, 36 years of cup finals, cup victories, and league titles, the football club with the best record and the best support in the English Football Association was to be relegated.

'Candidly,' wrote the editor of the *Sunday Sun* in a lead article the next day, 'we do not think that the club did enough to try and stave off this failure. For the past few months we believe the "writing on the wall" has been there for the club and all the world to see, yet not sufficient action was taken to erase those warning signs. The proof of this is in yesterday's defeat . . . The whole North-east looks to all concerned for the quick restoration of its lost prestige.'

They would look in vain. Cunningham bought Tony Leach, a 31-year-old centre-half, from Sheffield Wednesday, while a 19-year-old ex-England schoolboy international centre-forward named Jack Smith from Huddersfield Town came in to replace Ronnie Williams. Smith would turn out to be a superb goals-corer, collecting 73 in his 112 games, but United had a dismal introduction to Division Two in the 1934–35 season, losing 5-1 to Nottingham Forest, 4-1 to Blackpool, and 5-2 at home to Brentford, who had only just come up from the Third Division (South).

A young forward called Tommy Pearson arrived from Murrayfield Amateurs in Scotland, and the Toon experienced something of a revival, climbing to finish in sixth position.

But sixth in Division Two was no cause for celebration on Tyneside, and in the close season manager Andy Cunningham was sent on his way. He was replaced by Tom Mather from Stoke. Mather was lucky to inherit Pearson and Smith: he did precious little himself for the club. Smith hit 26 goals in 36 games in 1935–36, helping United to eighth position. But their defensive record was the worst in the top half of Division Two, as was indicated by the one spark of the old days in that dismal period: their fifth-round cup-tie at home to Arsenal in 1936. Some 65,484 success-starved Geordies turned out to see a 3-3 draw; and Arsenal duly won the replay 3-0. To crown the humiliation, Sunderland won the league title that year, scoring 109 Division One goals with a forward line that included their own Patsy Gallacher and the great Raich Carter.

Newcastle invested in defence. Yet another centre-half, Jesse Carver, was signed from Blackburn, and St Mirren's Bob Ancell, who would soon become a Scotland international, was brought in to replace the ageing David Fairhurst (although Fairhurst would prove difficult to supplant: he stuck around at the club until 1946!). Jimmy Gordon from Wishaw Juniors made his début at right-half – and in the 1936–37 season Newcastle made a serious bid for promotion. Their away record was fine – they won 11 out of 21 on foreign territory – but actually managed to drop 17 home points at the once almost impregnable Fortress St

James's, finishing fourth, six points adrift of the top two. The one bright pointer to the future was that Jack Smith, still only 22 years old, scored 24 goals in 28 games.

And then came near-disaster. The 1937–38 season was the worst in the history of Newcastle United. Dismissed from the cup, they sank down the Second Division table. Jimmy Richardson was finally transferred to Millwall, and Jack Smith, to the astonishment of all of the North-east, was suddenly sold to Manchester United.

Newcastle paid the price. They lost seven of their last nine matches and slumped to the bottom of the table. Unbelievably, the Third Division (North) loomed on the near horizon like a thunder cloud. At the season's end they were on 36 points – exactly the same as Nottingham Forest and relegated Barnsley.

Newcastle United and Forest stayed up on goal average. United were assisted in their survival by two astonishing strokes of luck. Firstly, an away game at Stockport was abandoned when Newcastle were losing 2-0, and United won the rear-ranged fixture 3-1. Secondly, the league fixture list brought fellow-strugglers Forest and Barnsley together on the last Saturday. They drew, and Barnsley took the drop as the result of a difference in goal average of 0.002. Newcastle themselves were saved from the Third Division (North) by the slightly more comfortable margin of 0.098 of a goal.

At the end of that terrifying season the retired winger Stan Seymour got a message at his sports outfitters shop to go and meet the directors at St James's Park. Expecting to be asked to let bygones be bygones and start supplying the club with shorts and shirts once more, Stanley ankled along to Gallowgate. There, vice-chairman George Rutherford put an arm around Seymour's shoulders and said: 'Do you fancy being manager at Newcastle United?'

No, said Stan. Then what about a directorship? continued the board. Yes, said Stan. He was allotted five shares, and he joined the board. Tom Mather kept his job for the moment, and Mister Newcastle was on his way.

He may at first have been no more than a very busy talisman, a man the fans and players alike knew and could trust, but after Seymour's appearance on the bridge things did start to look up. Some excellent purchases were made. Dougie Wright, a left-half, was signed from Southend for £3,250 in 1938. Jackie Milburn would later rate Wright as the best half-back he played with in a Newcastle shirt: 'He had four cartilages out but always succeeded in slowing the game down to his pace and beating man after man with sheer skill. Dougie often used to feint throwing the ball one way, then throw it the other. He could always outthink the opposition.'

Jimmy Denmark settled in at centre-half, and at the other end of the field two footballers made their mark. Locally born Billy Cairns, who had been on the books for five years, was given a run of first-team games and became top scorer, and a young man named Albert Stubbins was given 23 matches at insideforward.

Newcastle finished the 1938–39 season in ninth position in Division Two. They had played just three games of the following season, and recorded their first victory in beating Swansea 8-3, when Adolf Hitler invaded Poland, and Britain, for the second time in the century, declared war on Germany.

Once again a kind of wartime league was organised, with final placings dependent upon goal average rather than points. This time Newcastle United were involved in the fixtures of the North Division. The bare statistics tell us little of the full, chaotic story. They indicate that Newcastle finished tenth out of 36 clubs in 1941; 15th out of 38 in 1942; 26th out of 48 in 1943; 39th out of 50 in 1944; 35th out of 54 in 1945; and sixth out of 22 in 1946. (By 1945–46, with the war effectively over, the wartime league had become quite a sophisticated affair, with two proper north and south First Divisions and four regional Third Divisions, all teams playing each other for points home and away.)

But the statistics do not tell us the tales of strange feats, the eccentric ups and downs of wartime sport. Certain clubs, for instance, were abnormally favoured by wartime conditions. Blackpool, which had finished in the bottom half of Division

One in the two seasons before hostilities, won the wartime North Division for the first three years thanks to the club's geographical closeness to the air arm and to several military camps, and its consequent access to such conscripts as airman Stanley Matthews.

Portsmouth were able to use a sprinkling of international footballers from the fleet, although they were less favoured, there being fewer seaman footballers, and those that existed being often away at sea.

The club which benefited most was undoubtedly Aldershot of the old Third Division (South). This mediocre club from the army town was, at the outbreak of war, managed by that old Newcastle stalwart, the king of the off-side trap Bill McCracken. The former United full-back could hardly believe his luck, when told he could have the pick of the British army . . .

'I got myself a pass into the barracks,' McCracken remembered later in life. 'So as soon as those chaps came down, I collared them straight away. And I must say this about the officers down there, there were one or two good chiefs. I remember one of them was Michael Green, the cricketer. When I went down to the camp I'd see the officer, and he'd say "Morning, Mac." And I'd give him a big salute back. "Morning, sir."

' "Who do you want for Saturday?" he'd say.

' "Well, sir," I'd reply, "it might be a bit difficult for you because the chara's leaving at so and so, you see."

' "You just tell me the players you want," he'd say, and he would work it for me.'

And so it was that, when they were not fighting Hitler, internationals such as Frank Swift, Tommy Lawton, Jimmy Hagan, Wilf Copping, Stan Cullis, Joe Mercer and many others turned out for Aldershot of Division Three (South).

McCracken, understandably, loved it. 'They were a great set of lads. I said to them once, "You're all kidding. You're not the set of internationals you think you are. You're not bringing the crowds in. Let's have something a bit more spectacular" . . . Or other days I'd say, "This is a bad team you're playing today. I suggest you keep the ball up in the air and don't let them have a kick at it."

'Sometimes when they came in for their money I used to say, "What money? You told me you'd play for nothing." That really used to upset them. Mind you, a sergeant once asked to be put on the pay list to make sure the players were free! But I wouldn't have it. And I always kept a few boys standing by in case someone couldn't get away to play, but usually they could.'

Weird and wonderful things happened in wartime football. One Scottish soldier famously told Chelsea that he had been a pre-war professional with Motherwell. The London club promptly fielded him – only to discover after half a minute that he had plainly hardly kicked a ball in his life before. In the years before substitutions were allowed, they were stuck with him for the remaining hour and a half.

At least one of United's players found himself in the famous Stalag IVB prisoner-of-war camp in Germany, which was celebrated for the quality of its soccer team.

Back in Blighty, teams were frequently thrown into matches against each other more often than in the discipline of peacetime football. In the winter of 1942–43 Newcastle met Leeds United six times, and a grand total of 47 goals were scored. At Elland Road Newcastle won 7-1 and 3-1, and lost once, by 7-2. At St James's Park Leeds won 5-3, Newcastle won 9-0, and in the last game of this sequence, on Tyneside, Newcastle were leading 4-0 with 20 minutes to go before Leeds scored five goals to win 5-4 and level the series!

St James's Park itself was not, as in the First World War, commandeered by the military, though the ground was used for several wartime internationals. The first was in the first winter of the war, on 2 December 1939, when England played Scotland before a crowd of 15,000. Newcastle United's footballers featured more memorably in this match than on any previous occasion. Two England players, Sam Barkas and Eric Brook, were injured in a car crash on their way to the game, and so two Newcastle men were pulled into the England team at the last minute. They were the locally born defender Joe Richardson, and the forward Tommy Pearson – who was actually a Scot. Nine years later, in 1947, Pearson was capped for Scotland against England and Belgium. The achievement would have given him a unique collection of headwear had wartime internationals counted as full caps by the home countries – but, sadly for him and many others, they were not.

In 1947 Tommy Pearson's Scotland team failed to beat either England or Belgium. In 1939 his and Richardson's England XI defeated Scotland 2-1, and one of the England goals – a diving header from a Stanley Matthews cross – came from yet another club team-mate, Harry Clifton, whom Newcastle had bought from Chesterfield for £8,500 a year earlier. Neither Clifton nor Richardson would ever gain a full peacetime England cap.

Clifton's Newcastle career, like that of so many others, was badly disrupted by the war: he made only 35 peacetime appearances and scored a promising 17 goals, and was transferred to Grimsby Town when peace was declared.

But perhaps the most sensational wartime footballing record was that of big Albert Stubbins, the red-haired forward from Wallsend who had made his début in the last full season before the war. Stubbins had hardly been given the chance to prove himself in peacetime. During the war, against defences which were admittedly disorganised and under-strength, he seized his opportunity with both hands. Like so many others on Tyneside he was a worker in a reserved occupation, a draughtsman in a Sunderland shipyard, and so was not called up, and was usually free to play.

There is understandably some dispute about the number of games played and goals scored by Stubbins for Newcastle. But whichever way it is read, the record was nothing less than sensational. Some said it was 245 goals in 199 games; others put the tally at 230; yet others at 231 or 232 in 188 matches. We do know, however, that the carrot-topped hero in one purple patch in 1941 hit the net 15 times in five consecutive games, scoring firstly four, then three, three, three, and two – and that on five occasions during the war Albert Stubbins scored five goals in a game.

Stan Seymour rated the uncapped Stubbins as highly as the legendary England centre-forward Tommy Lawton. 'The only advantage Lawton might have over Stubbins is with his heading,' said Seymour. 'Stubbins is cleverer on the ball.'

The young Jackie Milburn recalled being picked in the same side as Stubbins. Usually a modest fellow, he leaned over to Milburn and surprisingly said quietly: 'I'll score three today, Jackie . . .'

'He did, too,' remembered Milburn. 'All in the first half, and each one brilliant in its own way.'

Stubbins was the most extreme example of a footballer whose career was blighted by the war. He had achieved little before 1939, and shortly after the conflict's end he would be transferred. That exceptional goal ratio, unequalled by anybody, was never repeated.

There were strange guest appearances in those unusual times. Both Tom Finney and Stan Mortenson turned out for Newcastle, and Eddie Carr of Bradford played for United against Bradford City on 18 November 1944 – and scored six times in the club's 11-0 win.

Many of United's footballers joined the armed forces, but the Roll of Honour of the dead of the Second World War includes the name of just one of them. Doubly tragically, it was the name of the son of the popular director Stan Seymour. Colin Seymour was killed in an air crash near Perth in Scotland.

Behind the scenes, the club quietly built for peacetime. Several new names were added to the roster during the war. The forward Charlie Wayman was a miner from Bishop Auckland who became an asbestos roofer, and who as a young inside-left with Chiltern Boys achieved local renown by picking up 65 goals. Wayman joined the Royal Navy as an Able Seaman, served for three years, and then went back down the pit before taking a trial at St James's Park and being snapped up by new manager Stan Seymour.

The most significant signing of them all, however, took place in the summer of 1943. That 19-year-old pit engineer from Ashington who had been christened John Edward Thompson

Milburn had gone along with a friend to a wartime match at St James's Park, and had not been impressed. 'I says, "Raymond, we could play better than this, surely," ' Milburn recalled. 'It was the last game of the season, and it was terrible . . . if we'd played as bad as that [for the Northumberland Air Training Corps team] we'd 'a been booed off . . .

'Then the new season came in, and there were adverts in the paper for writing to Newcastle for trials. So I said to Raymond [Poxton – Milburn's friend, who later had a trial for Derby County before returning to Ashington, where a cartilage injury finished his career in 1949], "Hey, we could play better than this lot. You write the letter." '

Milburn and Ray Poxton were given a trial. Milburn – who had previously played in virtually every position on the field other than centre-forward, which he hated – counted himself fortunate to be put on the same scratch trial side as two wartime first-teamers, Charlie Woollet and Bobbie Jacques. He scored six goals, and as he left the training field a posse of directors headed by Stan Seymour made for the 19-year-old from Ashington. Seymour, who had taken over as acting manager since Tom Mather had left in the second month of the war, invited Jackie Milburn and his father Alec into the office at St James's Park on Monday, 23 August 1943. The two Ashington pitmen duly arrived; Seymour brought out the whisky bottle and two five-pound notes, thrust the former at Alec and the latter at Jackie; and J.E.T. Milburn became a professional footballer with Newcastle United.

He made his début five days later, at Valley Parade against Bradford City in the 50-team-strong North First Championship. Saturday, 28 August 1943, was an auspicious afternoon in more ways than one. The young Milburn found himself part of a Newcastle side which lost 2-1 to Bradford City, both of whose goals were scored by their 25-year-old inside-right, a sergeant in the Army Physical Training Corps named Joe Harvey. 'I headed two goals for City that day,' Harvey would remember in later years, 'and Stan Seymour never forgot.'

On the following Saturday Bradford City travelled to play

United in Newcastle. This time, Jackie Milburn broke his duck. With his first touch of the ball he hit a left-foot shot from ten yards out at the Leazes End, and scored his first goal for the club. Newcastle won 3-2.

Many other youngsters were launched in the wartime black-and-white shirt. Manager Seymour used the war years to introduce local footballers to the club. Goalkeeper John Garbutt, who was unlucky enough to have signed from Billingham in 1939, stayed on Newcastle's books throughout the war. Full-back Bobby Cowell ('totally dedicated, and a man who literally cried with frustration and anger every time we lost. He headed more shots off the line than any other defender I can remember,' said Jackie Milburn of Cowell) came from Blackhall Colliery. Ernie Taylor, a future England international, made his début on the wing during the Second World War.

Half-back Charlie Crowe, who had been born in Byker, was signed from Wallsend St Leonards in 1944, and made his début in a 9-1 wartime thrashing of Stoke City (Stanley Matthews and all) before 48,000 Geordies who saw Albert Stubbins collect another five-goal haul. Outside-left George Hair arrived in 1943. Tommy Walker signed from Netherton immediately after the war, and full-back Bobby Corbett came from Throckley Welfare, making his début in 1943 and signing on full-time after the German surrender. Another full-back, Ron Batty, came from East Tanfield Colliery. Inside-forward Tommy Thompson, who would be sold to Aston Villa after a disappointingly small number of first-team appearances for United, but who became an England international after his transfer, came from Lumley YMCA . . .

It was an impressive record of activity by a manager who was not only working in the chaos of wartime, but was also mourning the death of a son. None of those footballers could be counted as full-time professionals during the war. If, as most of them were, they were in an essential 'reserved occupation' such as mining or shipbuilding, rather than in the armed forces, their reserved occupation came first. They worked their shifts, and only then could they train or play. For most of the local boys such as Milburn, this meant getting away to train on an average of two or three evenings a week for the duration of the war, and playing on most Saturday afternoons.

Seymour completed his task towards the end of the conflict, with a signing which was arguably almost as momentous as that of Jackie Milburn. That sergeant in the Physical Training Corps who had scored twice against United for Bradford City on Milburn's début back in October 1943, had by the autumn of 1945 become a sergeant-major and moved to Catterick. Seymour – who indeed had 'never forgot' his man – made inquiries about Sergeant-Major Joe Harvey that autumn, when the end of the war, peace and the resumption of normal competitive football were in sight. Bradford City asked for an impossible £10,000. 'Not on your life,' responded Stan. 'We only want him as a reserve.'

On 20 October 1945 Seymour got his man. Bradford City relented and dropped their asking price to £4,500; Newcastle shelled out, and Joe Harvey began his long and hugely eventful relationship with St James's Park.

He had made his first impression on Stan Seymour at inside-right. Seymour had other plans for the granite-jawed, nail-hard sergeant-major. Just as Jackie Milburn would, after a year or two and after the departure of Albert Stubbins, be moved from the wing and inside-forward positions to the number 9 slot which he had earlier so disliked, so inside-right Joe Harvey was converted to the half-back line.

That is where he played his first game for Newcastle, just two days after signing. It was another wartime North First Championship match, at home to Blackpool. Milburn was on the right-hand side of the forward line, and he remembered later that the new right-half, Joe Harvey, made an early impression. 'Within seconds of the start,' recalled Jackie, 'I pushed a ball back to him. It was a mile off the mark and went out of play. Now, I was working at the pits, and I thought no one could teach a miner how to swear. But never in my life have I heard such a torrent of abuse. All the lads heard it too, and got the message. Army man Joe was in charge.'

Newcastle United won that game 2-0. Joe Harvey returned to Doncaster afterwards to tell his wife all about his new club. When he got back to St James's Park for his second game, he was told that he had been made captain. 'Running into Harvey,' his team-mates would reflect, 'was like hitting a bag of iron.'

There were just a couple of major pieces of Stan Seymour's wartime jigsaw left. He slotted the first one in in May 1946, just three months before the resumption of normal Football League activity. A 21-year-old man-mountain named Frank Brennan, who had just been capped for Scotland at centre-half in the Victory International against England at Hampden Park (which the Scots won 1-0), was signed from Airdrieonians for £7,500. Brennan, who was virtually unknown when he arrived, would become a Newcastle legend over the next ten years. Len Shackleton – normally no fan of hulking centre-halves – would rate big Frank as the best centre-half he ever played with or against. 'Brennan takes the field for every match with one idea on his mind,' Shackleton said after leaving Newcastle, 'the subjugation of all attacking moves down the centre of the field. And what a magnificent job he makes of it.'

Joe Harvey, who dubbed Brennan 'the Octopus', swore that forwards had to make a detour of 20 yards to get past him. Jackie Milburn, who in his turn called Brennan 'the Rock of Gibraltar', told a story of the formidable Scot playing cricket – 'he was running between the wickets when a wayward return headed straight for him. Big Frank never broke stride as he nodded the cricket ball down and completed his run laughing all over his face. That's the sort of teak-hard fella he was; a man who, unlike a lot of centre-halves, never squealed for cover. He'd tell his full-backs: "Piss off out of the way and let me get on with the job." '

Brennan's initial impression on his new comrades, however, was that nobody had ever seen an appetite quite like that. 'Many's the time on the morning of matches,' recorded his captain Joe Harvey, 'I have seen him demolish grapefruit, cornflakes, three or four eggs, bacon, sausage, tomatoes, fried bread, toast and marmalade – and then polish off the mixed grills other players left.' Jackie Milburn's version of the tale was similar, but with Frank sucking back 12 fried eggs, half-a-dozen rashers of bacon, fittingly heroic amounts of toast – and then leading the rest of the squad in training. Brennan had been born, he told everybody, a three-and-a-half pound starveling. By the time he arrived in Newcastle he had a six-foot-two-inch, 14-stone frame to support.

One month later, in June 1946, Roy Bentley, a versatile forward with a reputation for heading ability, was bought from Bristol City for £8,000. By that time the Newcastle players, directors, staff and fans all knew that the club would resume its Football League career, after six long wartime winters, with a game against Millwall in London in the early September of 1946.

Newcastle United had, in those months after the end of the Second World War, one simple, overarching ambition: to get out of Division Two.

CHAPTER SIX

SHACK, STORMS AND GOODBYE TO THE SECOND: 1945–48

❖

The Football League restarted proper competitive soccer by faithfully replaying the abandoned fixture list of 1939–40 in 1946–47 – as if normality had not been turned on its head by Adolf Hitler, but merely interrupted.

But only two of the Newcastle United team which journeyed down to Cold Blow Lane to face Millwall in 1946 had undertaken the same journey in 1939. They were left-half Douglas Wright and left-winger Tommy Pearson. Of the others, Harvey, Brennan and Bentley had, as we have seen, been bought shortly before the league kicked off again. The rest – Milburn, Wayman, Cowell and the others – were Stan Seymour's Northeastern wartime harvest.

There were early disruptions. Albert Stubbins, that wartime scoring sensation, had been unhappy on Tyneside for a while, and on 12 September, shortly after the season's start, he was transferred to Liverpool for £13,000. Sadly for all concerned, he never repeated in peacetime his striking feats of 1939 to 1945.

The money received for Stubbins was well used. One month after the centre-forward's transfer, on 2 October 1946, Seymour paid Bradford Park Avenue exactly £13,000 for a unique inside-left named Len Shackleton. According to Shackleton, he was simply told by two United directors, Seymour and Wilf Taylor, 'You're coming to Newcastle' . . . 'I said, "Aye, okay, I'm going to Newcastle." I had thought that if I ever got transferred I would want a share of it, so I'm thinking, well, the record transfer fee is the £13,000 that Wolverhampton had got from Arsenal for Bryn Jones the last season before the war, and Newcastle have got £13,000 for transferring Albert Stubbins to Liverpool, so, £13,000 for them two, oh, I'll be worth about £5,000 or £6,000.

'Stan Seymour said, "You'll be coming to Newcastle." I said, "Oh yes, and what do I get out of it?" He said, "We're prepared to give you £500," which met what I thought was my standard, about 10 per cent of the transfer fee, so I signed.'

Shackleton's début game, like so much else about this cocky iconoclast, has passed into legend. The 24-year-old Yorkshireman, who had netted close on 200 goals for Second Division Bradford, who was known as much for his Tyke cheek as for his footballing flair, who was already celebrated for his impertinent opinions as well as for a beautiful talent, signed on a Wednesday. Three days later, on 5 October 1946, he turned out for United at St James's Park in a league game against struggling Newport County.

'As I ran onto that great playing area,' Shackleton would later record, 'I felt somehow that Newport County just had to be another chopping block in the career of Len Shackleton.'

If the new inside-forward felt good at 2.50 p.m., he felt even better two hours later. After just five minutes he had laid on a cross for Charlie Wayman to score. 'What a forward line we had at Newcastle,' Shackleton would reminisce a few years later. 'Jackie Milburn, Roy Bentley, Charlie Wayman, myself and Tommy Pearson. We were a happy bunch against Newport County!' He was not to know that, within less than 18 months, only one of those five musketeers would remain at St James's Park – one of them having left because of a missing clothes peg, and another because of a dirty bath.

Jackie Milburn would be equally complimentary about his mercurial Newcastle and England team-mate – while simultaneously suggesting that the little genius could be a trifle difficult to anticipate. 'Shack was the greatest ball player of all time,' judged Milburn. 'He could balance a ball on a snowflake. He was a born entertainer, and always original and inventive. Shack didn't know what he was going to do next, so what chance had us mere mortals playing with him?'

Wayman, who also missed a penalty, collected three more goals that afternoon. Milburn weighed in with two, and Roy Bentley got another.

But Len Shackleton, in his first game as Newcastle's inside-left, scored six goals in a 13-0 victory. It is a standing club record, and Shackleton's double hat-trick remains the biggest haul by any United player in a senior match. He also had a hand in laying on five of the others.

'Six-Goal Shack' caught the train back to his Bradford home the next morning. Being Len Shackleton, however, there were other things on his mind besides being the new hero of St James's Park. Thanks to his impish, intelligent refusal to be cowed by authority or 'tradition', we have a clear idea of the life of a professional footballer in the 1940s and 1950s. Shackleton exposed in writing the hypocrisies, deceits, illegal payments and other corruptions of a world in which some of the most popular entertainers in Britain were held in poorly paid bondage by the tradesman-directors of football clubs. It was an antiquated system of employment and management, and it would shortly crash around the feet of those directors – and first of all, as we shall see, around the feet of the directors of Newcastle United.

But in 1946 the vassal-footballer seemed a creature of great tradition, and few other than Shackleton thought to question his life. It was, after all, better than working at the coal face.

Shackleton, who had a bitter experience of being cast out penniless and seemingly futureless on to the streets of London by Arsenal FC while he was still a teenager, did question the system. (He also, as an adult professional footballer, put in extra training in the week before his club visited Highbury.) And by the time he took the train back from Newcastle Central Station to Bradford via Leeds on the morning of Sunday, 6 October 1946, the morning after his rout of Newport County, Len Shackleton had learned his actual transfer fee. It had not been £5,000 or £6,000, but £13,000 – £13,000 0s 3d, he was told. His 'standard' – illicit, but standard – 10 per cent signing-on fee should therefore have been not £500, but £1,300.

Len was unhappy. Club secretary Frank Watt had given him the £500 in five bundles of £100 upon signature of his contract, but as he picked it up Stan Seymour asked the footballer what he planned to do with the cash.

' "I'm going to put it into the building society."

' "Oh," he said. "You can't do that, because if you put a lump like that into a building society people are going to make two and two add up to four, and they'll know where you've got it from." '

So Len Shackleton was persuaded to take just one of the bundles of £100, and leave the rest in Frank Watt's safe, from where it could be discreetly withdrawn in £20 lots until the remaining £400 was exhausted.

On that train between Tyneside and Yorkshire the morning after his début – 'You couldn't dream a better thing, could you, really?' – Shackleton was in two minds. He fingered the bundle of notes amounting to £100 in cash. He had never held so much money. He counted it 'four times before we reached Durham'. And he was simultaneously rankled by the thought that his £500 should have been more than £1,000.

Shack would be rankled even further before his time at Newcastle was out. After collecting, over the weeks, a further £100 in £20 instalments, he was told by Frank Watt one day that no more money was available – 'Mr Seymour's been for it.' He took his complaint to another director, John Lee, who substantiated the story and promptly delivered the remaining £300 in the form of a cheque. Like so much else in Len Shackleton's football career, it was a bittersweet experience. On the one hand, he had been given £500 when legally he should have been given nothing. On the other hand, he perceived the manager-director Stan Seymour as attempting to do him out of £300 of the £500 – and as successfully tricking him out of £800 from a merited £1,300. His mood may not have been helped by the fact that an old lady had approached him after the game and – clearly unfamiliar with the details of the retain-and-transfer system – said: 'You're a lucky lad, getting £13,000 for joining Newcastle!'

'This,' he would sigh in later years, 'is what these guys do to you.'

Just as in 1946 even though the war had been over for a year not all servicemen were demobbed, so the men in reserved occupations were expected to keep working. That included footballers. Len Shackleton found himself, to his surprise and chagrin, firstly descending in a pit cage at Fryston near Castleford in Yorkshire ('a terrifying experience: it is like being suspended on a piece of elastic') and after his move to Tyneside working as a labourer for the fitter Jackie Milburn at Hazelrigg Colliery.

'Can you imagine that?' Milburn would smilingly request. 'It's hard to think of the highly skilled and artistic Shackleton being skivvy to anyone.'

It was certainly hard for Len himself to consider being a colliery labourer. The winter of 1946–47 was notoriously long and cold. Shack reported for his first day in the pitch dark, with six inches of snow on the ground. 'Jackie kept insisting he was on a "smashing job" so I went along to see what it was all about. "This way," said Jackie, leading me into a snow-covered field. The two of us waded through the snow and ice, eventually reaching a half-submerged pile of steel girders. Our "smashing job" involved lifting those girders and carrying them across the field. Nowadays, whenever I want a good nightmare I just go to sleep thinking about Hazelrigg Colliery . . . I suppose I was not cut out to be a miner.'

Newcastle United, with that dynamic new forward line firing on all cylinders, seemed set to raise themselves out of the Second Division in 1946–47, the first season after the war.

If it had been all down to the forwards, they would have done so. Newcastle finished the season as runaway top scorers in the division with 95 goals. Charlie Wayman got 30, Shackleton 19 and inside-right Roy Bentley 18. (Jackie Milburn, whose goals-coring potential was yet to be realised, was stuck out on the right wing.)

But they conceded 62 goals. Playing before enormous crowds which averaged almost 50,000 – *in the Second Division* – they won their first three matches before losing at Shackleton's old club, Bradford Park Avenue. Shackleton missed a crucial penalty that day because he suddenly recalled that the Bradford keeper Chick Farr had practised countless spot kicks with him. Surely Farr would know to dive to his right? Or would expect to be second-guessed, and dive to his left? Or . . . in his confusion Shack mishit a weak shot straight at the surprised Chick Farr.

Nonetheless, Newcastle led the table until Christmas, and then lost three league games on the trot and never recovered. In January 1947 a big freeze commenced, which was especially severe in the North-east, and coincided with United's loss of form.

But as they slipped down the table, eventually to finish in fifth spot, a full ten points off the promotion places, an old friend appeared to lift the gloom. The FA Cup had, of course, also been revived. Newcastle went for it like men inspired. Crystal Palace were despatched from the third round by 6-2 at St James's. Then Southampton arrived on Tyneside in the fourth round, and took the lead before a Charlie Wayman hat-trick saw them off – and, in the process, Tommy Pearson gave Southampton's new right-back, Company Quarter-Master Sergeant Alf Ramsey, a humiliating 90 minutes: Pearson, the future England manager would say later, 'had ball control I have never seen since'. (Pearson seems to have introduced Ramsey to a degree of paranoia about Newcastle left-wingers. His replacement, Bobby Mitchell, gave Alf such a hard time that on one occasion before a game at St James's Park Ramsey was seen inspecting the pitch for puddles, so that he could jockey his opponent into the water during the match.)

Leicester were next to be sent packing, and Bentley and Milburn saw off First Division Sheffield United in the quarter-finals. So, with promotion clearly missed, Newcastle travelled to Elland Road, Leeds, to meet Charlton Athletic in the semi-final of the FA Cup. United were used to winning semi-finals, and on paper there was no reason to suppose that they would lose this one. Charlton Athletic were a Division One side, but were struggling, whereas Newcastle had ridden high in Division Two and had just defeated championship contenders Sheffield United.

Add to that the fact that on the Friday before the game the Charlton players were given contaminated sausage-rolls at a Leeds pie factory, and the whole team became violently ill during the night . . . and Newcastle's job looked easy.

But Newcastle also had their problems. If Charlton's squad had what their doctor diagnosed as gripe, the United players simply griped. All was not well at St James's Park. Joe Harvey and Len Shackleton had not been given adequate accommodation – 'adequate accommodation' to top footballers in 1947 being a rented semi-detached house – on Tyneside, and were frustrated by commuting from Yorkshire.

Stan Seymour had stepped down as manager in March, and the directors were running the team themselves while they considered his replacement. They were not up to the job. Charlie Wayman had lost form, but they played him in one unsuccessful league game after another, hoping that the centre-forward would recover.

Between the quarter-final and semi-final matches they closeted the squad at Seahouses on the Northumberland coast, 'like a bunch of atom scientists,' said Shackleton, 'permitted to break camp for league matches once a week.' Grievances festered, more players form was lost, the whole team stuttered and squandered its rhythm. Harvey and Shackleton began to put it about that after the cup run they would never again play for Newcastle, due to the directors' refusal to find each of them a semi-detached house.

Some of them were also unhappy about money. They were on a regulated maximum wage of £10 a week, with the occasional illicit £25 win-bonus in important matches such as that cup semi-final. But they were not stupid men. Len Shackleton (it would, of course, be Len Shackleton) remembered walking to the ground on match days with half-back Dougie Wright. They would reach St James's Park at ten o'clock, and the queues for yet another attendance of 50,000-plus would already be form-ing. Shackleton would say to Wright: 'It's not right, this, you know. There's people queueing up at ten in the morning, and they're paying us a tenner!' Those were the financial and other discontents which were ticking away, and which would explode in the offices of St James's Park within 13 short years.

The final straw in 1947 came when the directors finally woke up to Wayman's loss of form and dropped their top scorer from the semi-final itself, replacing him with George Stobbart who had signed from Middlesbrough just eight months earlier and had been given precious little chance to prove himself in the first team. The players were in a state of near-mutiny when they walked out onto the Elland Road pitch. And just as divided political parties do not win elections, so mutinous football teams rarely win cup semi-finals. Newcastle saw Charlton defender Peter Croker (the brother of the future FA secretary Ted) twice clear off his line before the Londoners hit back with a devastat-ing two-goal burst from their captain Don Welsh. Charlton made it 3-0 before half-time, and eventually sailed into the FA Cup final (which they proceeded to win) by 4-0.

The Newcastle United changing-room was not a happy place. Club captain Harvey and Shackleton left Leeds and returned to their homes elsewhere in Yorkshire pledging to go on strike until the directors settled their housing grievances. All the players – who had been questioned by anxious fans before the semi-final about the reasons for Wayman's exclusion – were convinced that Charlie should have played, that he would have made a difference, and that regardless of his poor form, to drop a 30-goal striker from a cup semi-final verged on the suicidal.

Amazingly, all of those complaints were ironed out. Harvey and Shack were suspended by the club for a couple of matches (matches which they had sworn to boycott anyway), and were called before the board on the Thursday after the disastrous semi-final. Willie McKeag, a solicitor, future Lord Mayor of Newcastle, and future chairman of Newcastle United, led for the prosecution, blaming the footballers for any difficulties, but John Lee – 'a very good friend of all the United players' and another future chairman – offered to negotiate a settlement. Finally the two rebels were given a press statement to approve. It told the public that Harvey and Shackleton had apologised to the board. No sooner had they signed it than the players and their wives were taken out by the club to hunt, successfully, for semi-detached houses in Gosforth.

And in May, just a couple of weeks after Charlton Athletic had beaten Second Division runners-up Burnley in the FA Cup final, Newcastle announced the appointment of a new manager. He was George Martin, a former First Division forward who had been managing Luton Town, a Division Three (South) club which had gained promotion to Division Two shortly before the war and had managed to stay there. Luton had finished below Newcastle in the 1946–47 season, but they were comfortably in mid-table, and Martin's side had impressed the United directors by coming back from being 3-0 down in the league fixture at Kenilworth Road to beat Newcastle 4-3.

Although clearly a good motivator, Martin had his eccentricities. Left-half Charlie Crowe caricatured a George Martin team talk as going something like: (To Harvey): 'Joe . . . keep 'em going.' (To Crowe, bashing one fist against the other): 'Charlie . . . give 'em the usual.' (To Milburn): 'Jackie . . . show 'em your arse.' (To Ernie Taylor, ruffling the subject's hair and nodding emphatically): 'Aha! . . . The little man!' (To all): 'Right then, lads, out you go!'

But he was possibly just the balm that United needed in the disturbed close season of 1947. The pressures upon those players were enormous. The biggest and most fanatical following in the land expected them to get out of Division Two in the shortest time possible, and to stop losing FA Cup semi-finals. That relentless pressure alone could have destroyed a team, and cracked a less amiable manager.

'George was a very likable man whose main concern was the welfare of his players,' said Jackie Milburn. 'In my day we all lived in club houses, not the four-bedroom detached jobs in the posh part of town which today's stars can afford, and George was always ready to help us get over any little financial difficulties.'

Martin would help with getting cracks in the kitchen ceiling repaired; he would telephone sick wives to inquire after their health; he would entertain the squad with his excellent singing voice. George Martin 'worked on the assumption that if you get the little things right, the big things would fall into place'.

One of the first of George Martin's big things to fall into place was a goalkeeper who was signed from Preston North End in July 1947. Jack Fairbrother was a former policeman who insisted on playing in a copper's white gloves, which he persuaded Newcastle's Market Street police station to supply. He was also an extraordinary student of his position, well in advance of his time. Fairbrother was obsessed by angles. Convinced that if a goalkeeper was in the right place few shots would beat him, he developed an elaborate training routine. He would tie a long rope to each goalpost, and then persuade a Newcastle forward – preferably Jackie Milburn – to come racing in with the ball from a variety of angles.

'He would shout "STOP!". I would be tearing in, and as soon as he shouted I put my foot on the ball and kept running out of the road, so the ball was left at an angle where he was in comparison with the posts.'

The ropes were then extended to reach the ball. If Jack was seen to be standing exactly in between the ropes, he was happy. If not, they did it over and over again until he got it right. 'This took hours,' recalled Milburn, but the result was that 'Fairbrother was the only keeper I've ever known whom I always felt would save any shot.'

Jack Fairbrother, echoed his friend Len Shackleton, was 'the outstanding British goalkeeper of the time . . . [he] never played a poor game and I know of no other goalkeeper of whom that could be said.' Fairbrother was never capped for England, in the view of many, because he rarely made extravagant saves; he did not need to: the rope exercises took care of that. 'Spectacular goalkeeping,' ruled Shackleton, 'is the result of bad positional play', and Fairbrother's practised positional play was so perfect that the ball would more often hit him on the body than go into the net, and an uneducated spectator such as the average England selector would put it all down to luck.

(Fairbrother would also have an early experience of Stan Seymour's wily, insistent meddling behind the scenes. When the goalkeeper failed to discover his form after his arrival in 1947, Seymour approached young Jack after a reserve game and suggested that he apply for a transfer. 'Being a new boy,' Fairbrother recalled years later, 'I thought that was what was expected of me.' He wrote out his request and took it to a bewildered George Martin, who gently persuaded the goalkeeper to tear up the letter and forget the whole incident.)

In September a youngster called Bob Stokoe who had come up through the junior ranks signed professional forms at Newcastle, and shortly after the start of the 1947–48 season George Martin made arguably the most momentous decision of his managerial career. The unhappy Charlie Wayman was sold to Southampton for £10,000 in October. His discontent with the club after being dropped for the cup semi-final had eased, only to be replaced by another. Bizarrely, the straw which broke Charlie Wayman's back was the fact that he could not find, in both of the two palatial St James's Park changing-rooms, a peg upon which to hang his clothes. He walked in one day, found all the pegs occupied, and said: 'Bloody hell! I can't even get a peg in the dressing-room now. I'm off.' So Martin sold him to the south coast.

But that was not the momentous decision: it was only a contributary factor. George Stobbart was injured, and so Wayman's departure left United with no recognised first-team centre-forward. Shortly after the peg incident a group consisting of Martin, Stan Seymour, Joe Harvey, trainer Norman Smith and Jackie Milburn were sitting around chatting, and the question of Wayman's replacement arose.

'Jackie's the man,' asserted Martin.

'Naw, keep him at inside-left or on the wing,' said Smith.

'Aye, he's not good enough in the air for centre-forward,' said Seymour.

Milburn himself was nodding his head in violent agreement

with the last two. He had played centre-forward just once before, while at school, and had missed so many chances that the memory haunted him.

'They're right,' he ventured. 'I'm not cut out to lead the attack. I'm happy where I am.'

But George Martin was not to be deflected. 'You're wrong, all of you,' he said, and followed it with one of the great football predictions of the 20th century. 'Not only will Jackie make a centre-forward, but he'll get a cap into the bargain.'

The next match was against lowly Bury at Gigg Lane. A terrified Milburn, having spent a sleepless night, kicked off for the first time in the Newcastle United number 9 shirt. He need not have worried. After five minutes the Bury goalkeeper, George Bradshaw, broke his leg. In the days before substitutes a defender, Harry Catterick, who later became famous as manager of Everton, went between the posts. Suddenly Newcastle were playing not only against a side which was struggling against relegation, but also one with only ten men and no recognised goalkeeper.

Milburn made the most of it. He promptly scored a lucky opener, and then went on to complete his hat-trick. United won 5-3, and the legend of Newcastle's most worshipped centre-forward – some would say, Newcastle's favourite son in any walk of life – was born. When George Stobbart returned from injury, he was handed the inside-right's number 8 shirt. Number 9 was taken.

By December United were up in second place and clearly challenging for promotion. They were an extravagantly gifted side – too extravagant, some thought, for the blood-and-thunder of a Second Division battle. In a 4-1 defeat of Cardiff City in November, Shackleton took advantage of the cushion provided by a ten-second Milburn goal to spend 90 minutes offering the delighted crowd the full range of his skills. 'He and Tommy Pearson gave an exhibition,' said Milburn. 'They kept the ball between them with six or seven defenders around them, frightened to death to tackle. And this happened for 90 minutes.'

As ever, this variety of exhibitionist football had its enemies.

Joe Harvey, the club captain, was one. 'We'll never win anything with Shackleton in the team,' Harvey told Martin. 'We've got to get rid of him.'

A part of the uncomplicated Milburn agreed. 'Len was a smashing fella, but he had no interest other than entertaining the crowd. He would rather beat three men than lay on a winning goal.'

And Len himself, aware of the muted ill-feeling, was uncomfortable at the club. He still harboured resentments over the missing £800 from his signing-on fee, and the unnecessary delays in finding him a suitable house. He found the regulations and pomposities of the club oppressive and stultifying. He hated the neat little coloured books, the printed guides to behaviour, training and discipline which were handed out to players and which had to be carried all times and even shown to the commissionaire before all home matches! He hated the restrictions on motorcycle riding, on dancing between Wednesday and Saturday, on talking to the press (for Len Shackleton loved to talk). He disliked having to wear a uniform of blazer and flannels for away matches. He was angered by the club's assumed control of his private life – its insistence on approving any place in which he stayed for the night other than his own house, its refusal to allow him to spend weekends away when there was no match, its insistence on submitting him to medical examinations at will. 'How many other workers,' Shackleton wondered aloud, 'excluding those in the armed forces, have to comply with such regulations?' And all for just £10 a week (soon to rise to £15) – excluding, of course, illegal kick-backs, favours and bizarre treats in lieu of a decent wage.

Riding high in the Second Division, in season 1947–48 Newcastle United were playing before the biggest crowds in the Football League. Their average gate over the whole season was 56,299. It is still a Newcastle record, and it stood as an English record for two decades until Manchester United narrowly improved upon it (in Division One) in their European Cup-winning year of 1968.

That kind of thing may have made the directors happy. It

sustained a huge playing staff of around 70 men, and it paid for ground expansion and improvements. But, as we have seen, the idea of 50,000-plus people paying to see Shackleton on a Saturday afternoon, and Len himself pocketing perhaps just £10 from the deal, was not designed to make the Yorkshireman jump for joy.

This second winter of discontent climaxed at Christmas 1947. All was seemingly well. Newcastle were still nicely poised for promotion in second position. Jack Fairbrother and Len Shackleton had each made separate arrangements to spend the festive holiday in the Midlands – Fairbrother with family, and Shackleton with friends.

Then the draw was made for the third round of the FA Cup, and Newcastle were placed away against the cup-holders, and their nemesis in the previous season's semi-final, Charlton Athletic. It was clearly a big game, a grudge game, and George Martin was delighted to notice that Charlton had a league fixture in Middlesbrough at Christmas. The players, he announced, would all travel to Ayresome Park to watch their cup opponents.

'I am not,' declared Shackleton, 'spending Christmas in Middlesbrough.'

And nor, echoed Fairbrother, am I. 'Martin seemed to think we had taken leave of our senses, insisting that football was our bread and butter,' Shackleton recorded later.

'The only reason we want the bread and butter,' snapped Fairbrother at the time, 'is so that we can look after our wives and families. Unless they are happy, this whole football business is meaningless.' Fairbrother, who had by his own admission lost form, was briefly replaced in goal by the veteran John Garbutt. He did, however, fend off a half-hearted attempt to transfer him to Blackburn.

Both players missed the appointment at Middlesbrough. And, when the cup-tie itself came round, an unfortunate incident widened the gulf between Shackleton – although not, this time, Fairbrother – and the club.

The squad was playing golf at Tynemouth on the Wednesday

afternoon before the game at Charlton. That morning Shack's 15-month-old son was taken ill. On Thursday he deteriorated, and by the Friday morning, when the players were due to take the 10 a.m. train from Newcastle Central to London, the child's condition worsened dramatically.

Shackleton left reluctantly for the station that morning, with the doctor promising to keep in touch by telephone. After calls to his London hotel throughout the night and the Saturday morning, which informed him that young Graham had been operated upon to untie a knot in his intestine but was still suffering, Shackleton told George Martin that he would play against Charlton only if a taxi was available immediately after the game to take him to Kings Cross to catch the 5.35 Newcastle train. Martin happily agreed.

At half-time it appeared that Martin had not made the arrangements, and Shackleton asked a Charlton official to take care of the taxi. At full-time, at which point Shackleton hardly cared that United had just been knocked out of the third round of the FA Cup by 2-1, he raced away and back home to his child.

The episode rankled with Newcastle's brilliant inside-left, not least because he later had difficulty in reclaiming his £15s 0d taxi fare, plus half-a-crown tip, while being simultaneously denied his pound-note London overnight bonus as he had not spent Saturday night in the capital. (Newcastle thought that Shackleton was over-charging them for the taxi. They were perhaps right to be suspicious, although not so much on this occasion. 'I'm no saint,' admitted Shack, 'but this was different – a case of illness. I wanted no profit from that.')

The result of all this was that the January and February of 1948, when Newcastle United, playing before the biggest average gates ever recorded in English football, were making their big sustained push for promotion, were also stormy, unpleasant months in the changing-room and on the training pitch.

On the pitch, the New Year started wonderfully, with two home wins and Milburn netting five times. Luton Town arrived from mid-table to face 64,931 fans and a Jackie Milburn blitzkrieg. Milburn's hat-trick (a fierce left-foot drive, a placed shot from 15 yards, and a right-footer) was added to by a late clincher from Stobbart as United won 4-1 to move one point clear of Cardiff City in second position.

Meanwhile, off the pitch, striker Roy Bentley was on the move after another of those bizarre carry-ons which would plague Newcastle in the 1940s and 1950s. Bentley, a single man, had been living in a flat belonging to the sister of a United director. In November 1947 he complained about the condition of the bath. George Martin duly trooped around to inspect it, but this time decided that nothing more than a fresh coat of paint was necessary. Bentley took umbrage, indignantly put in a transfer request, and in the middle of January 1948 was sold to Chelsea for £11,000.

In the short term he was replaced by Bert Sibley, who had arrived from Southend the previous year. But Martin used the cash to go out and buy the winger Billy McCall from Aberdeen. (At one point it was suggested by the local press to Bentley that he might become part of an exchange deal with Aberdeen. The forward, who had arrived in Newcastle from the south-west, gave 'an expressive shudder. "No thanks," he said, "I definitely want to go south." ')

Shackleton, meantime, was making no secret of the fact that he got more satisfaction out of a few rounds at Tynemouth Golf Club than helping Newcastle United to promotion.

The situation was clearly untenable. It was brought to a head by two bad defeats in January, which took Newcastle out of the promotion zone. Firstly a shot deflected by Frank Brennan past the unfortunate Garbutt – who was between the posts in one of his periodical replacements of Fairbrother – led to a 1-0 defeat at Brentford: a scoreline which actually flattered United, as both inside-forwards Shackleton and Stobbart were marked out of the match and were quite ineffectual.

Then, on 24 January, Newcastle travelled to lowly Leeds United and were eclipsed by 3-1. Milburn's goal was no consolation for another ineffective showing, in which Shackleton started well, feeding Pearson cleverly, but then both the inside-forward and the veteran winger faded from sight. By the end of

Fashions change but the passion stays the same... the Toon Army through the ages: (*top*) a group of fans arrive in London for the 1924 Cup Final; (*middle*) complete with mascot their descendants turn up for another final in the 1950s; (*bottom*) a group of bell-bottomed youngsters in Trafalgar Square before a match in the 1970s.
Getty Images Sport

The first cup final team. The 11 team members (in the years before substitutes) pose with their trainer and 'secretary'/manager for a pre-match snap before the game against Aston Villa at the Crystal Palace ground in Sydenham in April 1905. Left to right: trainer James McPherson, Peter McWilliam, Jackie Rutherford, James Howie, Alec Gardner, Andy Aitken, Colin Veitch, Jimmy Lawrence, Bill Appleyard, Andrew McCombie, Jack Carr, Albert Gosnall, and on the far right the man who made Newcastle United, the legendary Frank Watt. Eight of the 13 men in the photograph, including Watt and McPherson, were Scots. *Getty Images Sport*

Newcastle's bogey ground: the wide open bowl of the ground at Crystal Palace, packed with spectators, during the 1905 cup final which Newcastle lost 2-0 to Villa. *Getty Images Sport*

Above. The team of all the talents. Three of Newcastle's internationalists pose together in 1908. On the left, the Irish full-back and offside trap specialist Bill McCracken; in the middle the club's most successful captain and England forward Colin Veitch, and on the right the Newcastle and Scotland inside forward Jim Howie.
Getty Images Sport

Left. Newcastle United won their first, and the old trophy's last, FA Cup Final in 1910. After United beat Burnley to claim the cup at their fourth attempt, the vase pictured above wearing the club's colours was retired, and the FA Cup, which is still in use, was cast for the 1911 season. Newcastle would, on several occasions, take that one home too... *Getty Images Sport*

There were more ways than one of getting to Wembley. Some Newcastle fans sail up the Thames on the SS Bernicia in time for the 1924 cup final against Aston Villa. Their mascot Felix the cat was modelled on a cartoon character in a local newspaper of the time. *Getty Images Sport*

The seafaring fans and Felix the cat will have enjoyed this: Stan Seymour buries Newcastle's second goal in a 2-0 win over Aston Villa in the 1924 final. It was sweet revenge for the disappointment of 19 years earlier. *Getty Images Sport*

Above. The Maradona of his day, and probably the greatest Newcastle player of all time: Hughie Gallacher leads out the team. When Gallacher was signed from Airdrieonians in 1925, the Geordie fans were aware of his goal-a-game record, but in the pre-television era were unaware that Hughie was only 5' 5" tall. As he ran onto St James's Park for the first time, he remembered, 'the deafening cheers turned to an... *oh!*' But the cheers soon started up again, and for Hughie Gallacher they never stopped.
Getty Images Sport

Left. Getting back to normal after the war. The hero of the 1948 promotion struggle. Frank Houghton is sized up in his new kit, watched by one of Newcastle's great servants and 'the outstanding British goalkeeper of the time', Jack Fairbrother. *Getty Images Sport*

The 1950s FA Cup hat-trick. (*Top*) Captain Joe Harvey is held aloft by his team-mates after the 2-0 victory over Blackpool in 1951; (*middle*) Jackie Milburn watches as George Robledo's header bounces into the net for the only goal of the game against 'unlucky' Arsenal in 1952; (*bottom*) Milburn scores what was then – and would remain for a further 42 years – the fastest FA Cup final goal, after 45 seconds in a 3-1 win over Manchester City. *Getty Images Sport*

The last major trophy of the 20th century. Captain Bobby Moncur shows off the Inter-Cities Fairs Cup (which two years later would become the UEFA Cup) from an open-topped bus in June 1969. On the previous evening the Magpies had completed a 6-2 aggregate hammering of Hungarian champions Ujpesti Dozca – or 'Oopsy Daisy' as they were known on Tyneside. *Getty Images Sport*

The stalwarts of the early 1970s: player-turned-manager Joe Harvey with captain Bobby Moncur and the brash young goalscorer Malcolm Macdonald. *Getty Images Sport*

Three comings and goings of King Kevin. (*Above*) A youthful Keegan celebrates after scoring the winning goal on his debut for Newcastle United against Queens Park Rangers in a Second Division match at St James' Park on 28th August 1982. (*Opposite top*) A slightly more senior Kevin with his assistant manager Terry McDermott on the touchline at St James's Park in January 2001. (*Opposite bottom*) After his 'constructive dismissal' a cardboard cutout of the great man is carried in front of protesters before the Hull City Premier League game on 13th September 2008.
Getty Images Sport

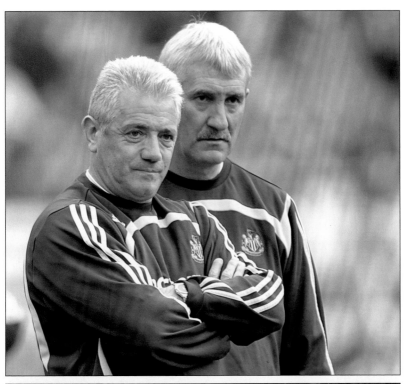

That trademark celebration. Newcastle United's record goalscorer Alan Shearer salutes the air after scoring against Middlesbrough in 2004. *Getty Images Sport*

'A truly warm and passionate human being.' Manager Bobby Robson watches with Alan Shearer from the sidelines at Villa Park on 28th August 2004. Two days later Robson was sacked. *Getty Images Sport*

Alan Shearer and Terry McDermott join other luminaries of European football at Sir Bobby Robson's memorial service in Durham Cathedral in September 2009. The service was also shown to thousands on big screens at St James's Park and Portman Road, Ipswich – the first the club of his heart, and the second the club of his head. *Getty Images Sport*

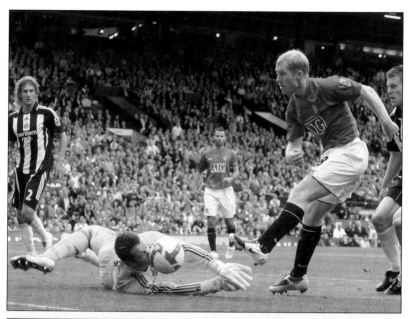

Steve Harper, pictured below making a save against Watford in February 2010, joined Newcastle United before Shay Given, pictured above saving from Manchester United's Paul Scholes in 2008. But Harper had to wait 16 years to nail down his first-team place. When he did, nobody was disappointed. *Getty Images Sport*

St James's Park, past and present. (*Top*) The mostly standing only terraces are full for the visit of Huddersfield Town in 1954. (*Bottom*) The all-seater stadium is packed once again, for the visit of Ipswich Town in April 2010 – a season in which Newcastle United averaged the fourth-highest gate in England, while playing in the second tier. *Getty Images Sport*

Redemption song... manager Chris Hughton takes the Championship trophy from Nicky Butt after the Ipswich Town match. Newcastle United have bounced straight back to where they belong – the Premier League. *Getty Images Sport*

the 90 minutes only some fine saves from Garbutt – still replacing Fairbrother – kept the scoreline halfway respectable.

But George Martin had had enough. Newcastle had slipped behind both Birmingham and Cardiff City. One February afternoon at Tynemouth Golf Club Shackleton, Fairbrother and Pearson were putting in their 18 holes when a messenger appeared from the clubhouse with the words: 'Mr Shackleton must report immediately to St James's Park.'

They knew the game was up. They finished the 18 holes, and then Pearson drove Shackleton into Newcastle. There he learned that Sunderland had offered £20,050 for the temperamental forward, and that the bid had been accepted. Shackleton was resigned, if not entirely happy. He would miss his golf with Jack and Tommy, and at one stage he had certainly been 'determined to stay to the end of my playing days at St James's Park'.

But it had all turned sour, and was unsustainable. The fans, when they heard, were outraged and appalled – not least by the fact that Shack was off to Wearside. The local papers were flooded with letters, and workers at the huge Vickers Armstrong factory held a 'Keep Shack' protest meeting, but it was no good. In his own heart, Shackleton knew that he was ready to go; and Newcastle United itself was no longer big enough for a discontented Shackleton and a frustrated, anxious George Martin who was eager to create his own team. In Shackleton's words, 'Plenty of little, nasty things were happening at St James's Park.'

As Tommy Pearson dropped Shackleton off outside the ground that fateful February afternoon he said: 'You're doing the right thing, Len. I'll probably follow you soon.'

He was right. Martin judged Pearson to be Shackleton's partner-in-crime not only on the field, where the two vied with one another in trickery, but off it too, where Martin suspected Pearson of assisting Shack in fomenting discontent. In the latter, Martin was wrong. Tommy Pearson, who had been with Newcastle since 1933, was fully committed to his club. He made a point of preaching to younger professionals about club loyalty. His reward was a transfer back to Aberdeen.

The result was the dismemberment, halfway through the

1947–48 season, of the swashbuckling forward line which had started the campaign, and which was at that stage the highest-scoring unit in the Football League. Of the famous five, only Jackie Milburn remained, flanked now by the workaday talents of Stobbart, Sibley, McCall, and a big brave £5,500 signing from Ballymena in Ireland, Frank Houghton.

The goals dried up a bit (United, once top scorers in the league, would finish the campaign as fifth-highest scorers), but the points were slowly accumulated. Newcastle began a steady haul back towards the promotion places. By early March, with 11 games to play, a single close-range goal from Milburn gave them a 1-0 win over Bury – the side which had suffered Milburn's centre-forward début hat-trick earlier in the season. They were in the middle of a sensational home run which saw the Tynesiders win ten league games on the trot at St James's Park, and fail to concede a single league goal at home for three months. They were also comfortably positioned in third place in Division Two, a point behind Cardiff but with a game in hand.

On 4 April a 2-0 home win over Bradford Park Avenue thanks to strikes from former reserve half-back James Woodburn and George Stobbart, while Cardiff were losing 1-0 at Coventry, meant that Newcastle went two points clear of the Welshmen in second place (Birmingham, at the top of the table, were six points ahead and almost out of sight) while a new threat, Sheffield Wednesday, moved into third place. Newcastle were now playing undistinguished, even dour football, but they were grinding out results. 'Constructively unimpressive,' judged the *Sunday Sun*, but 'a grand fighting effort, and grand result.'

A week later they travelled to south Wales knowing that they could not afford to lose to Cardiff. Fairbrother was reinstated in goal, but at the other end of the pitch Newcastle made their mark early in the game. Milburn had adapted his wing play brilliantly to the centre-forward's role, and embarked upon a series of fast, powerful runs ending in drives which somehow missed the net.

But the opening goal came from another source. In the 25th minute left-winger McCall slung a cross over beyond the far post, where right-winger Houghton headed it back into the middle, and inside-right Stobbart met it with a glancing header to give United the lead.

They hung on grimly, with Frank Brennan spending a good part of the second half heading out Cardiff through balls, until shortly before the final whistle when Cardiff gave their 49,000 crowd some cause for cheer by equalising from the penalty spot.

But the draw was almost enough. Seven days later third-placed Sheffield Wednesday were due to play second-placed Newcastle at St James's Park. Both sides had three games remaining, and Wednesday were two points behind United with an inferior goal average. Another home win would virtually clinch promotion . . .

Wednesday travelled north early, and watched United make up their game in hand by beating Fulham 1-0 in midweek with a late Stobbart penalty. The Yorkshiremen then retired to Tynemouth to prepare.

When 66,483 had crammed into St James's Park on the afternoon of Saturday, 17 April 1948, the gates were locked, and director William McKeag announced to the thousands shut outside that he would keep them informed of events by loud-speaker commentary.

In the changing-rooms captain Joe Harvey read in the paper that the Wednesday team had relaxed on the previous evening by attending a variety show. 'The real show starts this after-noon,' he growled at his team-mates, 'and we're top of the bloody bill'.

At first it did not seem that way. After ten minutes Dougie Whitcomb slammed home a penalty to give Wednesday the lead, and destroy United's three-month home defensive record. George Stobbart equalised 30 seconds before half-time, but Harvey was still furious. 'Now, listen,' he bawled during the break, 'I'll never forgive you if we lose this one.'

He then took over on the field itself, moving up to head home a Tommy Walker corner after 16 minutes of the second half. But with nine minutes to go Sheffield's Jackie Marriott made it 2-2.

The ground fell silent, but for Harvey screaming at his players that 'We can still beat this lot!'

And with just three minutes to go Houghton ran the ball in at the post from a low through ball. Pandemonium erupted, and the pitch was briefly invaded – but Houghton was not finished. In the last minute of the match he completed a wall pass with Milburn, collided with Wednesday keeper Dave MacIntosh, spun into a post and collapsed . . . to see the ball trickling over the line to make it 4-2. Houghton suffered a broken arm, a gashed thigh and severe shock. He later went down with a bout of tuberculosis which was linked to the accident, and had to recover in a Swiss sanatorium. They were still stretchering him around the side of the pitch when the final whistle went.

The players fought their way off the pitch through joyful fans, 'most of us crying like babies,' admitted Joe Harvey, past manager George Martin who was standing by the tunnel with both arms raised high.

United were virtually promoted; almost returned to Division One after 14 years away. They required just one point from two remaining games to clinch it, to make sure that goal average was not needed. They got that point a week later at White Hart Lane. While elsewhere in north London 99,000 people were watching Manchester United beat Blackpool 4-2 in the Cup final, 44,000 saw a Sibley goal straight after half-time win Newcastle the point in a 1-1 draw which enabled celebrations truly to begin.

George Martin had built the team to his own specifications, and had won promotion. It was not, at the end, a pretty sight. For the last 15 minutes of the Spurs match everybody but Milburn crowded back around big Frank Brennan to defend the point. And when Newcastle came to play their last, irrelevant league game of the season a week later, at home to Millwall, their lowest crowd of the season – 44,328 – turned out to see the newly promoted side win with a goal from Joe Harvey, the captain's third of the campaign. It was perhaps a signal that they, the fans, had given their all, and were also due a holiday.

Martin had sold some of the most skilful footballers ever to wear a black-and-white shirt. But he had also discovered Jackie Milburn's true position, and in so doing had uncovered one of the greatest English centre-forwards.

And he and the directors could breathe huge sighs of relief at the end of April 1948. They were back in Division One.

CHAPTER SEVEN

WEMBLEY MASTERS: 1948–55

❖

They enjoyed themselves back at the top. Some players reckoned that Division One was actually easier than Division Two, after the lower flight's desperate scramble for the precious pair of promotion places, and with its Chesterfields, Burys and Brentfords fighting hard to keep Newcastle down and keep that lucrative visit to St James's Park on their own agenda. These were impossible to ignore: the First Division found the club's gates as irresistible as had the Second – although the average, as United cruised to a comfortable fourth spot in the league, was down a couple of thousand on the previous, record-breaking promotion year.

And the players achieved recognition. The players past and present. On 20 September 1948 both Newcastle's Jackie Milburn and Sunderland's Len Shackleton were chosen for the Football League Select (a kind of full international second team, in those days before under-23s and under-21s) to play against the Irish League in Liverpool.

Shackleton – who a few months previously had helped his new club to escape relegation while his old club was winning promotion – found himself on the same train from the Northeast as the Newcastle director George Rutherford. 'You can get Jackie into the England team, Len,' urged Rutherford. 'You know the sort of passes he likes. Give them to him all the time and we'll have Jackie in an England shirt.'

Shackleton smiled to himself at this director, one of the men who had sold him just eight months earlier, calling upon him to display such selfless loyalty. But he did the job for Milburn. Jackie (who, incidentally, shared a Liverpool hotel room that weekend with yet another débutant, the Tottenham full-back Alf Ramsey, who insisted on staying up half the night talking tactics) got a hat-trick for the Football League, and later paid tribute to Shack's service.

And so two weeks later, on the evening of Monday, 4 October 1948, Milburn picked up the *Evening Chronicle* and read that he had been picked for the full England side to face Northern Ireland in Belfast that Saturday. A few days after that the official letter confirming this arrived from the FA's International Committee, who naturally informed the media of their decisions before writing to the players.

He scored once in a 6-2 thrashing of the Irish. It was the beginning of what would, in the end, be a somewhat disappointing international career. Hampered by injury (which he reckoned cost him some 20 caps), and obliged to compete for his place with such as Manchester United's Jack Rowley, his old team-mate Roy Bentley of Chelsea and, later, the formidable Nat Lofthouse, Jackie Milburn won only 13 England caps. But in those 13 matches he managed to score nine goals – a superb ratio which, had it been allowed to be spread over a greater number of matches, would have made Milburn one of the most celebrated England strikers.

As it was, Jackie settled down to becoming a hero of Tyneside. It was always enough for the Ashington boy, in between the transfer scares. The first came immediately after his England début. On the boat back from Belfast Milburn was convinced by some of his new team-mates that the streets leading to southern clubs were paved with gold. His wife, Laura, although a Glaswegian, had lived in Willesden Green, London, since the age of 16 (Milburn had met her when the Newcastle squad put up in a Luton hotel), and she was not altogether happy with the North-eastern climate. So Jackie put out a statement which read: 'I need to get away from the North-east because my wife's health is suffering'; Tyneside went into panic at the prospect of losing the last and best of the five musketeers; Stan Seymour stepped in for a few quiet words about contracts and prospects; and Milburn stayed where he was – 'among the good people of Northumberland, the best in the world'.

Steadily, as United consolidated their First Division place, he was joined by other footballers of note and potential. The reserve centre-forward Andy Donaldson, who had come to the club from Vickers Armstrong works team during the war and made just 19 first-team appearances in six years, was sold to Middlesbrough in January 1949 for an astonishing £17,000. (This footballing inflation – Hughie Gallacher himself had gone for only £10,000 just 20 years earlier – was due less to a decline in the real value of the pound than to the immense amounts of money which were being netted by soccer clubs in the football-hungry years after the war.)

Two days after the bonanza of Donaldson's sale, on 27 January 1949, Newcastle splashed out £26,500 on two Chilean brothers who were playing for Barnsley. United had really only wanted the inside-forward George 'Pancho' Robledo, who had become something of goalscoring sensation in Yorkshire, but George insisted that brother Ted, a relatively inexperienced half-back, come too.

They were quickly joined by another of the great historical names of Newcastle United. Bobby Mitchell moved from Third Lanark to Tyneside that February of 1949 for £16,000. Twelve years, 408 games, and 113 goals later, the brilliant little left-winger was still there – still as mesmerisingly skilful as ever, still the favourite of the fans, and still with his curious pre-match ritual of getting fully changed into his kit one whole hour before kick-off, and then killing the remaining 60 minutes by sitting down and doing crossword puzzles.

Mitchell made his début in the first league derby with Sunderland since 1934. George Robledo was also on the pitch for that emotionally charged fixture early in 1949, and the Chilean made his mark – and gave an early indication of the birth of one of the great goalscoring partnership – by sharing the goals with Milburn in a 2-1 victory. Pancho, Frank Brennan would say, would score 'hat-tricks all over the place. But most of them were down to Milburn. Jackie would have a crack from 20 or 30 yards, and they would come off the woodwork or a defender's body, and there would be George to put them away. He was always poaching around the goalmouth.'

That assessment of Robledo's contribution was lightly meant and slightly unfair. Pancho could, as Milburn would attest, and as the whole world would eventually see in the biggest club cup final of them all, lay on as many goals for Jackie as Jackie did for George.

Bradford had knocked United out of the FA Cup in 1949, and so the club sat back and concentrated on the league. A Milburn hattrick saw off Aston Villa by 3-2, and set the fans to wondering if Hughie Gallacher himself could have done any better.

And as the season drew to a close, United were actually in with an outside chance of the championship. They were just three points behind leaders Portsmouth, and Pompey were due to play at Fortress St James's. Pompey arrived, and the fortress walls collapsed. The south-coast team raced to a 5-0 hammering of United. Portsmouth's first league championship was clearly just weeks away. Newcastle, on the other hand, stunned by that defeat, promptly lost again at home to Derby County by 4-2, thereby relinquishing not only their hopes of the title, but the runners-up slot as well.

There was at least one happy Newcastle United footballer at the end of the 1948–49 season. Jackie Milburn finally got out of underground work at the pit. It was a well-kept secret at the time, but he escaped the worst of his reserved occupation with the help of a dodgy medical examination which diagnosed external otitis, or inflammation of the ear. Jackie was forever picking his ears with a matchstick. He knew it was dodgy, but he didn't care. For the rest of his time at the colliery he would be assigned to 'light' surface work, instead of grinding away on late shift at the coalface the night before an important match. External otitis, or chronic ear-picking, came as a blessed relief to Milburn. 'They got us out of the pits with that.'

As if to celebrate, he ducked out of the summer England tour of Scandinavia and France, and went instead with Newcastle to the USA and Canada. Stan Seymour, who had only recently been fielding transfer requests from his star striker, was impressed – the International Committee of the Football Association less so. Fortunately for all concerned, they did not write the Newcastle man out of their plans.

Fourth place had been good, but not good enough. George Martin strengthened his squad halfway through the 1949–50 season, when Newcastle were once more showing promise without actually topping the table, by purchasing two fine new talents from the Irish club Linfield. George Hannah and Alf McMichael would both turn out to be inspirational signings. Inside-forward Hannah would, despite being born in Liverpool, become an Irish international: an early example of the ancestral claim ruling. He would also stay with Newcastle for 167 games and eight wonderful years. Full-back McMichael became Newcastle's most capped footballer of all time with 40 appearances for Northern Ireland while on the club's books, which he was for 13 years until 1962, making 431 showings in a black-and-white shirt.

The two Irishmen made their début together in January 1950, helping United to a 4-2 victory over Manchester City. Hannah scored in this match, but twisted his ankle later and had to be helped from the field to a roof-raising endorsement from 58,000 fans. United had slipped to the middle of the table, and although they had got their FA Cup campaign off to a useful start by hammering Oldham of the Third Division (North) 7-2 in Lancashire, courtesy of another Milburn hat-trick, they were knocked out of the fourth round 3-0 by Chelsea at Stamford Bridge.

Without much of a chance of winning the title, they nonetheless embarked upon a promising run of league successes, beating Stoke 4-2 and West Bromwich Albion 5-1, with the help of an increasingly confident Jackie Milburn. The centre-forward finished the season with 18 league goals, and a useful hat-trick for England in a 4-1 win over Wales – Shackleton again helping his former team-mate – and yet another for the Football League in their 3-1 trouncing of the (Northern) Irish League in Belfast. As the Sheffield Wednesday inside-forward Eddie Quigley was sold in the close season to Preston North End for a world record fee of £27,000, pundits estimated Milburn's value on the market as being in the region of £80,000.

United began their 1950–51 league campaign by shooting to the top of Division One in the most convincing fashion, with ten undefeated matches. They were finally beaten 3-0 on 7 October at Villa Park in a match which top-scorer Milburn missed because – to loud complaints from the Newcastle directors – he was called to Northern Ireland as a non-playing England reserve by the Football Association. While he sat uselessly on the bench at Windsor Park watching England win 4-1, Newcastle were knocked from the top of Division One.

By December they had slipped to fourth position, and after a 7-0 defeat at Tottenham George Martin decided to pull down the curtain on his three-and-a-half-year reign at St James's Park by accepting the manager's job at Aston Villa. Some were sad to see Martin go; others considered that it made little difference. Stan Seymour moved from his director's chair into the manager's office once more, and, as Jackie Milburn said: 'Actually, Stan was always the big noise in the club whoever else was around.'

Seymour and trainer Norman Smith were recognised as the true powers behind even Martin's throne. Seymour had a large say in team selection and player purchase and sale, and Smith organised the squad, kept the lads in line, rollicked them for misdemeanours in front of the other directors, and enjoyed a pint with them in private. Not even Seymour and Smith, however, confident and familiar as they were, could have expected such enormous success so quickly.

When struggling Bury arrived from the depths of Division Two to face United in the third round of the FA Cup on 6 January 1951, Newcastle were in fifth place in Division One, five full points behind leaders Tottenham. The pitch was terrible that day: in the opinion of some possibly the worst ever to be played upon at St James's Park. A lake of thawed ice and rain sat on a surface which was frozen to the consistency of concrete. Both United's and Bury's officials argued that it was unplayable, but the referee insisted upon going ahead.

When his decision reached the Newcastle changing-room, George Robledo – displaying a far-sightedness unusual in British football of the time – proposed using the new rubber-studded boots which had arrived from South America following the 1950 Brazil World Cup, which England had entered for the furst time. He was dissuaded, and the whole team stuck with the large, screw-in studded footwear of their forebears. Robledo was truly ahead of his time. Stanley Matthews, who had also experienced the new boots in Brazil the previous summer, was about to market his new eponymously named boot in Britain. The 'Stanley Matthews', the adverts read, unlike the old Manfield Hotspur cobblery, weighed just 10 ounces and 'You can bend it double!'. Within a decade the Manfield Hotspur tackety boot was virtually obsolete, and the lightweight bendy plimsoll – often with moulded rubber studs – was all the rage.

The old boots did not let Newcastle United down on 6 January 1951, however. Within 19 minutes on that flooded skating rink of a surface, they were 4-0 up and Bury were effectively out of the cup. In the 11th minute Milburn flicked a low corner home at the near post with his right instep. He then drew the keeper and presented Tommy Walker with an open goal. Then George 'Pancho' Robledo collected a Joe Harvey free-kick and scored from ten yards. And, finally, just eight minutes after the first goal, Harvey knocked a Walker corner on to Ernie Taylor, who fired under the crossbar. Bury made it 4-1 with a penalty before half-time, but that was the way the scoreline stayed.

A week later Newcastle's failing league title hopes took a further knock when they travelled to play second-from-bottom Chelsea, and lost 3-1 thanks to a pair of goals from a 17-year-old wonderboy from Redcar called Bobby Smith. As if to rub salt in the wound, a certain Roy Bentley laid on both of Smith's goals. Newcastle could only console themselves with the thought that, as Redcar was nearer to Middlesbrough than to Gallowgate, Smith had technically been stolen from under the shadow of Ayresome, not St James's, Park.

Newcastle, not so long ago league leaders and favourites to regain their old Division One title, were suddenly fifth in the league. Stung, they turned to the cup. A gate of 67,659 paid £6,893 3s to watch First Division Bolton Wanderers, Nat Lofthouse and all, in the fourth round on 27 January. They anticipated a keen match. Wanderers had the best away record in the league (they had more points away from Burnden Park than at it), and they were just one place beneath Newcastle in Division One.

Frank Brennan was injured, and it was left to his recently signed Scottish understudy Matty McNeil to mark Lofthouse. McNeil could not cope. His inadequacy, however, only contributed to a stunningly thrilling contest. Bobby Mitchell gave United the lead after just three minutes when a Pancho Robledo shot was blocked and rebounded to his feet. Then McNeil fouled Lofthouse, and from the free-kick Bolton's inside-right Moir equalised. Four minutes later Lofthouse turned McNeil inside out and laid on an easy chance for Moir to make it 2-1.

In the hothouse atmosphere, it was clearly up to Jackie Milburn to make a point against his contender for the England number 9 shirt. He did so. He almost always did so – that is why he was loved. One minute after half-time Bobby Mitchell headed a through ball on to Milburn who, with his back to goal, spun around and shot home from 15 yards. Ten minutes later he had made it 3-2, and Newcastle were ahead for the first time in the match: Ernie Taylor played a low ball into the flying centre-forward's path. The whole Bolton defence – goalkeeper included – stood appealing for an offside decision that never came. Milburn raced on, and from 12 yards scuffed his shot so that if keeper Hanson had been doing his job instead of looking expectantly at the referee, he might have saved it. But he did not.

Then things got nasty. Lofthouse was being fouled beyond endurance by McNeil. After one scything tackle the Bolton and England man turned to the Newcastle half-back Charlie Crowe and asked: 'Who the hell is this fella? Does he think he's playing rugby or what? He'd better watch himself or I'll have him.'

McNeil, outclassed, could not and did not watch himself, and Lofthouse did have him. With 20 minutes to go Newcastle's stand-in centre-half went for a 50-50 ball with Lofthouse, and received Nat's boot on his ankle. As he lay on the turf being treated by Norman Smith, McNeil yelled threats at Lofthouse. The centre-forward strode over and informed him: 'Lad, you're not going to get up. You're out of this match.'

So he was. McNeil limped out time on the wing and was later rushed to hospital for X-rays. He played a sum total of 11 first-team matches for United before being transferred to Barnsley eight months later.

To everybody's relief, Frank Brennan was back for the fifth-round match at Stoke on 10 February. Another useful First Division team of the time, Stoke City were seriously handi-capped after just five minutes of this tie when their rightback Mould badly injured himself in a vain attempt to tackle Mil-burn. United cashed in their dividend against ten men, Pancho Robledo scoring twice to give them a 2-0 half-time lead. Stoke got one back shortly after the break, but Milburn nipped in to restore the two-goal advantage. A penalty brought the home side back to 3-2, but a Mitchell header shortly before the end concluded matters at 4-2.

Having disposed of two good Division One teams, nothing was more typical of United's cup form than that they should proceed to struggle against a side from the Third Division (South). It had actually taken Bristol Rovers three games to dispose of non-league Llanelli in the first round, and since then they had hardly been stretched, having drawn Second Division Luton and Hull in rounds four and five.

Bristol travelled to Newcastle as long-odds underdogs – and proceeded to draw 0-0 a match which they almost snatched at the very end, when Fairbrother could only watch a low shot whistle past his right-hand post. Fortunately the replay at Eastville four days later was a more comfortable affair, Taylor, Crowe and Milburn winning the game 3-1.

The semi-final was equally fraught. United drew Wolves at Hillsborough and, after running riot in a first 20 minutes that saw Milburn and full-back Bobby Cowell both come close and Milburn have a goal disallowed for offside (although 60 seconds earlier Swinbourne, his opposite number with Wolves, had also had one chalked off), the match settled down to a 0-0 draw. Once again, though, the opposing side could have snatched it at the close, when Hancocks twice missed in front of goal.

So to another midweek replay, this time at Leeds Road, Huddersfield, on a waterlogged pitch which, when the players kicked off, was surrounded by piles of emergency drainage pipes. Wolves took the lead early on and Newcastle came under pressure, particularly down their own left flank, where Wolves' goalscorer Walker and right-winger Hancocks gave Newcastle's left-back Bobby Corbett a torrid time ('I was too cocky,' said Corbett later, 'but I've learned my lesson.')

And then, 1-0 down and with their opponents on the war-path, disaster struck Newcastle United. Rising to clear a corner, Frank Brennan misjudged his landing, stumbled off the pitch, and cracked his head against a stacked drainage pipe with such ferocity that Stan Seymour said he heard it in the directors' box.

Under the substitution rules of 20 years later, Brennan would instantly have been replaced. As it was, Norman Smith treated Frank, who was grey-faced and clearly concussed, and urgently implored the centre-half not to head another ball until his vision was restored. Brennan mumbled something, lurched back into play – and immediately collected a fierce drive on his forehead, sending it back to the halfway line. He blinked, shook his head, and smiled fondly at his astonished team-mates.

After that, how could they lose? Little Ernie Taylor – who was having a wonderful season – found a way through the Wolves defence and laid on a tap-in for Milburn to equalise (a goal which meant that he had scored in every round so far), and then Milburn set up Bobby Mitchell to make it 2-1 and send Newcastle United through to yet another FA Cup final. The fans packed up their outsize rattles (one was five feet long) and 'souvenir magpies', bizarre mechanical birds which actually doffed their hats, and waited for the big day.

Once more, United had a rocky time in the seven weeks between the semi-final and the date at Wembley with Blackpool: United's desired opponents, for as Seymour said, 'Now we have two good-class teams who can play top-class football.'

There was immediate press speculation about the possibility of a league and cup double. After the semi-final victory, Newcastle were fifth in the table, just six points behind leaders Tottenham with 13 games to play and three games in hand.

Not only did they not win the league; they virtually threw their chances away. United took just 11 points from a possible 26 out of those 13 games, while Tottenham took 16 from their last ten and stormed to the title. What would become a familiar malaise was born: once in the cup final, Newcastle forgot about everything else.

Understandably unaware that the same pre-cup final malaise had affected the team back in the 1900s, many in 1951 blamed Stan Seymour. Immediately after the semi-final win over Wolves, the delighted manager had burst into the changing-room and excitedly announced: 'There's going to be no worrying about who plays in the cup final. Whatever happens, you fellows who've brought us this far will play at Wembley.'

He was as good as his word: the same 11 did turn out on 28 April. And he may have been right, for they probably comprised his strongest team. But the intervening seven weeks were crucial in the league, and 'quite unconsciously,' as one of them said, 'every man who is going to play in a great match doesn't put everything he possesses into ordinary league games before the great day.'

As a consequence, the huge support had little to roar about between early March and the end of April. There was a 'cup-final preview' when United visited Blackpool in the league, but both sides considered themselves by then to be out of title contention, and Stanley Matthews, Joe Harvey and Ernie Taylor were all rested. (Harvey's place was taken, incidentally, by the local lad who had progressed through the juniors, Bob Stokoe.)

The game finished 2-2, to the satisfaction of both teams, with Milburn scoring and then laying on a second-half equaliser for Robledo.

On 7 April, three weeks before the cup final, champions-elect Tottenham Hotspur visited Newcastle in the league and completed their double over the Tynesiders with a deserved 1-0 win. Newcastle's league hopes were, finally, dead and buried. They had, in the words of Jackie Milburn, 'tottered from one defeat to another'. Their form had been pathetic. They were demoted from cup favourites, and the bookies elevated Blackpool.

Blackpool were not only the bookies' favourites: they became the nation's darlings. This was largely due to the fact that their beloved ageing winger Stanley Matthews had, in the course of a distinguished 20-odd-year career, never won the one trophy which he coveted: the FA Cup. Three years earlier, at the age of 33, he had experienced his first final, and lost. Time was running out. Stanley's reward was overdue. This would, the papers crowed, be 'the Matthews Final'. Newcastle could certainly expect no support from the tens of thousands of neutrals at Wembley.

And their own preparations swung from tragedy to farce. The Newcastle players were genuinely resentful at the prospect of competing for just £12 a head in a football match which would raise £40,000 in gate money alone. Their mutinous feelings were not quelled by Len Shackleton, who wandered over from Sunderland one day to tell his old team-mates: 'You want to refuse to go on the bloody pitch!' This notion of a boycott was seriously, if briefly, discussed by the players, but they (probably correctly) decided that strike action would only persuade the board to field 11 reserves in the final.

In a ludicrous attempt to cash in, these First Division footballers, many of them internationals, were reduced to bringing out a brochure which they themselves attempted to sell for two shillings a time from a trestle table outside St James's Park on the match days before the final.

The club, in its thoughtless, high-handed behaviour, did not help matters. The players' wives were duly issued with tickets, but Ida Harvey noticed that they were for standing on the terrace! Ida told Joe: no seat, no Wembley. Stan Seymour was approached by the club captain and persuaded to find the ladies more comfortable accommodation behind the Royal Box.

Still the ructions rumbled on. A week before the final the team was taken to Buxton Spa, a venue which had proved lucky for them before other big matches. For the first three days they were allowed a loose rein. From Wednesday onwards, however, a no-drinking curfew was in force. Two players instantly broke it; Stan Seymour caught them sneaking like truant schoolboys back into the hotel; and they were told that they would be dropped and sent home. The whole Newcastle party spent an anxious night, until Seymour woke up in the morning and, relenting, allowed them to stay for the price of an apology.

The rest of the world knew little or nothing of Newcastle United's attempts to defeat themselves in the 1951 cup final. One or two little things, however, worked in their favour. They were an independently minded crew. They knew that they had ditched their own league chances, but they did not much mind; they were happy to sacrifice the league for the cup. 'We stopped playing league games after the semis,' Milburn admitted later – but so what? Wembley was the place. The league was a comparatively workaday affair, won and lost on cold dark grounds in midweek. You could win or lose the league without even playing the decisive game. The league had less glamour than the cup – and there was not even, in 1951, the prospect of European competition for the champions and runners-up.

But Wembley, 'with a crowd of 100,000 people and millions more looking in on television, is a setting second to none'. 'I have no excuses to make,' Joe Harvey would say soon after the collapse in his team's league form. 'All that concerned us was winning at Wembley.'

In other words, Wembley excited and motivated this group of individualists. 'We always had to have a reason for winning,' said Jackie Milburn. 'I remember the lads once reading in the papers that Derby County had gone 12 games unbeaten. From that moment they were dead . . . we just had to take their record. Right or wrong, that's the sort of team we were.'

And Stan Seymour, for all his unorthodox promises to the semi-final team early in March, the promises which tied his hands and blunted his league campaign, retained a degree of cuteness. He, after all, had won the cup back in 1924, and he never stopped reminding his players of the fact. 'He was crafty, was Stan, and he knew how to egg us on. It certainly worked!'

They had the best support in England, 12,000 of whom would be at Wembley. And no fewer than six of the Newcastle United team were the local boys whom Stan Seymour, with brilliant foresight and superb selection, had signed on during or immediately after the war. There was right-back Bobby Cowell, a quiet man, a keen gardener, who nonetheless led the coach choir on away games. There was left-back Bobby Corbett whose job would be to mark Stanley Matthews, and who, when asked about the prospects for Wembley, replied: 'Aa'll dee me best.'

There was talkative, sociable Charlie Crowe, a Newcastle United fan and footballer since boyhood. There was right-winger Tommy Walker, the former sprinter from Cramlington. Inside Walker there was five-foot-four-inch Ernie Taylor – Ernie of the size-four boots; Ernie who, after any match, would want to discuss the game and United's tactics, moving salt and pepper cellars and mustard pots about the table. And, greatest of them all, there was Jackie Milburn. Softly spoken, chain-smoking Jackie, who signed every autograph, whose only weakness was a round of Canasta and records of popular music, and who was the fastest, deadliest forward in Great Britain.

Those six men, all brought in and up by Stan Seymour, would have been on the terraces had they not been on the pitch. They were Geordies. They had cost the club nothing. And they did not intend to let Newcastle United – fractious, rebellious, discontented Newcastle United – lose the 1951 cup final. Or any other cup final.

So the team which travelled from Derbyshire to Weybridge outside London on the Friday afternoon before the final; the team which was entertained by big, comical Jack Fairbrother commandeering the coach's microphone all the way south – the team was in better shape than might have been expected. They were prepared to play not for the directors who exploited them, but for themselves, for each other, for Newcastle, and for the fans.

And they were prepared to win because they were annoyed by Blackpool's favoured status in the press, because they wanted nothing more than to 'spoil Matthews' Wembley party', as the normally good-natured Milburn put it, and because they knew themselves to be one of the best teams in the Football League. They were formidable opposition.

They proved it, of course. Stan Seymour introduced them to the Wembley turf for an hour on the Friday afternoon, 24 hours before kick-off. They were woken at seven on the morning of Saturday, 28 April, by fans singing 'Blaydon Races' outside the hotel. George Robledo, who was terrified of travelling by bus, left to catch a train to Wembley after lunch – the rest followed him by coach. Seymour told his players that he was not going to tell them how to win the game: as adult professionals with Newcastle United they should know that already. The pale, sickly King George VI, who would die nine months later, was introduced to the squad by Joe Harvey (who had that 1901 penny deposited safely in his pocket).

'Have you played here before?' the king asked the captain.

'No,' replied Harvey, and jerked a thumb at Seymour at the end of the line, 'but our chief has.' Then Newcastle United's eighth FA Cup final, and third at Wembley, kicked off.

Matthews gave them trouble in the first half despite the attentions of both left-half Charlie Cowell and full-back Corbett, and Cowell was obliged to clear a Stan Mortenson header off the line.

But the second period was dominated – and the cup was won – by two sensational goals. Blackpool had, in an attempt to deal with the threat presented by J.E.T. Milburn's speed, employed an offside trap. For all of the first half it worked well. It seemed once to have resulted in an apparently good Milburn goal being chalked off, although the players later learned that it was disallowed for a mistaken hand-ball. Newcastle discussed the offside trap at half-time and decided on a ploy. In the 50th minute, the ploy worked and Blackpool's offside trap was blown apart.

Milburn received the ball under pressure on the halfway line. He instantly played it back ten yards to George Robledo. Robledo held off a challenge just inside the centre circle and pushed the ball back strongly into Milburn's path. Jackie's acceleration took him immediately clear of Blackpool's centre-half Eric Hayward; he actually had time to pause on the ball and check that the linesman's flag was still down. It was: if there was any doubt about Hayward being between him and the goal, right-back Shimwell had definitely played him onside. Shimwell was now racing to cover, but it was too late. 'I knew he would score,' reflected Joe Harvey afterwards, 'and so did Jackie.' Milburn – who once clocked 100 yards in 9.7 seconds – set off again, left Shimwell dawdling in his wake, and, as George Farm advanced off the Blackpool goal-line, he tucked it neatly into the net below and beyond the goalkeeper's right hand. Flustered and wrong-footed, Farm was not even given the chance to dive.

Milburn had now scored in every round of the FA Cup – every round available to him, of course, as First Division Newcastle did not enter until the third. He personally rated that first goal against Blackpool as his best, 'a goal for the connoisseur', and a goal which had stemmed from intelligent discussion at half-time, but it was his and United's second which attracted the plaudits.

It came just five minutes later, in the 55th minute. Tommy Walker swept down the right wing and played the ball to Ernie Taylor in the inside-right position at the edge of the Blackpool penalty area. 'I was wondering whether to try a shot or not,' Taylor recalled, 'but out of the corner of my eye I saw a black-and-white shirt streaking along . . .'

Milburn was moving in from behind Taylor, screaming, 'Backheel it!' By the time Ernie did so, the centre-forward was 25 yards from goal, and slightly on top of the ball. He hit it left-footed, and fell over. Once again Farm had no time to leave the ground: Milburn's shot shrieked into goal inside his top right-hand corner. It was moving with immeasurable force, but still managed to curl slightly inwards. Taylor missed it all, shot and goal. Having delivered the backheel he turned his back to goal, heard the roar, and saw Milburn 'sitting on the ground, grinning!'.

It was, Stanley Matthews said later, 'the greatest goal I have ever seen, and certainly the finest ever scored at Wembley'. As Milburn returned to the centre circle the Blackpool centre-forward Stan Mortenson – who came originally from South Shields, and who had actually turned out for Newcastle in a couple of wartime matches – shook his hand and said: 'That's just about the greatest goal I've ever seen. It deserves to win the cup.' 'It's ours,' muttered Joe Harvey to himself, clapping his hands together gleefully. 'It's ours.'

At the final whistle a drained 36-year-old Matthews grabbed Milburn by the hand and said to the man who had 'spoiled his party': 'You deserved it, Jackie. Well done.' From the Royal Box the young Princess Margaret told the passing Jack Fairbrother: 'A lovely day for you!' Joe Harvey collected the cup, clattered down the steps and sprinted across to the massed choir of Geordies waving the trophy and shouting: 'It's yours! It's yours!' Tommy Walker and Bobby Corbett sneaked out of the changing-room to cut off a piece of Wembley turf. 'I'll water this every day,' Corbett told Joe Harvey. 'You might as well put it back,' said Harvey. 'I'm coming back next year.'

To most of the players, that 1951 cup-winning side was the best of the lot. It was a proud outfit, quirky, perhaps, but single-minded when it chose to be. It played a measured passing game which could explode into life around the opposition's penalty area. It was hard in defence, and fast and direct up front. It was a well-balanced team, with the brilliance of Taylor, the workrate of Crowe, the stature of Brennan, and Joe Harvey, not the most skilful of footballers or the most elegant of captains, but . . . 'It never mattered to Joe how much of a rollicking he got from the crowd: he made his own decisions and he knew his players were always 100 per cent behind him,' said Milburn. 'And that's not usual, I can tell you.' And the team had him, 'WOR JACKIE,' headlined the *Sunday Sun*, 'THE TOAST OF LONDON'. Wey aye.

The directors, naturally, succeeded in creating some ill will out of all this glory, all this happiness and joy. Once more, the situation veered towards farce. Back in Newcastle a celebration dance was laid on at the Oxford Galleries, and the directors told the players to bring their wives, as a 'special presentation' would be made to the ladies.

Every footballer knew of the undercover payments made to professionals. One cup-final opponent of Newcastle United had promised to slip each of its players £750 in the event of a victory. The Newcastle lads did not object to any of this – they just wondered where theirs was. For the Newcastle directors were famously tight-fisted when it came to payments, legal or illegal.

Now, however, it was obviously all going to be put right. The rumours confirmed that the presentation to the wives would be 'handbags'. And what could be in those handbags, but . . .

Come the big night, and one by one the wives trooped up on to the bandstand to be presented with their fashion accessories. Tantalisingly, the brand new handbags were bulging – so much so that the handle snapped off Mrs George Hannah's before she got back to her table. Salivating, the players seized the handbags, tore them open, and found . . . old newspaper stuffing. Not a pound note anywhere. What you saw was what you got, and the handbags were it. The club had bought them all in a cut-price job lot for £17. 'That was what we got for winning the cup! Oh, it's unbelievable! We never got a penny. The lads never forgave the club for that.'

Some of the lads quickly got out. The team that money could not buy split itself up. After a short tour of Europe, United had a pre-season warm-up game against Celtic. With no warning and little explanation, Seymour dropped Taylor, Corbett and Crowe. Ernie Taylor slapped in a transfer request; the Newcastle board pompously refused to be 'blackmailed'; Joe Harvey's anguished pleas were ignored ('Stan, for God's sake don't give the little fell a transfer. Transfer me! Anybody! But keep Ernie.'); and Taylor went to the team he had just beaten at

Wembley, Blackpool, for £25,000. It all happened so quickly that it seemed hardly credible. Taylor, naturally, was later capped for England.

Bobby Corbett was the next to go, supposedly after an onfield bust-up with Joe Harvey at Bolton early in the 1951–52 season, but it was really just another manifestation of discontent with the club when the boy from Throckley Welfare moved on to Middlesbrough.

Even Jackie Milburn, who had fallen out with the directors when they stopped him from taking a £1,000 job in the close season as a football boot manufacturer's representative, had to issue a press statement insisting that he had no plans to depart – 'if I leave Newcastle it will be because they have kicked me out'.

Charlie Crowe, upset by his gradual replacement by George Robledo's brother Ted, kept asking for a transfer and being refused. Jack Fairbrother, who when Ronnie Simpson had arrived from Third Lanark earlier in 1951 had been reassured that his own goalkeeping position was secure, was instantly replaced by Simpson at the start of the 1951–52 season, and shortly afterwards moved on to non-league Peterborough, later returning to Tyneside with Gateshead.

New boys were bought in, of course. Third Division Chester City were relieved of their Welsh international inside-forward Billy Foulkes, who was bought to fill the enormous gap left by the departure of Ernie Taylor; and another Welsh international forward, Reg Davies, arrived from Southend. Alf McMichael was promoted to the first team, and Ted Robledo became something of a regular. And Bill McCracken, the veteran of the great days of three and four decades earlier who had returned to Newcastle as chief scout, had his eyes on a 21-year-old serviceman named Vic Keeble, who was turning out as centre-forward for Third Division (South) Colchester United. If Keeble was bought – and that was thought to be unlikely, as his army commitments made him a risky investment – just who was he supposed to replace?

But this remarkable football club, riven from base to apex by discontent, suspicion and dissension, just kept on winning. It was bizarre. They seemed to feed off their own bitterness, to take energy from their disputes. With Milburn injured early in the season, George Robledo took the opportunity to start cracking in the goals as if there was no tomorrow. By January 1952 the Chilean had hit 26, compared with Milburn's 16. Robledo did not of course score as many goals for Newcastle United as did Jackie Milburn. George got a total of 91, and Jackie netted 198. But Robledo played far fewer matches – just 164 against Milburn's marathon 395 peacetime fixtures; and so Pancho's goal ratio of 0.55 goals a game was actually better than Jackie's ratio of 0.50. Statistics do not prove greatness, of course, and if we're talking decimal figures here, neither of them came close to Hughie Gallacher.)

Between them, once Milburn regained fitness, they would score 61 league and cup goals in 1951–52, Robledo getting 33 and Milburn 28. Newcastle scored an astonishing total of 113 goals in 49 league and FA Cup games. Twice United hit seven goals, and four times six goals in the league. In their first four home matches they scored 20 and conceded just three.

Once more, then, they hurtled to the top of the league in the first four months of the season, and once more the newspapers were excitedly tipping Stan Seymour's team for the league and cup double.

The press could hardly be blamed. By the time the draw for the third round of the FA Cup sent Aston Villa to St James's Park on 12 January 1952, United were fourth in Division One, five points behind leaders Portsmouth with a game in hand. They had scored 38 goals in 13 home games, and 39 goals in 13 away games. They were phenomenal. They warmed up for that third-round tie with Villa – who were managed by Newcastle's old boss George Martin, and had three former United reserves in their forward line – in typical form, murdering Preston North End 3-0 with goals from Milburn (racing in at the far post), Robledo (pressing in to convert a low cross), and Foulkes (flicked skilfully in off the post). Frank Brennan ended the game with his right instep heavily bandaged, but pronounced himself fit for next Saturday's cup-tie.

Almost 57,000 fans saw a stunning match that afternoon. Villa's Hebburn-born inside-left Jackie Dixon, whom George Martin had taken with him from St James's Park to the Midlands, gave the visitors a dream 0-2 lead within 13 minutes of the kick-off. Twice Dixon beat Ronnie Simpson with consummate ease, leaving the Geordie supporters wondering exactly why their club had released him. After 20 minutes George Robledo nodded down a Mitchell cross for Billy Foulkes to make it 1-2, but that was the way the scoreline stayed for another 60 minutes – and in fact, Villa were judged unlucky not to have made it 1-3 when their North-eastern centre-forward (and another United old boy) Tommy Thompson had the ball in the net in the 38th minute but was ruled offside.

Then, with just nine minutes remaining, all hell broke out in the Aston Villa penalty area. Firstly right-back Bobby Cowell pushed forward and caused havoc on the edge of the Villa box: the ball ran loose and Bobby Mitchell slammed it home from 25 yards. One minute later Mitchell ran onto a Robledo pass to make it 3-2. And before the hubbub subsided, Robledo himself converted a cross from Milburn. United had come back from the dead to win 4-2. Villa trooped unhappily home.

After Villa, it was high-flying Tottenham Hotspur at White Hart Lane in the fourth round. Spurs were league champions and United were cup-holders: the London club were presently sixth from the top of the league, and the North-easterners were fourth. Newcastle's old good fortune in drawing teams from the lower divisions appeared to have temporarily deserted them, but nobody complained. 'The world's greatest showman,' enthused the *Sunday Sun* 'could not have brought together two more colourful teams for what should be the match of the year.'

'We seem to be set for the greatest cup clash since the war,' commented Stan Seymour. 'I see no reason to unduly worry about the Spurs.' Joe Harvey added that he was confident at least of forcing a draw, 'but we are capable of winning at the first attempt, and that is our goal'.

United prepared for their trip to Tottenham by thrashing Charlton Athletic 6-0 with two apiece from Milburn (each of them a beauty from distance) and Robledo, after Walker and Foulkes had made it 2-0. Newcastle were flying: they sat just four points behind Manchester United with three games in hand.

And Spurs suffered. Newcastle trained for a week at Brighton before moving up to north London and – fielding an unchanged 11 for the 11th consecutive week – annihilating the champions by 3-0. Tottenham's famous 'push-and-run' game was entirely eclipsed by United's fast, hard, direct game which saw Pancho Robledo finish off a move started by brother Ted in the 13th minute; Mitchell hit a 20-yarder 15 minutes later; and Robledo finished things off halfway through the second half. 'Well played, Bobby,' said Spurs' right-back Alf Ramsey to Mitchell straight after his third-round tie. 'All the best for Wembley.'

The result was front-page news. Geordies packed the streets of the West End, singing and chanting and boasting that this was their best result in London since . . . well, since the previous April's final. We want Arsenal, they chanted. Send the Gunners up for the next round . . .

They would have to wait for the Gunners – and for the fifth round. In the meantime there were league points to win. 'All the lads,' announced Milburn to the press immediately after the Spurs match, in an attempt to head off mentions of the previous year's slide, 'say they are going for league points just as hard as for a cup bonus.'

Whether they were or they weren't, they failed to win them. In the two weeks between the fourth and fifth rounds Newcastle played three league games and won just one point. On 16 February, the Saturday before they were due to travel to Swansea for their fifth-round tie, they crashed 3-0 at mid-table Wolves. Suddenly they were seven points behind Manchester United with just one game in hand. The rot had set in once more. Stan Seymour took a risk and finally bought Vic Keeble from Colchester for £15,000 in that month, but one centre-forward, no matter how good in the air, was not going to correct this strange failing.

They beat Second Division Swansea at the Vetch Field, of

course, a Bobby Mitchell volley just before half-time proving enough to clinch a 1-0 win and save some blushes, for the Welshmen missed an uncomfortable number of chances. The Swansea match was, Joe Harvey said later, the toughest game in their 1952 cup run: 'We had to fight every inch of the game, and I make no apologies for saying we were lucky that day.'

The quarter-final draw on 8 March 1952 looked like the hardest of the lot: a 674-mile round trip to play Portsmouth, who were third from the top of Division One and – unlike Newcastle – still going strong in the league.

In the event, that tie was possibly the club's greatest success of the season. It was also, according to some spectators, the finest cup quarter-final that Wembley never saw. Portsmouth took the lead in the fourth minute, and then Jackie Milburn – aware of young Vic Keeble breathing down his neck from the proximity of the reserves – set off on a number of scintillating but fruitless runs. In the 36th minute Milburn went off for treatment of agonising stomach cramps, and returned to flick home a 40th-minute equaliser.

After 17 minutes of the second half Billy Foulkes surged through the middle and released Milburn, who lobbed the keeper and saw the ball hit the angle before dropping onto the line and rolling into the net. Portsmouth made it 2-2 shortly afterwards, but Milburn was on fire. He completed his hat-trick in the 81st minute, drawing a fiery Scottish half-back named Jimmy Scoular out of position before thumping his shot home by the far post. Robledo completed the scoring at 4-2, thanks to a move started by Milburn. 'I should say,' reported the *Sunday Express*, 'that Milburn turned in one of the best centre-forward displays of all time.'

'Everything he did,' announced the *Sunday Sun*, 'bore the stamp of class, and so outstanding was he that some folk might have forgotten just how good was this Newcastle team.'

This Newcastle team was astonishingly unchanging. Since the disruptions at the turn of the year, Seymour had stuck as faithfully as possible to a set 11 players. They were Simpson; Cowell and McMichael; Harvey, Brennan and Ted Robledo;

Walker, Foulkes, Milburn, George Robledo and Mitchell. Unless obliged to do so by injury or sickness or suspension (and there were hardly any of those) Seymour never deviated from this line-up. Superb talents such as George Hannah, Charlie Crowe, Bob Stokoe, Reg Davies, Vic Keeble, and the home-grown Alex Tait and Ron Batty, were left in the reserves, week after week.

They were an effective, settled side, but there was some dispute as to their actual merit. Joe Harvey rated them as 'scientific, swift and brilliant' when they were allowed to play, and 'the stubbornest, hardest-to-beat 11 in football' when the chips were down. But many of the players, Milburn included, rated the vintage of 1952 well below that of 1951. It was not as enjoyable a side to play with. Something irreplaceable had gone when Ernie Taylor left for Blackpool.

Len Shackleton (who else?) thought their 'direct, go-ahead' style was boring and monotonous – 'although Ernie Taylor and Bobby Mitchell helped to relieve the monotony to some extent. Perhaps Newcastle's plan was inspired by the director who once told the United lads, "Kick the ball as hard as you can, and chase like mad after it".'

Good or bad, they were indisputably settled. Not even another, predictable spell of appalling league results by this cup-obsessed squad could induce Seymour to drop one of them. Two weeks after the Portsmouth quarter-final Newcastle travelled to Liverpool, where two vengeful goals from Albert Stubbins helped the Scousers to a 3-0 win which effectively finished United's 1952 league title hopes.

As in 1951, the statistics are damning. On 26 January 1952, a week before the Spurs fourth-round cup-tie, Newcastle United had taken 34 points from 26 Division One games and were, as we have seen, strongly placed in fourth spot. Between the Tottenham game, which got their cup campaign rolling once more, and the end of the season they took a mere 11 points from 16 games. They finished in eighth position. They were the division's top scorers with 98 goals, but they were 12 points shy of the championship.

They drew Second Division Blackburn Rovers in the semi-final of the FA Cup, and the bookies instantly made Newcastle favourites to become the first club in the 20th century to retain the trophy for two consecutive years (Blackburn Rovers themselves had last done it in 1889–90 and 1890–91).

The first semi-final at Hillsborough resulted in a 0-0 draw, which United considered themselves lucky to attain after a wonderful save from Simpson in the dying minutes kept them in the hunt. And the faithful consoled themselves with the thought that it had taken the unrepeatable combination of Newcastle at their worst and Blackburn at their best to produce a stalemate. The replay at Leeds would be a different story.

It was, but only just. Robledo headed home a Milburn cross to give United the lead early in the second half, but Eddie Quigley grabbed an equaliser for Rovers. The end of the match was pure drama. A Robledo shot was handled in the box; the referee gave the penalty; captain Joe Harvey put the ball on the spot and looked around for his regular penalty taker. But Jackie Milburn was walking away from the area. Harvey chased him, and Milburn rubbed his knee, indicating an injury. In truth the great centre-forward, who made no bones in private about his own lack of footballing confidence, did not want to take this crucial penalty. Harvey looked around in desperation until little Bobby Mitchell stepped forward without a word and slammed the ball past the static Blackburn keeper. It was 2-1, and Newcastle were at Wembley once more.

There, in a month's time, they would meet Arsenal, who had disposed of Chelsea in another replay. It gave them time for a bit more internal conflict. Charlie Crowe continued his regular applications for a transfer, until being bought off by Stan Seymour offering him 100 cup final tickets (three times his normal allocation as a reserve) and a guaranteed place in the close-season trip to South Africa.

Shortly afterwards Newcastle were fined 50 guineas by the FA for giving their footballers twice as much spending money as was allowed. United had been in the habit of slipping the lads two pounds a day pocket-money on away trips. This should, said the FA, be only one pound. United's directors promptly concurred, topping up the quid with a compensatory bonus packet of cigarettes – which suited Jackie Milburn, who pocketed his non-smoking colleagues' rations.

Charlie Crowe's 100 tickets was the standard allocation to a player who was in the cup final team. The professionals would, of course, keep a dozen or so for friends and family, and sell the rest at an inflated profit. This was illegal. Shortly before the 1952 final rumours swept Tyneside that Newcastle CID were investigating a £350 ticket deal involving a Newcastle player. Immediately after the final Joe Harvey, the Newcastle captain, was prosecuted, and shortly after that the FA imposed a limit of 12 tickets per player. This merely impoverished the professionals: it did not prevent abuse. The directors and club officials still had their own limitless allocations. During the 1952 final, said Len Shackleton, 'some of the smartest spivs from the seamy side of the city of Newcastle occupied the best seats behind the Royal Box.' That state of affairs would not change.

In contrast, Jimmy Nelson, Newcastle's Scotland international captain for the 1932 final against Arsenal, wrote to St James's Park asking for a ticket – one ticket – for the 1952 final. He received in reply a telegram which read:

'NELSON ROYAL GEORGE HOTEL MACKINTOSH PLACE CARDIFF. REGRET NONE AVAILABLE. NEWCASTLE UNITED.'

Jimmy Richardson, Newcastle's outside-right in the 1932 final, sent the club a postal order for six shillings and asked for two of the cheapest Wembley seats in 1952. His postal order was returned intact, with no tickets and no further comment.

'We are the happiest side in soccer,' Joe Harvey told the press a week before the final. 'United today are a real family party.' Happy they might have been; a family they were not.

By 26 April, a week before the cup final, the league had been well and truly won by Matt Busby's Manchester United, and Newcastle were doomed to finish no higher than eighth. So they promptly beat Aston Villa 6-1. Seymour rested George Robledo and Billy Foulkes for this last league match, giving Reg Davies and George Hannah a run-out in the inside-forward positions. Frank Brennan put United ahead with a rare goal in the fifth minute. He scored it, he said, to spite Hughie Gallacher, who had joined the Tyneside media and had written a newspaper column accusing Brennan of being nothing more than a stopper. 'That bugger's for you, Hughie!' Frank yelled at the press box on his way back to his own half. Davies got two, and Hannah, Mitchell and Milburn shared the others.

Both Davies and Hannah put in exemplary skilful performances, revolutionising United's forward play, and giving Milburn 'his happiest afternoon for some time'. But they knew, and the fans knew, and Seymour knew, and the rest of the squad knew, and Robledo and Foulkes knew who would be walking out at Wembley, despite that what-might-have-been cuffing of Villa in the league.

For a record-making occasion, the 1952 cup final, despite being won by Newcastle 1-0, was generally accepted as being something of an anti-climax. It was partly the sense of déjà vu, the been-there-done-that feeling of so many of the players. 'I for one did not feel the satisfaction of the previous year,' said Milburn sadly. 'It was nothing like the first time,' agreed Frank Brennan. 'Nothing ever is. First time is always best.'

There was also something about the match. For once Arsenal – lucky Arsenal, boring Arsenal – were deemed to be slightly unfortunate, and won public affection. Not because they were the better team. United were below form, but were still the better team. But because of an incident in the 24th minute, and its repercussions . . .

It all began cheerfully enough, with the newly re-elected prime minister Winston Churchill doing the pre-match honours; and with former army buddies Joe Harvey and the 38-year-old left-half Joe Mercer – now the captains of Newcastle and Arsenal – chatting amiably in the centre circle before kick-off. Harvey would later say that his most vivid and happiest memory of that day was of 'a bandy-legged little man in a red shirt, sweat pouring down his craggy face, his chest heaving' laughing, as

Mercer (for it was he) shook a fist at Harvey and shouted: 'That's as far as you come, you big lanky . . .'

Not much had happened until the 24th minute. Then Arsenal's right-back Wally Barnes, chasing the ball and under no pressure, stuck his foot in the thick Wembley turf, twisted and fell to the ground in agony. For a few minutes he limped on, and then he hobbled off the pitch and out of football forever.

Arsenal were reduced to ten men with more than an hour to play, and that condemned the match. All the players hated it: Newcastle because of the unfair pressure, and Arsenal because their remaining nine outfielders had to run until they literally dropped. Joe Harvey remained convinced that Newcastle would have won more easily had Barnes played on. 'My team was full of pity,' he said. 'I had the hardest job I ever had as skipper. I cursed, I swore, I cajoled, I pleaded. "You're a set of babies," I told them at half-time. "You're feeling sorry for Mercer's lot. You'll feel even sorrier for yourselves if I don't get that cup." '

But the chances were few. Milburn, having a quiet game, saw one back-header cleared off the line, and Arsenal twice came close towards the end. Then, with five minutes remaining, from the left wing Bobby Mitchell swung a long cross over to beyond the back post, where George Robledo ran in and headed it down and – flicking the post on its way – into goal.

'There was a lack of drama about the goal,' was Milburn's verdict. Everybody else chose, in the absence of any great spectacle, to praise Arsenal's 'heroism'. 'It was a valiant game by Arsenal,' said Gateshead councillor Norman McCretton, 'for they were struggling most of the game against injuries.'

One young pair of eyes at least found the contest inspirational: 17-year-old Ray Wilson, who was just about to sign professional forms with Huddersfield Town, and who would 14 years later win the World Cup on that very ground, was attending his first Wembley final. 'There was the fabulous Bobby Mitchell,' Wilson recalled, 'skating with speed and effortless skill down Newcastle's left wing. There was Jackie Milburn, so quick and lethal in the middle, and George Robledo's goal . . .

'Poor Arsenal. Everything seemed to be going against them. Men were collapsing with cramp as they tried to cover too much ground after the injury that ended the career of their Welsh international Wally Barnes. Joe Mercer, the oldest man on the field, was playing magnificently in the losing cause. It seemed a pity he had to be on the defeated side.'

But he was, and the cup returned to Tyneside for the second successive year, and toasts were drunk in the North-east to 'United – the Team of the Century!'

They returned, hot, tired and happy, from a 16-match tour of southern Africa. They had promptly to greet yet another new arrival, a Northern Irish half-back called Tommy Casey who was signed from Bournemouth, and who at first looked like just another example of Stan Seymour's compulsive desire to have every available footballer in Great Britain on Newcastle United's books. Casey or no Casey, a poor start to the 1952–53 season (they took only seven points from their first eight games) was complicated by another Milburn transfer request in September.

This incident appears to have begun with a light-hearted suggestion by the new United director Lord Westwood that anybody who wanted Jackie should 'start bidding at £30,000'. It is possible that the cute, dispassionate Seymour might have accepted such a record sum for his 28-year-old striker. Stan Seymour could be quite unsentimental when it came to players – and, after all, he had Vic Keeble (who had scored both goals in Newcastle's 4-2 Charity Shield defeat by Manchester United) itching in the wings.

Certainly, when Milburn approached the manager-director, Seymour told him to put a transfer request in writing. Taking this to be a strong hint that his Newcastle career was on the rocks, Milburn did so. But the board instantly considered his written request, and rejected it.

The next 24 months were a time of flux. In January 1953 United beat Swansea in the third round of the cup, but were astonishingly knocked out of the fourth round 3-1 at home by Second Division Rotherham United. The Yorkshire side had a talented young forward named Len White and, true to form, Seymour pursued his if-you-can't-beat-'em-buy-'em policy by instantly grabbing White for £13,000. The cup, incidentally, was finally won by Blackpool: Stanley Matthews had his medal.

On 25 February St James's Park celebrated its newly installed floodlights by hosting a showpiece match with Celtic. United won 3-0 (Robledo, 3). There was little other brightness on the horizon. Ted Robledo left for the Colo Colo club of Santiago, the reigning champions in his native Chile (who also, coincidentally, played in black and white), soon to be followed across the Atlantic by his free-scoring brother George. By April United were struggling in the relegation zone, and a 3-2 home win over Bolton in the last league match of the season made them seem more secure than they actually had been. They finished in 16th place, safer than it seemed, for they were actually just three points clear of relegated Stoke City.

In the close season Joe Harvey retired from playing to become club coach. His replacement was that hard-working half-back whom United had encountered in the cup at Portsmouth a year earlier. Newcastle paid a club record fee of £25,000 for Jimmy Scoular. His legacy was mixed. He turned out to be a solid, faithful, disciplined and reasonably successful captain. But there could be no doubt that Harvey's passing marked the end of an era. Scoular, said Jackie Milburn, just was not what Newcastle were used to – 'mainly we were all just local lads who'd got together after the war'. The Yorkshireman Harvey had become, of course, an honorary local lad. Scoular, on the other hand, was clearly as Scottish as it was possible to be, and he enjoyed the company of other Scots, and some of the Englishmen accused him of divisive clique-ishness. United's long and honourable Scottish tradition, the immense and unrepayable debt which the club owed to Scotland, could at times conveniently be forgotten.

At first, Scoular made little impression. After a good start to the 1953–54 season, United set a miserable new record by losing six consecutive home league games. Following the sixth, a 2-0 beating by Huddersfield, Seymour went out and paid

Manchester City £20,000 for their 29-year-old forward Ivor Broadis. It was not perhaps so rash a signing as some suspected, for the ageing Broadis actually gained his six England caps while on United's books. At the time, however, along with the purchase of the Stockton-born centre-forward Alan Monkhouse from Millwall, it looked suspiciously like a panic measure.

The team struggled to get through the third and fourth rounds of the cup against non-league Wigan Athletic and First Division Burnley, but went out honourably in the fifth round at West Bromwich Albion – who would eventually win the trophy and finish as runners-up in Division One.

Scoular was promptly dropped, and Alf McMichael given the captaincy. Over the following couple of months, as Newcastle trailed in to 15th place in Division One, no fewer than six disgruntled first-team players asked for a transfer. They were Bob Stokoe, George Hannah, Billy Foulkes, Ron Batty, Reg Davies and Tommy Walker. Walker was promptly sold to Oldham. The other five would not only stay but would astonishingly, within 15 months, be part of yet another FA Cup-winning squad.

Behind the scenes it is clear in retrospect that all of the big football clubs who were milking the profits from the huge gates of the 1950s were sowing the wind and preparing to reap the whirlwind. Because of the fixed low-wage system, clubs such as Newcastle usually had more money than they knew how to spend. In 1952 the top Newcastle players were all on the maximum £12 a week. In the 1951–52 season the club made a profit of £42,637. The total gate money from the cup final that year was £40,000 – the winning Newcastle team each took home a £20 bonus.

By 1954 the players' maximum wage had crept up to £15. But because United had managed to make an unusual annual loss of £38,619 – thanks largely to Stan Seymour's cavalier approach to the transfer market – several top players were actually told to take a wage cut! Ronnie Simpson saw his packet reduced to £13, and Billy Foulkes and the recently signed Len White were also trimmed.

On top of that, as we have seen with Jackie Milburn's venture, the board were frankly schizophrenic about any effort by players to improve their own lot by starting a business. Back in 1952 Stan Seymour, recalling his own time as a player who opened a sports outfitting shop, had stated that: 'I do not think the United board would raise the slightest objection to any player, even today, doing the same as I did, so long as he . . . gives his full time to all calls made upon by him by the club.' But when in 1954 Frank Brennan did just that, opening a sports business, he was promptly and inexplicably dropped, and Seymour went off on a highly publicised search for a new centre-half which resulted in Bill Paterson being signed for £22,000 from Doncaster Rovers in October 1954.

By then Stan Seymour had become chairman of the board as well as manager, and it was decided that this was too much for one man. Seymour's record as manager was speckled. In his first term, between 1939 and 1947, he had certainly held the club together through the difficult period of the war and, more than that, had astutely signed a brilliant backbone of playing staff which laid the foundations for success in peacetime. It was effectively Stan Seymour's team which won promotion back to Division One, and it was certainly Stan Seymour's side which won the first two cups of the 1950s.

As a team manager he was wonderfully effective. It is possible that he mistook his vocation: if Seymour had never been a club director, he might have become a great manager. He was not a coach. His capacity for motivating players was strictly limited. Because of Newcastle's habit of turning lost causes around in the second half, Seymour's half-time talks became a press legend. But they were a myth, a media fabrication. Seymour rarely talked to his teams. 'In five years as a Newcastle player,' Jack Fairbrother said years later, 'I never heard Stan Seymour deliver one tactical talk to the team at half-time – that includes our promotion season and the cup final year of 1951' (when New-castle United were in fact drawing 0-0 at half-time against Blackpool at Wembley). Stan Seymour's strengths lay in selec-tion – the selection of good young players from local sides and from other league teams, and the selection of an effective 11 players, all in the right positions, and all in a black-and-white shirt. There was a time – Stan Seymour's time – when this was enough.

But he also built faults into his own foundations. Cheque-book-happy, Seymour's answer to virtually every difficulty at Newcastle was to buy, and too often – as in the cases of Len Shackleton and Ernie Taylor and others – to transfer-and-buy. He would argue that he always put the club first; that if he was high-handed with players; if he treated their financial claims with contempt; if he got rid of them rather than debate with them; this was because nobody was bigger than Newcastle United. But in the process of establishing the club's great super-iority over tiny, mortal individuals, he left too many of those individuals with the (justifiable) sense that the club cared for them not one jot, and that no matter how much they cared for the club, they might be better off away from it. But one thing was certain at the end of 1954: despite his resignation as manager, Newcastle United had not seen the last of Stan Seymour.

The club's directors approached Dugald Livingstone, the Scottish former full-back who had attracted some attention in Britain by coaching firstly Sparta Rotterdam and then the Belgium international team (which had, in the autumn of 1954, achieved two notable victories over world champions West Germany and Holland).

Livingstone arrived in December to find a team which, after a bright start in the league, was once more slipping back. His 'modern' continental coaching and training techniques instantly irritated the players. 'He had us,' said Jackie Milburn, 'jumping over high hurdles then ducking under them and leaping into the air to head the ball. After the first week there were no fewer than ten players on the treatment table with groin strains. When we went to Sheffield United for our first game under the new Livingstone régime we lost by six goals with Jimmy Hagan, a Geordie we used to call The Stroller because of his style, tearing us to bits.'

The score at Bramall Lane on 1 January 1955, for Dugald Livingstone's first game in complete control, was actually 6-2. It was hardly the first time that Newcastle had crashed to such a scoreline in recent years, but it was true that the casual Jimmy Hagan ran riot. It was also true that two local youngsters promoted to the first team by Livingstone, half-back Joe Cooper and inside-forward Billy Curry, were destroyed by Hagan, and that some observers reckoned that Newcastle were fortunate to escape a 'double-figures humiliation'.

That destruction dumped United into the bottom half of Division One and, perhaps more damagingly, it rubbed salt in the wounds of the older players. They did not feel that they needed all of this fancy training and tactical discussion anyway. There was in the 1950s a strong reaction amongst many British footballers against the new methods. The grand old man of English football, Stanley Matthews, raged against the England coach Walter Winterbottom for his team talks: 'You just cannot tell star players how they must play and what they must do when they are on the field . . . You must let them play their natural game.'

Len Shackleton, always with a mischievous eye open for trouble at his old club, wrote that: 'It came to my ears that Newcastle United, putting the accent on coaching in 1954–55, held one session at which every player on the club's books – many of them internationals – was taught to kick the ball correctly. I can just picture my old team-mate Jackie Milburn being taught how to shoot . . . after scoring more goals than his instructor had probably ever dreamed of.'

The coaching session to which Shackleton was almost certainly referring became famous on Tyneside as the one in which Dugald Livingstone told Bobby Mitchell how to kick a ball with his left foot. Jackie Milburn explained: 'It sickened me. The most educated left foot I ever saw in my life was Bobby Mitchell's. The manager had us coaching at Fenham, and he drew a chalk mark on Bobby Mitchell's left foot, demonstrating how to side-foot a ball to the rest of us. "That's exactly the point where you catch it," he says. Well, the lads, like Frank Brennan and them, were looking at me, and we couldn't believe it! I mean . . . that's kid's stuff. I says: "Hey, that's me finished with him. That's the end as far as I'm concerned." Everybody started to laugh about it, because they said Mitch's left foot was bloody dynamite! He could do anything with it. He could open a can of beans with his left foot, and . . . this chalk mark!'

Dugald Livingstone encountered at Newcastle United a squad of senior footballers who were convinced that he could teach them nothing. They had set a record for consecutive FA Cup wins in the 20th century; they had dragged themselves up from the Second Division; they had been through the war. 'We needed new training like a hole in the head . . . We were naturals, and all the new techniques simply upset the balance.'

To the younger, ambitious players, however, Livingstone represented not only the man who would determine their future, but also a manager who was introducing new and interesting techniques. At their age they benefited from teaching; they appreciated the attention. And so two camps were formed among the playing staff at Newcastle United – 'For the first time,' said Milburn, 'there was a rift in the club.'

So there was Scoular's clique, and Livingstone's clique, and Seymour's clique, and the clique of those who followed nobody at all . . . and somehow Newcastle United set off once more on the road to Wembley.

Seven days after that league thrashing at Sheffield, United had the opportunity to make amends when they travelled all the way south to play Plymouth Argyle in the third round of the cup. It was a good opportunity: Plymouth were at the bottom of the Second Division. Livingstone left out both Cooper (who would only make six first-team appearances in his five years on the club's books) and Curry, but as Charlie Crowe was injured he tried out another reserve half-back, Stanley Keery. And Bob Stokoe was retained at centre-half, despite the 31-year-old Frank Brennan's puzzled public insistences that he still had five years of first-class football left.

Newcastle won 1-0, but had thoroughly deserved to lose. Plymouth outplayed them from front to back, beginning to end.

'We stole the match,' admitted chairman Seymour afterwards. Only a series of miraculous saves from Ronnie Simpson frustrated the south-coasters. Just once in the whole 90 minutes did Newcastle launch an attack of substance – and they scored from it. Even there they were fortunate: Vic Keeble's optimistic hook towards goal struck a defender and landed beautifully in Keeble's path once more, for the big centre-forward to smack it home. For the rest of the game Argyle's 21-year-old left winger Peter Anderson put Newcastle through the wringer, without reward. United's four train-loads of fans went home not knowing whether to celebrate or mourn. In the end, they decided to celebrate.

The next round, on 29 January 1955, promised to be a lot easier. Brentford of the Third Division (South) had got past Bradford City and were suddenly in the rarefied atmosphere of the fourth round of the cup. Sadly for them, they were drawn away against the greatest cup team of the age: Newcastle United.

Luckily for them, though, Newcastle United were still not quite themselves. After a first half which 'struck a new low for Gallowgate football', according to the *Sunday Sun*, the recalled Billy Curry headed United into the lead. But Newcastle old boy Geordie Stobbart promptly equalised for the Londoners. After 71 minutes Bobby Mitchell hit a long, low shot which crept in to make it 2-1. Mitchell leapt delightedly in the air, as if he had won the cup itself instead of taking the lead over a team from Division Three (South). But 30 seconds later Stobbart, determined to enjoy his swansong at St James's Park, immediately released Brentford's inside-left Rainford, who struck a rising shot which beat Simpson under the bar. Stobbart's and Rainford's joy was shortlived, however. Three minutes later George Hannah completed the scoring and won the game 3-2 for United. Once again, the feeling in town was that the boys had stolen it.

These knife-edge results, on top of the recurring discontent within the club which, in such a city as Newcastle, was quickly broadcast about the town, resulted in a huge meeting at the City Hall. It was called by the Shareholders' Association, and more than 2,000 fans turned up. When a vote of no-confidence in the board of directors was called, an estimated 2,000 hands went up in favour. When those who still had confidence in the board were asked to show themselves, three hands were raised.

Back on the pitch the team prepared for their fifth-round game away to Second Division Nottingham Forest by losing 4-3 in a thriller at Chelsea. Ex-United centre-forward Roy Bentley maintained the honourable tradition of Newcastle cast-offs against their old side by getting a hat-trick. Despite the result, Newcastle were judged to have performed well against a championship-chasing team (Chelsea would indeed finish the season with the Division One title), and one newspaper regretted that Duggie Livingstone had preferred the reserve full-back Arnold Woolard to Bobby Cowell before the Stamford Bridge match, because the team had played so creditably that it would now be impossible to make changes – 'It is difficult to see how Newcastle can make a change after the Chelsea display. And yet Cowell should have been the right-back.'

They were forgetting that Livingstone was of the new breed of manager: scholarly and diffident, and unafraid to change his side. He picked horses for courses, and had no doubt noticed Woolard's disturbing tendency to be left stranded upfield and out of position during counter-attacks. Cowell was recalled; as was Vic Keeble at inside-left. George Hannah was dropped from the forward line and instantly put in a (rejected) transfer request. Jackie Milburn, displaced from the centre-forward spot by Len White, found himself once more out on the right wing – not a position which he disliked, but not one to encourage a sense of stability in the veteran striker.

In the end it was Milburn who scored United's only goal that afternoon of 19 February 1955. It was 0-0 with five minutes to go when Forest dramatically took the lead. Two minutes later Milburn, who had switched from the right to the left wing, and had just seen a brilliant cross headed wide by White, took a hand. He chased a through-ball from Keeble and, with typical electrifying pace, outstripped the Nottingham defence to roll it past the stranded keeper.

The replay was postponed for a week due to a sudden fall of snow, and in the meantime United lost the home league derby with Sunderland (who were second in the league) by 2-1. Once more Milburn was on the right wing, and once more he scored.

The first replay was drawn 2-2, but a toss of the coin took the third match safely back to Tyneside. For the second FA Cup replay with Forest Livingstone continued with his shake-up, introducing the reserve centre-forward Alan Monkhouse and playing Milburn at inside-left. And Jackie continued with his practical reminders to the manager, running riot against a demoralised Forest defence and laying on both goals for Monk-house in Newcastle's 2-1 win.

And they did it again in the quarter-finals. This time it was the turn of old rivals Huddersfield Town, who were just a couple of places above Newcastle in the First Division table, to put the fear of God into the travelling Geordie support. Huddersfield took the lead in the 62nd minute, then hit the bar, and then saw two penalty claims for hand-ball against Stokoe and Tommy Casey turned down. Newcastle were on the ropes and should have been counted out. But in the 87th minute a long Simpson clearance found Bobby Mitchell. The left-winger jockeyed for position before pin-pointing a cross to the far post, where an onrushing Len White had only to stoop and head the ball home from three yards for the equaliser. The replay was drawn 0-0 in normal time, but Mitchell and Keeble clinched it in extra-time.

'They must have a good-luck fairy in their side,' the Forest manager Billy Walker had said after his side's defeat at St James's Park in the fifth-round second replay.

If so, that fairy was not about to desert a winning team. It played probably its most important game in the semi-final of the 1955 FA Cup, where Newcastle were drawn against York City of the Third Division (North).

No Third Division team had ever been to Wembley, and more than a fifth of York's 100,000 population made the journey to Hillsborough to see them take on Newcastle. Vic Keeble – to whom Livingstone gave the centre-forward spot, sending Len White out to the left wing – gave United the lead in the 13th minute. But York equalised in the 29th minute through inside-right Arthur Bottom, who had scored in each of York's seven cup rounds, and, despite White crashing a header against the bar with two minutes to go, the 14-1 underdogs held on for a replay at Roker Park, which United won 2-0 with goals from White and Keeble.

For the third time in five years, Newcastle United were in the FA Cup final. It would be their tenth final in all, a new English record. They had arrived there by the most tortuous of routes, playing nine matches in five rounds. They had scraped past lowly Plymouth and Brentford, and had been taken to at least one replay by every other opponent. They had played 15 hours of cup football, instead of the scheduled seven and a half. Manchester City, their cup-final opponents (who had eliminated Sunderland in the other semi-final, thereby dashing the best chance ever of a Tyne versus Wear final), must not have known whether to rub their hands with glee, or look nervously out for the good-luck fairy in a black-and-white shirt.

'Still,' wrote Jackie Milburn in the *Sunday Sun*, 'we are *there*, and what a wonderful feeling it is . . . Bobby Cowell, Bobby Mitchell and myself can be well excused if we have a certain pride in the fact that if we are selected to play and are on the winning side we will join only seven other players who have collected three winners' medals.'

With Dugald Livingstone as manager, however, Jackie was by no means guaranteed his third Wembley medal. Nor was Cowell. Only Mitchell, if he escaped injury, seemed secure. The days of Stan Seymour promising a cup-final place to each member of a victorious semi-final team were gone. After his heroics in earlier rounds, Milburn had failed to score against York City, and had in fact put the ball over the bar from three yards out. There were five Saturdays between the semi-final replay and the cup final, and Livingstone announced that he would be using the breathing space to 'make changes regularly' and 'seek the most effective line-up for Wembley'.

This meant, most obviously, dropping Milburn. After cruising with various degrees of comfort from one side of the forward line to the other, Wor Jackie suddenly found himself in the stand. Livingstone's ruthless approach had at least one beneficial effect: in contrast to recent years United actually won most of their pre-cup-final league matches, steering themselves clear of the relegation zone and up to a respectable eighth position in Division One.

A lot of the time, however, his selections seemed very strange. The long-serving full-back Alf McMichael, for instance, was played on the left wing in the last home match of the season. McMichael took the opportunity to score his only goal for United in 13 years and 431 games, but that was hardly the point. This was not 'seeking the most effective line-up for Wembley'; this was tomfoolery.

And a lot of the time, Milburn was not there. His familiar name was missing from the team-sheet when United played relegated bottom-of-the-table Sheffield Wednesday at Gallowgate on 9 April. This was more important than it might have seemed. Wednesday would concede 100 First Division goals that season of 1954–55; their defence was a colander, and therefore an ideal warm-up for a cup-final forward line. Livingstone selected White, Davies, Keeble, Hannah and Mitchell to penetrate that colander, and in a 5-0 victory they all scored but Keeble. Reg Davies got two.

And so it came about that, on the weekend before the 1955 cup final, while Jackie Milburn was telling the press how 'lucky and fortunate' he felt to have escaped injury and therefore be available for the final; while Milburn was informing the fans that he had 'no fear' of the so-called 'Revie plan' – the orderly style of play masterminded by the deep-lying Manchester City centre-forward Don Revie; while all this was happening, Dugald Livingstone was presenting the Newcastle United board of directors with his proposed cup-final team.

It excluded Milburn. It was the same forward line as in the thrashing of Sheffield Wednesday. The man whose goals had won the cup in 1951; the player who, before 7 May 1955, had scored 164 goals in 319 league and cup games since 1946 was missing from Newcastle United's cup-final line-up.

It was, simply, inconceivable. The directors could for once appreciate what would have been the reaction of the fans. It would have been like Newcastle United ditching their black-and-white shirts, or asking the supporters to refrain from singing 'Blaydon Races'. Milburn's appeal transcended the day-to-day tactics and schemes of football management. He was loved not only for his soccer genius, although there was enough of that, but also because the people of the area saw in Jackie Milburn the image of their favourite son. He was modest, witty, warm and honest. He was effortlessly, unaffectedly dashing and handsome. He was hard when necessary, but always ready with a grin and a conciliatory word. He was a canny lad with a passion for his homeland. Dropping Jackie Milburn, the best-loved character in the North-east of England, from a Newcastle United cup-final team was out of the question. Dugald Livingstone was told by the board of directors of Newcastle United Football Club to reinstate him.

So the manager did as he was told. He opted to drop Len White, but then Reg Davies went down with laryngitis and could not play, so White also was reinstated. As the players were preparing to jog down the Wembley tunnel to receive the applause of 30,000 travelling Geordies, Stan Seymour nudged up to Milburn and said, 'Go out and show them, Jackie.'

Jackie did. After just 45 seconds of the match United won a corner on the right. Len White took it and flighted an out-swerving ball which dipped to head-height some 15 yards out from the near post. Milburn and Keeble had been loitering with intent around the penalty area when the Manchester City captain and left-half Roy Paul decided to leave Jackie alone and concentrate on marking big Vic – 'Bloody hell,' Milburn heard Paul exclaim as White placed the corner-kick, 'I should be marking Keeble.'

Thus liberated, Milburn loped unattended towards the near post, leaned backwards slightly to meet the ball with his left temple, and despatched a header of sublime quality in at the angle of post and bar, right on what footballers call the postage stamp. Milburn was not, it should be remembered, renowned for his heading ability. His chronic fibrositis made him reluctant to jump or stretch himself in the air – crowds at St James's Park had been known to cheer ironically when their favourite nodded a ball. It is doubtful, however, whether Wembley had ever before, or has ever since, seen a headed goal of such brilliance. 'I could head as well as the next fella,' Milburn would explain, 'as long as I was on my own.' Duggie Livingstone, watching his team go 1-0 up in the final in record time, but with a goal scored by a player whom he considered not fit to be on the pitch, cannot have known whether to smirk or to sneer.

Livingstone was proved partly right for the remaining 89 minutes. The pulled stomach muscle which had troubled Milburn all season began to play up again, and the 31-year-old forward did little else for the rest of the game. Fortunately, Manchester City were also down to ten men. In an uncanny résumé of the Wally Barnes incident three years earlier, at almost exactly the same time – 18 minutes into the game – the City right-back Jimmy Meadows also wrenched his knee in almost exactly the same area of the pitch. The injured Meadows struggled on for the rest of the first half, but did not reappear after half-time. He would be in plaster for six weeks after the match. United's good-luck fairy had not deserted them.

City did, however, equalise after a typically complicated series of passes around the edge of the Newcastle penalty area, Bobby Johnstone finishing the classical 'Revie Plan' move by diving to send a looping header over Simpson. But in the second half Newcastle proceeded to dominate Manchester City's ten men in a way that they had never dominated the reduced Arsenal side of three years before. It was the best of the three finals of the 1950s, and the finest Newcastle United performance of the three, although arguably it was achieved – as some of the players themselves considered – with the weakest management, the weakest team, and the lowest all-round morale.

They made it 2-1 in the 53rd minute, when a move begun by the authoritative Jimmy Scoular resulted in a Len White cross towards the far post which deceived City's right-winger Spurdle, who had dropped back to help out his stricken defence. The ball fell behind Spurdle, and Bobby Mitchell controlled it and shifted forward in the one deceptive, dangerous movement, drawing keeper Bert Trautmann out to cover his expected cross before thumping the ball directly home between Trautmann and the near post from the narrowest of angles. Five minutes later Scoular released Mitchell, whose cut-back finally fell to George Hannah in space 12 yards from the goal-line. Hannah had time to pick his spot, and United were 3-1 ahead.

'You have broken a record,' said the young Queen Elizabeth II to Stan Seymour as the final whistle blew. (Several records, actually, Ma'am – quickest goal in a Wembley final; first club to ten finals; first club to win six in the 20th century; easily the most wins – five – at Wembley; only regular finalists undefeated at Wembley . . .) Her escort, the Duke of Edinburgh, happily made it known that he had once commanded a frigate named *Magpie*. Milburn, Mitchell and Cowell, two of them the sole survivors of United's harvest of local wartime talent, and the other the greatest left-winger thus far in the history of the club, had joined the élite Three Cup-Winners' Club. The 1955 final was their last great hour; but it also signalled the arrival of the Jimmy Scoular era. The Scot had been immense throughout the match. His strength, vision and discipline finally banished the ghost of Joe Harvey. 'He is,' said two female fans picked at random by a newspaper reporter from the streets of London, 'the finest half-back in the country.'

Back on Tyneside the years of gathering outside the *Evening Chronicle* offices to hear the wired scoreline had long since passed. The 1951 and 1952 finals had been appreciated on the radio. The 1955 final was the first featuring Newcastle United to be broadcast in black and white on BBC television. April and early May of 1955 saw an unprecedented surge in sales of the newfangled TV sets in the area.

Four days after the cup final, manager Duggie Livingstone was told that he would no longer be allowed to pick the Newcastle United team. Shortly after that, his office at St James's Park was taken from him, and he was asked to work out of a spare referee's changing-room. He went on the club's summer tour of Germany, but upon their return Livingstone seems finally to have got the message when a club house which he had been promised was suddenly given instead to Bob Stokoe. Duggie Livingstone was pushed out of a position of power at Newcastle United seven eventful months after joining the club, and two months after winning the cup. Strangely, he lingered on for several months, a humiliated sight, coaching youngsters and ignored by the seniors, until he moved to Fulham in February 1956.

He was quickly followed on the road out of Newcastle by coach Joe Harvey, albeit in slightly different circumstances. Stan Seymour was temporarily back at the helm, and when he heard that Harvey wished to make a break for freedom and have a crack at an independent reputation by taking the manager's job at Division Three (North) club Barrow, Seymour tried to dissuade his old captain. 'It will break your heart, Joe,' said Stan.

The odd thing was, reflected Joe Harvey many years later, pondering on his seven years of exile from St James's Park – the odd thing was, given what happened to Newcastle United in those seven years, Seymour had been right. It nearly did break Harvey's heart.

CHAPTER EIGHT

SWORD-DANCING WITH CHARLIE: 1956–61

❖

For two and a half years after Duggie Livingstone's departure, the team was supposedly selected by a directorial committee and coached by Norman Smith, the faithful Geordie who was trainer at St James's Park between 1938 and 1962 (and whose career at the club was only ended after he made the fatal error of accepting the poisoned chalice of management).

But, in reality, for the third time Stan Seymour, the man who could not properly relinquish control, took over the manager's tasks. He immediately celebrated his return to the manager's chair with one of the shoddiest actions in the club's history. Big Frank Brennan, unlike some others, had failed to get the message that he was no longer wanted. The Doncaster Rovers centre-half Bill Paterson had been bought for £22,000. When Paterson struggled, Bob Stokoe was brought up from the reserves and given the cherished stopper position. But Frank, despite some grumpy comments, stayed put and insisted that he was ready to add another couple of hundred games to his 340 appearances for Newcastle.

Finally, early in 1956, Stan Seymour cut Brennan's wage from the legal maximum of £15 a week to a risible £8 a week. Market forces justified it: Brennan had, after all, become little more than a third-team player. But the fans, who loved the big man, hated it. Brennan refused to accept the cut and was instantly transfer-listed. In March he went to North Shields in the North-Eastern League. It was a disgracefully humiliating end to the league career of one of United's greatest servants, and arguably the finest centre-half to wear the shirt.

In January 1956, at the same time as Brennan's wage was being slashed, his old defensive partner Bobby Cowell, who had sustained a bad injury in the 1955 tour of Germany, was told that he would never kick a football again. That odd character Seymour kept Cowell on full wages for the remainder of the season and gave him a £4,000 testimonial match. People did keep saying: if only Frank Brennan had not opened a sports outfitters' shop to rival that of Seymour . . .

On the pitch, Newcastle enjoyed something of a honeymoon with the fans after that record-breaking 1955 cup final. Their league form was neither better nor worse than indifferent middle-of-the-table (they finished 11th); but they did put on a spirited cup run in 1956. The gates remained reasonably high and – for all the very public annoyance about such issues as the shameful treatment of Brennan – the fans remained optimistic.

They enjoyed one more record in the 1950s. In the January 1956 third-round tie United were drawn away to Sheffield Wednesday. Ever since 1871 those winter Saturday afternoon cup-ties had kicked off at two o'clock or even one, to defeat the early dusk. In 1956 the Sheffield Wednesday versus Newcastle United third-round clash at Hillsborough became the first of its type to kick off at three, because it was the first ever FA Cup-tie to be played under floodlights. Newcastle responded to the big occasion as suitably as ever. Wearing a special 'floodlight strip' of white shirts and black shorts, they beat the Division Two leaders 3-1.

Fulham at Craven Cottage in the fourth round did not, on paper, promise all that much. Just as Newcastle were a middle-of-the-table Division One side, so Fulham were a middle-of-the-table Division Two side. But what followed was later described by the Fulham right-winger, a tall, gawky young man named Jimmy Hill, as 'the most memorable match of my life. Anyone who was there will tell you that it was the most exciting cup-tie they ever saw.'

As well as 40,000 fans, the Pathé News cameras were there, and their grainy, stuttering film shows that within 27 minutes Newcastle seemed to have sealed the match. Milburn, once more out on the right wing, made it 1-0 with a fierce drive into the roof of the net; Bob Stokoe moved forward to see his shot deflected home; and Tommy Casey made it 3-0 with a scorching left-footer.

Just before the break Fulham's left-winger Tosh Chamberlain made it 3-1 with what seemed like a consolation goal, but which in fact gave Chamberlain the confidence to take on and beat Arnold Woolard, who was being given another chance to prove himself at right-back.

What followed was almost a disaster for Newcastle, and was certainly a disaster for Woolard. Thirteen minutes after half-time Hill put Chamberlain through on the left. Chamberlain waltzed past Woolard and hit an angled shot past Simpson – only to see it controversially disallowed for offside. A few minutes later, however, he repeated the exercise and this time the goal stood. Shortly after that Johnny Haynes set Chamberlain free again, he beat the humiliated Woolard at will, and it was 3-3. The 'Blaydon Races' died away from the terraces and the Fulham crowd went wild. Three minutes after that it was 4-3 to Fulham: Chamberlain crossing from the left and Bedford Jezzard heading home. 'Have you ever seen a pair of crutches hurled skywards at a football match?' asked the *Daily Mail*'s reporter. 'Well, I have . . .'

Sadly for the Second Division team's disabled supporters, Vic Keeble came to life in the dying minutes and forced home two goals which gave Newcastle a passport to the fifth round. Sadly for Arnold Woolard, his mauling by Tosh Chamberlain proved the last straw. His four-year career on Tyneside at an end after just ten first-team appearances, he was sold to Bournemouth in June. There was perhaps one happy ending. It was a month after this that Fulham put Duggie Livingstone out of his misery by taking him out of his referees' cubby-hole at St James's Park and making him their manager.

Bobby Mitchell and Bill Curry got the goals in a 2-1 defeat of

Stoke City which sent United once more into the quarter-finals. Newcastle, the cup-holders and new 4-1 favourites, were promptly given some compensation for Sunderland's failure to make it a Tyne versus Wear final the previous year, by drawing their oldest and deadliest rivals at home in the quarter-finals of the 1956 FA Cup. Some compensation! If anybody was going to spoil the party, it was Sunderland – and they did so, knocking United out by 2-0 before going on to demonstrate their own lack of true cup pedigree by losing yet another semi-final, 3-0 to Birmingham City.

The season was over. Newcastle lost nine of their last ten games on their way to an undignified 11th place in the league. Stan Seymour continued to tinker with the engine. It was while doing so that he made what would prove to be an immensely significant signing, for Newcastle United and for British professional football as a whole. In May 1956 he travelled to Northern Ireland to look at a Linfield inside-forward named Jimmy Hill (no relation to the lanky Fulham player). Having already provided Alf McMichael and George Hannah, Linfield had since the war proved a profitable nursery to Newcastle.

Seymour travelled back without Hill, but with a 20-year-old centre-forward who had been born in Blackpool but who was playing in Ireland for Ards. People had heard of this player's father, a professional footballer who had the same name, but as he had so far spent all his short career in Northern Ireland, in May 1956 not many had heard of George Eastham junior. They would, and not only because Stan Seymour signed him for £9,000. In the summer of 1956 he was picked for the Irish League, and scored in their 5-2 thrashing of the English League. But George Eastham was destined to be remembered for more than his footballing prowess. In September 1956 Seymour signed another Northern Irish player, Linfield's full-back Dick Keith, who would give wonderful footballing service to Tyneside before his tragic death at the age of 34. But not many people outside Newcastle would remember Dick Keith, whereas George Eastham would soon become a household name, and would shake the cosy world of professional football to its core.

In the short term, Eastham's main immediate effect was to contribute to Jackie Milburn's suspicions that it might be time to call it a day. Although he knew by 1956 that the number 9 shirt would never be his again, Milburn had finished the 1955–56 season with a respectable 21 goals from 42 games. But Vic Keeble had usurped the top-scorer's slot with 26 strikes. And then, on top of Keeble and Eastham, the 1956–57 season began with the Bedlington boy Alex Tait arriving from the juniors and reserves and picking up a hat-trick in a 6-2 trouncing of Sunderland.

Tait seemed at first to have a charmed life. The FA Cup third round in January took United to a replay at Manchester City's Maine Road. After 24 minutes the Tynesiders were 3-0 down. Their response was to do a Fulham – but to do it properly. Newcastle fought back magnificently, equalising in the 87th minute. Tait took Milburn's place in that game, and seemed to fit effortlessly into the old master's boots: he scored by running with the ball from inside his own half, outstripping four defenders before hammering the ball past Bert Trautmann in the City goal. City made it 4-3 shortly into extra-time, but Newcastle won 5-4 . . . and were then knocked out of the fourth round of the cup 2-1 at Cold Blow Lane, home to Millwall of Division Three (South).

Newcastle finished the season of 1956–57 in 17th position. Reg Davies was top scorer with 13 goals. Jackie Milburn got 12 from 33 games – not bad for a 33-year-old winger-cum-inside-forward. Excellent, in fact, for most. But not satisfactory for the great Jackie Milburn. It was time to move on. 'Get out while they remember you with affection,' his father Alec had wisely told him before his recent death. 'Don't spoil things.'

He went to Linfield in Northern Ireland as player-coach. He had been on £15 a week at Newcastle: Linfield offered him £25 a week and £1,000 down. It was his first signing-on fee, since that tenner and a bottle of whisky in Stan Seymour's office back in 1943. He went with a heavy heart. It was made even heavier when Stan Seymour stepped in with a typical piece of smart footwork. The Newcastle director-manager demanded a

£10,000 transfer fee for Milburn from Linfield – and the signature of the young forward he had looked at for a couple of years, Jimmy Hill. Linfield, their hearts set on Milburn, agreed. The £10,000 was a drop in the ocean of Newcastle United's coffers, and Hill would last only 11 games at St James's Park before being transferred to Third Division Norwich, but the player and the money had meant a lot to Irish football. 'They skint the club I was going to manage!' was Jackie Milburn's assessment.

The North-eastern press was full of protesting letters, many of them incredulous at Newcastle's astonishing insistence that the club would not give Milburn a testimonial match because he had not chosen to finish his playing career at St James's Park – a position which both chairman Wilf Taylor and Stan Seymour would publicly defend as right and proper. Not for the first or the last time, the supporters looked at the actions of the club they adored with feelings of disbelief, bordering on disgust.

They had another reason for mourning in that summer of 1957. Jackie Milburn signed for Linfield on 13 June. Two days earlier, at midday on 11 June, close by a spot known as Dead Man's Crossing on the London to Edinburgh main line just south of the River Tyne, two young trainspotters 'noticed a small man wearing a cap pacing up and down the footbridge. He kept looking up the line.'

The small man heard a train coming, left the bridge, brushed by one of the boys and, before walking up the trackside footpath, said: 'Sorry'.

They were the last words anybody ever heard from Hughie Gallacher. The 54-year-old footballing hero jumped in front of the Edinburgh express a few minutes later, and his decapitated body was found near the line. Gallacher had returned to his beloved Tyneside in 1938, firstly to play for Gateshead and latterly to work for the local press. He had become a familiar sight once more at St James's Park, hanging around the entrance steps on match days, swapping stories with the likes of Jackie Milburn, drinking heartily in the city pubs . . . On the morning of 12 June he had been summoned to attend Gateshead Magistrates' Court to answer charges of assaulting his 14-year-old son. On the morning of 11 June, before taking that walk to Dead Man's Crossing, he wrote and posted a letter to the Gateshead Coroner expressing regret at the trouble he had caused.

'HUGHIE OF THE MAGIC FEET IS DEAD' headlined the *Newcastle Journal*. 'I say without hesitation,' said Stan Seymour, 'that he was the greatest centre-forward I have ever seen.' Jackie Milburn, preparing to move to Northern Ireland, began to weep when he was given the news. 'How a man so loved and idolised,' he said, 'could feel so alone, I'll never know.'

Milburn took Linfield to a Northern Irish cup final in his first season. Back on Tyneside, 1957–58 was a dismal winter. George Eastham slotted in nicely at inside-left, and Arthur Bottom, the inside-right who had given United so much trouble in the semi-finals of 1955, was bought from York City in February 1958, and proceeded to score ten goals in 11 games before being sold on to Chesterfield ten months later.

But United slipped ever closer to the relegation zone, and in the end it was probably only the magnificent surge to form of Len White which saved them. After scoring 67 goals in 120 games in black and white, Vic Keeble was sold to the Second Division leaders, free-scoring West Ham United, in October 1957. While Keeble helped the Hammers to net 101 league goals and take the Division Two title, White put on the number 9 shirt for struggling Newcastle. Luckily, it fitted. In midseason he was averaging a goal a game. He was a short, stocky man, just five foot seven in his socks, but wonderfully effective nevertheless. A local schoolboy named Howard Kendall, who would later make his name as a player and manager, saw White at this time, and many years later would rate him in the top five British centre-forwards he ever saw. 'He was a muscular and solid centre-forward,' Kendall recalled, 'with the power and physical strength to pick up the ball inside his own half, run fully 70 yards, and then score. He managed to combine grace and brute force. A really top-class player who never really received the acclaim he was due.'

The likes of Jimmy Hill, Alex Tait and Arthur Bottom would prove to be of limited service to Newcastle United. Len White gave the club ten solid years, 269 games and 153 goals. He won nothing in the season of 1957–58. Newcastle were knocked out of the fourth round of the FA Cup in January 1958 by Scunthorpe Town of the Third Division (North) by 3-1 at St James's Park. They finished their league programme in 19th position with just 32 points, avoiding relegation only because their goal difference was much superior to that of relegated Sunderland, who also had 32 points. But United scored 73 goals, while Sunderland managed only 54, and this life-saving difference was largely due to Len White's leading of the forward line. His work in that dismal winter was hardly publicised, but it was worth more than the cup-winning corner which led to Jackie Milburn's record-breaking goal in 1955. And it is a revealing statistic that Len White's total of 153 goals make him the second-highest goalscorer ever for Newcastle United, behind Jackie Milburn, and just ahead of Hughie Gallacher.

But Len White's form aside, times were bad, on and off the pitch. In that eventful summer of 1957 the solicitor William McKeag had replaced Wilf Taylor as chairman of the club and begun his own two-year term of office. McKeag was possessed of at least one burning certainty: that Stan Seymour could not carry on being director-manager of Newcastle United. The disagreement boiled into a bitter and very public personality clash. It seemed to many that McKeag – whose family had a long connection with the club – and Seymour were vying for the title of 'Mister Newcastle United'. The two men were born to hate each other. McKeag had briefly been Liberal MP for Durham in the 1930s, had unsuccessfully fought Newcastle North twice after the war, but as a consolation prize became Lord Mayor of the city. He had an exaggerated personal dignity and a grand style of affected oratory. Seymour was a shopkeeper and former professional footballer whose accent cheerfully betrayed his origins, and who spoke conspiratorially out of the side of his mouth. Seymour also knew his football, and he looked with scorn upon the likes of McKeag, who did not. The issue of

Seymour's compulsive, possessive management of the team became a crucial battleground in this long and debilitating war.

The conflict ran on all season, and became national news. In March 1958 – while United's footballers were battling for their First Division lives – McKeag called Seymour a 'traitor' for wishing to continue in his role of 'honorary manager'.

'He never was honorary manager of this club,' asserted the Alderman. 'He just drifted into a position where he was allowed to claim the title. The only way to save this club is to appoint a manager who will have complete control. But who will take on such a job? We want a young, energetic man who will come here with a three-year plan – because it would require that spell to put the club back in its former place as a leading force in football. But who will blame a man who looks suspiciously at this searing hot seat? I frankly do not disagree with any ambitious manager who takes that view.'

The subtext of William McKeag's argument was plain: a manager was clearly needed by Newcastle United; but until Stan Seymour's insistent meddling was ended, nobody would do the job. If the solution was Seymour's departure from the club, then so be it. McKeag proceeded to pass a gagging order which forbade any member of the board other than the chairman to talk to the press.

The *Daily Express* sent its star reporter Desmond Hackett to Tyneside to explore and publicise the problem. His recommended solution was that both men must go – 'The power struggle has gone on too long and too far . . . Now the fans have had too much of McKeag and Seymour and too little of soccer success.'

Both men (and their families) stayed at St James's Park, but three months later McKeag won his battle for a manager. In June 1958, against the loudly expressed wishes of Stan Seymour, the Newcastle United board appointed Charlie Mitten as manager.

It was a curious decision, and not only because Mitten was, at 37, the youngest manager in the Football League. He had a celebrated interest in betting, and a chequered, rebellious history. In 1950 he had walked out of Manchester United and the English FA's maximum wage to play in the unaffiliated (some said outlaw) Colombian League for Bogota Santa Fé for £5,000 a year and a £35 per match win bonus. It was roughly ten times what the 29-year-old winger had been earning at Old Trafford, but some said that it would finish his career in European football.

Not so. Mitten returned in 1951 to a £250 fine and a six-month ban. In 1956 he became player-manager of Third Division (North) Mansfield Town, where his hell-for-leather brand of attacking football attracted some attention, without actually winning anything but affection for the Stags – although in 1958, when the old Third Divisions North and South were dissolved to create two new national Third and Fourth Divisions, Mitten's Mansfield Town finished sixth in Division Three (North), thereby qualifying for the Third rather than the Fourth Division.

The Mansfield directors were apparently not as impressed by this achievement as they should have been, and so their manager started casting around for a new job. In 1956 and '57 Mitten had bought for Mansfield the two Newcastle United half-backs Stan Keery and Charlie Crowe, and so established a connection with the Tyneside club. He applied, received the patronage of Alderman William McKeag, and was given the job, although even in Seymour's absence McKeag could not persuade his colleagues to offer the new man a three-year contract: Mitten was initially taken on for just 12 months. As things turned out, it was probably just as well.

Instantly there was a flurry of close-season activity. After his short stay, the Irishman Jimmy Hill was transferred to Norwich. Long-serving Irish international half-back Tommy Casey was sold to Portsmouth. Nobody of note was bought in immediately, but Mitten certainly introduced some new ideas, which cost the club nothing but its dignity.

Firstly there were the shorts with edging. This design, commonplace in South America where Mitten had picked it up, would become widespread in Britain 30 years later. The idea was that, by trimming Newcastle's black shorts with a ribbon of white, a hard-pressed footballer unable to raise his eyes too far from the ball, could see at a quick glance whether or not a nearby pair of thighs belonged to a team-mate. This, in 1958, was probably farsighted management. But it was also completely new to British players; its possible links to fancy-dan frippery worried the Newcastle footballers; and although they protested only under their breath, their suspicions were confirmed when United ran out for their first away game of the 1958–59 and a local wag bellowed at their tough Scottish captain: 'Hey, Scoular, your slip's showing!'

The second innovation, which may have confirmed many of the squad in their suspicions about Mitten, was the Highland-dancing training routine. For obvious reasons, not disconnected from the petticoat-shorts controversy, this was kept a tightly bound secret from the press and the fans – and, for equally obvious reasons, it turned out to be one of the very few soccer secrets which was not leaked by a player to the media.

Charlie Mitten was a big fan of Highland dancing. As a boy of seven his family had moved to Perthshire, and there he took up – and became a lifelong enthusiast for – Highland sword-dancing. There was nothing like it, he insisted, for balance, speed, agility and strength. So in the summer of 1958 the Newcastle United first-team footballers found themselves with their arms in the air, pirouetting over crossed sticks in the gymnasium. 'But after a month,' Mitten recalled with evident regret, 'I had to give it up. When we started you'd have thought they were shire horses trying to skip around the swords, bloody shire horses! Lads like Alf McMichael, Dick Keith, Lennie White, George Eastham – but could they master it? Could they hell! I tried to convince them sword-dancing was even better than jumping the spring-board and the horse – and not as sissy as it sounds. But that was the problem. I started putting it to music, but they thought they looked too much like a bunch of sissies. They couldn't see the point I was making.'

Plainly, nobody had told Mitten of the difficulties which had been faced by his predecessor when Duggie Livingstone had introduced the Newcastle players to gymnastic training – and

Livingstone had never tried to get them dancing reels. Mitten tried more orthodox exercises in the gym, and they ended up doing them (perhaps for fear that he would reintroduce the sword-dance if they did not), but: 'You'd have thought I was asking them to commit hara-kiri.'

None of this would have mattered if Mitten got results on the field. But the tone of his dismal time in Newcastle was set in his very first game. It was the opening league match of the 1958–59 season, and United were at home to newly promoted Blackburn Rovers, who had not seen Division One action for ten years. In the absence of fresh talent, the manager mixed tried-and-tested regulars – Dick Keith, Alf McMichael, Jimmy Scoular, George Eastham, Billy Curry and Bobby Mitchell – with a clutch of men newly promoted from the reserves. Stewart Mitchell was given a rare chance to supplant the injured Ronnie Simpson in goal. Malcolm Scott, who had been on the books for three years and spent them all in the second team, was given the centre-half's shirt. Jackie Bell, who had made his way up from the juniors, was played at left-half. Two more local boys, Ken Hale from Blyth and Gordon Hughes from Tow Law Town, were given the inside-forward positions.

The last three, Bell, Hale and Hughes, would turn out to be good professionals in time, but on 23 August 1958 Mitten's hastily assembled crew slumped to a nightmarish 5-1 defeat at home to Blackburn. The visitors were 2-0 up by half-time, and scored another two in as many minutes straight after the break. A 'strangely dispirited' Newcastle team, reported *The Times*, offered 'little organised resistance'. Blackburn 'sliced through Newcastle's ranks where and when they liked'. Blackburn even scored for Newcastle: right-back Whelan heading into his own net; but they converted a penalty in the 86th minute to restore the four-goal advantage.

Mitten clearly had to buy. In his hunt to replace Simpson – a hunt which was arguably a little premature, for after his sale in 1960 Ronnie Simpson would go on to win a series of Scotland caps, and a sackful of domestic honours and a European Cup-winner's medal with Celtic – he picked up Brian Harvey from non-league Wisbech. Early in October Mitten signed Ivor All-church, the brilliant 29-year-old Welsh international inside-forward, from Swansea Town in a part-exchange deal involving £28,000 and Reg Davies.

But Stokoe and White missed a series of matches through injury; United were knocked out of the third round of the cup 4-1 by Chelsea; after an improvement in league form had seen the team ascend the league late in 1958, the fans had to put up with a spell of two victories in 13 outings which sent them back down the table once more.

Newcastle finished the 1958–59 season in 11th place. His record had not been so startling that Charlie Mitten could, in his heart of hearts, have expected a lengthy new contract. But he asked for four more years; William McKeag was anxious to offer him three; and the board ended up giving him another 12 months.

He celebrated by attempting to re-sign Jackie Milburn. The old hero's honeymoon in Belfast was over, and he was anxious to return to England. There, the 35-year-old Milburn told himself, his old friend and almost exact contemporary Bobby Mitchell was still playing on the left wing. Why not Jackie?

Charlie Mitten appeared to agree, suggesting to Milburn that if he could sort out the small matter of an earlier 'signing-off' payment of £900 from the Football League Provident Fund, Newcastle would take him back. Stan Seymour publicly dis-agreed, stating with dubious diplomacy that Jackie would be a fine sight in England once more, as 'the little clubs of Ashington, South Shields, Berwick Rangers and Horden Colliery Welfare endeavour to secure his services in the autumn of his career'. Horden Colliery Welfare, fine club though they were, were not exactly what Jackie Milburn had in mind.

It was perhaps as well, however: Jackie would have taken no better than anybody else to the gymnastic workouts and the Highland sword- dancing. And his dream of himself running riot down one flank and Bobby Mitchell down the other was equally misplaced. It is true that Mitten still picked Mitchell, but he was just as likely to use the veteran at left-half. (Milburn saw

Mitchell play in midfield at Arsenal early in the Mitten era. 'I nearly killed myself laughing' at the selection, he said – but later admitted that, playing behind Eastham, White and Allchurch, 'Mitch was a revelation, the best man on the field.')

Charlie Mitten had in fact a serious problem with left-wingers. Having been one himself, he could never find another to suit him. In later years he would actually boast that the Newcastle players had 'tried to persuade me to turn out for the first team', and that he had been tempted. 'I thought I could have put myself on as outside-left – in training I was putting the ball into the far corner of the net from the edge of the box every time, a foot high and never touching the ground, no trouble . . .'

He did not pick himself, of course, because his job was to encourage the youngsters. So he pulled a far greater left-winger than Charlie Mitten had ever been, Bobby Mitchell, into midfield, and he scoured the country for replacements. He brought back George Luke – no spring chicken he – from Hartlepool United. When George disappointed he signed his own son, John Mitten, from Mansfield. John satisfied him for a while, but then the Mitten dream collapsed . . .

Backstage, Newcastle United were close to chaos. After the 4-1 cup defeat by Chelsea Stan Seymour (who, a month after Mitten's appointment, was wandering about Newcastle telling people: 'Only 11 months to go!', and four weeks later: 'Only ten months to go', and so on) told the press that the new manager's tactics were to blame. William McKeag promptly stated that Seymour's comments were 'unauthorised and ought never to have been made'. That old servant Jack Fairbrother, who had just arrived back in Britain after a spell of coaching in Israel, described Seymour as 'disloyal and trouble-making', and wondered whether 'a professional manager will again have to make way for an honorary manager'.

In June Jimmy Scoular tried to jump ship, asking for a transfer to take up a job as player-manager of Guildford City. He was refused. In August United kicked off the season in exactly the same way as a year earlier: losing 5-1 at home, this time to Tottenham – although at least in 1959 Newcastle did score their own goal, a dipping 58th-minute header from Eastham. In October Mitten and McKeag made a highly publicised swoop on two brilliant and expensive young Scottish internationals: the 20-year-old Motherwell striker Ian St John, and the Aberdeen outside-left George Mulhall. Newcastle entered the bidding waving £50,000. Both men rejected the club.

In November Wally Hurford, a dentist and keen bridge player, replaced McKeag as chairman of the board. Sitting in the no-man's-land between the spiteful trenches of McKeag and Seymour, the mild-mannered Hurford told *The Observer*: 'Let's just let things unroll. That's the best way. I don't mind a little difference of opinion in the board. It's good as long as it does not become sinister.'

But it had become sinister long ago. The only hope was that Charlie Mitten could screen the players from it all. 'I know there must be trouble in the background,' said Scoular disingenuously, 'but it never reaches us.' Before very long, however, in January 1961 Scoular would finally get his wish and be allowed to leave for the player-manager's job at Bradford Park Avenue.

From a safe distance, big Frank Brennan consoled the players of Newcastle United with the assurance that: 'We won the cup twice in spite of the circus up there'.

The problem was: there were no more Wembley victories, and none in sight. By February 1960 Newcastle were once more marooned in mid-table, and once more unable to attract quality players to St James's Park. Mitten made headlines by advertising his willingness to pay Huddersfield Town a sensational £100,000 for their two young prodigies Denis Law and Ray Wilson. Once more the deal fell through, and United drifted into eighth position in Division One.

They had money to spend: there was no doubt about that. In the summer of 1960 Newcastle invested £6,000 in a big, ultramodern medical room, which was built on top of a swimming-pool. Under the faithful eye of Sandy Mutch's son Alec, who had been masseur and physiotherapist at the club for 30 years, players could use these facilities, change in dressing-rooms with shuttered lockers and piped music, wash in a palatial, terrazza-floored bathroom. Come to The Toon, the directors seemed to be imploring, we will treat you like gods.

But in June 1960 the ground began to shake beneath that terrazza flooring. It started harmlessly enough, with George Eastham putting in a transfer request at the end of his standard 1959–60 contract on 30 June. He did not intend to become a martyr, he explained later. 'I just wanted more money, Newcastle could not give me any more, and they would not let me go to another club.' Eastham was already on the maximum wage with Newcastle; he wanted a substantial signing-on fee to boost his career income. That could only be gained by moving.

Having failed to attract anybody else to Tyneside, Mitten was not about to release one of his few genuine stars without a fight. 'At that time,' he would say, 'football was in a state of unrest – players knew that they were not getting a salary to compensate for their professionalism, not getting the rewards for their skills.' It is one of sport's great ironies that Charlie Mitten, one of the early rebels against the maximum wage and the retain-and-transfer system; a man who had actually fled to South America and put his British career in jeopardy to escape that system, should have been the manager who, in 1960, was in charge of the club whose resistance to change forced the law to act. Later Mitten would insist that he had sympathy for Eastham, and that he warned the Newcastle board: 'Gentlemen, you are wasting your money taking them to court, because he will win.' But in 1960 Mitten the manager admitted: 'I didn't want him to go – he was one of my top players.'

So in June 1960 George Eastham's transfer request was refused by United. Eastham then refused to re-sign. This meant that Newcastle were no longer obliged to pay him a wage, and they did not do so. But under the retain-and-transfer system it also meant that Newcastle United Football Club could keep Eastham on their books for as long as they wished, thereby preventing him from making a living with any other football club – and they did just that.

Eastham took a civilian job in Reigate on the south coast of England, and insisted that he would not re-sign for Newcastle.

In July he appealed to the Football League Management Committee, who rejected his claim, saying that it was entirely a matter for club and player.

George Eastham then had only two courses of action. He could, as so many had before him, have buckled under and resigned another 12-month retain-and-transfer contract for Newcastle. Or he could do what no professional footballer had ever dared to do before: test the matter in the courts of law.

With the backing of the Professional Footballers' Association, he chose the latter course. As Derek Dougan, an official of the PFA, would later say: '[The PFA] knew that one day we would have to have a guinea pig. The average life of a footballer is only eight years, and George Eastham, to his eternal credit, took almost one year out of his career. He made a stand at Newcastle.'

So on Friday, 21 October 1960, as the Newcastle United squad arrived in Manchester to play Manchester United on the following day, writs were served in their hotel rooms on Wally Hurford, the chairman of Newcastle United, and Charlie Mitten, the club's manager. Identical writs were also delivered to five other directors, including Messrs Seymour and McKeag, and to the Football League Ltd, the Football Association Ltd, and Newcastle United Football Club Ltd. The writs were served in the name of George Eastham, and they alleged that since the beginning of July all of the aforementioned bodies had prevented him from earning a livelihood in football.

Alderman William McKeag was a solicitor, and it is clear that he at least recognised that the defendants in this case were unlikely to win their legal battle. By any standards other than those of the looking-glass world of professional football, they had acted in unreasonable restraint of trade. They were caught bang to rights. Their only hope was to plead the special circumstances of soccer, and to pray. It was unclear which of the two would prove most effective.

The writs certainly concentrated the minds of the Newcastle directors. Almost immediately after receiving them, they transferred George Eastham to Arsenal in November 1960 for

£47,500. He was therefore able once more to begin playing. (He did not in fact sacrifice a whole year of his career, as is popularly supposed. He lost five months' wages and three months of the season. The admirable thing about him was that he – and nobody else – was prepared to sacrifice a year, or five years, or his whole career: nobody could say how long. He alone was ready to take the step into the unknown, on a massive point of principle.)

The Newcastle board almost certainly hoped that by agreeing to the transfer they would call off Eastham's legal dogs. They were wrong. The PFA was not prepared to let this action slip. Cliff Lloyd, the PFA's chairman, persuaded Eastham to continue his case. It was finally heard in June 1963, and Lord Justice Wilberforce agreed with Eastham's counsel Gerald Gardiner when he said that: 'I regard this as a system from the Middle Ages. It is really treating men like cattle, and really the position is that they are paid slaves.'

Justice Wilberforce pronounced the defendants in unlawful restraint of trade. None of them appealed. The retain-and-transfer system was dead and buried. From then onwards, thanks to George Eastham of Newcastle United, footballers were free to negotiate their own livelihoods once their agreed contracts had expired. Along with the abolition of the maximum wage, it was one of the great bombshells to hit British football in the early 1960s. The game would never be the same again. 'I only did,' Eastham would say, 'what I thought was right.'

Charlie Mitten must have wondered if his world had been stood on end. From being a roguish rebel, the Bogotá Bandit, he had become a losing defendant in a restraint of trade action.

And while the writs were raining upon him and his employers, Newcastle United FC were slipping precariously down the First Division table. By November the club was clearly in a relegation struggle. Mitten was still fiddling desperately with the line-up – United's first 30 league goals were scored by 14 different players! The Sunday Dispatch found itself wondering why Tyneside could no longer attract the star players necessary to lift the club to safety. The newspaper concluded that Newcastle, in a new age of glittering affluence and aspiration, had become seen as a dour, penny-pinching club. 'Newcastle had the reputation of being prepared to give their players the very best of everything. Now players talk about restrictions of out-of-pocket spending money when United play away; a change of hotel for London games – from Mayfair to King's Cross; the plan to make the team return from the south by overnight train, to save hotel expenses . . .'

Jackie Milburn, unable to tear himself away from the club, went to see the game which may have cost Newcastle United their Division One place in 1961. It was against Spurs in London, three-quarters of the way through the season, and if the players were bothered by staying in King's Cross on the Friday and catching the return train that Saturday night, they did not show it. United actually beat the champions-elect by 2-1. But after a vicious tackle by the Tottenham captain Dave MacKay on Len White, the Newcastle striker was carried off, and missed the rest of the season. Up until that point White had scored 28 goals in 33 games. After it they slumped into the bottom two for good, and were relegated to Division Two in 21st place, having scored 86 goals but conceded an astonishing 109. That was the legacy of Charlie Mitten's go-for-broke football: a team that scored plenty but conceded even more; that excited the neutrals but left the loyal fans watching Second Division football.

And yet such was the influence of the McKeag faction on the board that they could not at first fire Mitten. The process of his departure was purely farcical. He prepared his team throughout the close-season and kicked off in Division Two. On 10 September 1961 a 'Mitten Must Go' motion was put before a special board meeting. William McKeag and four of his supporters defeated Stan Seymour, Wilf Taylor and Lord Westwood in the vote. It was agreed that another meeting would be held to reach a decision on Mitten's contract before the end of October.

Confident that 'before the end of October' meant 'towards the end of October', on 26 September William McKeag flew to America on a lecture holiday. He was due back in 26 October. On 18 October Stan Seymour called another special board meeting. Stanley had used McKeag's holiday well: in the Alderman's absence he had converted one of his allies to the anti-Mitten cause. When the vote on Mitten's future was taken once more, in the absence of McKeag and with one defector, Charlie was axed by four votes to three.

'I am shocked beyond measure,' said McKeag from Maryland, USA, 'that this should have been done at this stage, without a full board meeting, and especially when it was known I would be back in the country in a few days.'

Over at Workington Town FC the manager Joe Harvey, on being told that Mitten had been sacked and the Newcastle board intended to advertise his job, said immediately: 'An approach would not surprise me. If I get an offer I will certainly take it. I am not on contract at Workington.'

CHAPTER NINE

RETURN TO PRIDE AND GLORY: 1961–75

❖

They did not immediately give Joe Harvey the job he longed for, and the job to which his destiny had led him. Harvey had actually left Barrow for Workington Town, not in order to improve himself, but so that he could be marginally nearer to his beloved Newcastle – nearer to its throes of agony.

But the board kept him waiting at the church. Upon the dismissal of Mitten and the furious committee-room arguments which followed it, they battened down the hatches. Between August and October 1961, seven players had asked for transfers. They were all refused. In a desperate attempt to stop a haemorrhage of footballing talent which could have resulted in Third Division football, the board now announced a ban on all transfers from the club until further notice. Norman Smith, the trainer since 1938, was once again made caretaker manager with just one brief: keep Newcastle United in Division Two.

Smith, a no-nonsense 64-year-old moulded by the football of the pre-war era (he had played for Huddersfield Town, Sheffield Wednesday and Queen's Park Rangers in the 1930s) succeeded with comparative ease. With the help of Joe Richardson, the full-back who had arrived from Blyth Spartans back in 1929, Norman Smith motivated his Newcastle players into 11th place in Division Two by the end of season 1961–62. The two old-timers, steeped in United's glorious past, served their club well in its hour of need.

But by the summer of 1962 Smith was talking of retirement (he would leave that November, although the remarkable Joe Richardson was prepared to stick around for another 15 years, not finally bowing out until 1977 – nine years before the even more extraordinary Sandy Mutch, whose 64-year career as club physio did not end until 1986!). The board took a deep breath and decided to invest in the future. For the same wage that they had given Charlie Mitten – £3,000 a year – they asked Joe Harvey to return to St James's Park.

He was delighted. Harvey's own future had not, in truth, looked all that bright – 'During my two years at Barrow I was interviewed for the manager's chair at Hartlepool and Mansfield Town. Funny – if I had got either job the chances are I might never have come back to St James's Park. It doesn't bear thinking about.'

Harvey was given a 12-month contract and told bluntly that the price of failure would be the sack. He discovered to his horror that his old club was £100,000 in the red. During each of the previous two seasons, for the first time since the war the average home gate had sunk below 30,000. 'They seemed to me,' he said, 'to have lost all the pride and glory I had known and loved.'

He needed time, he reckoned. 'It takes time to reorganise a football team. Time, patience, and a lot of heartache. You need luck on your side, and the backing of your directors.' Time he certainly did not have. Newcastle needed success, financially and morally, and they needed it quickly. Patience he did have – he proved it. Heartache he certainly suffered. And as for luck and the backing of the directors . . . only time would tell.

If he found a substantial overdraft, Joe Harvey also discovered that in his absence Charlie Mitten had built up an excellent youth team. There was a limited number of promising first-team players who wanted to stay in Newcastle – centre-half John McGrath, who had recently arrived from Bury in an exchange deal with Bob Stokoe, was a rare exception of a footballer who would successfully make the transition from the Mitten era to the Harvey years.

But, everybody was agreed, the youth team was bulging with promise. They would win the FA Youth Cup in 1962. (And to Charlie Mitten's fury, just months after his sacking, his old enemy Stan Seymour stepped up to collect the youth trophy after the Newcastle boys Mitten had tutored had seen off Wolves in a two-legged final.) Harvey acknowledged his luck in inheriting such an exceptional crop of youngsters. The youth product of the time (not all of whom were in the 1962 Youth Cup team) included the midfielder Alan Suddick, full-back George Dalton, inside-forward (soon to be centre-half) Bobby Moncur, defenders Colin Clish and Frank Clark (who had been spotted playing for Crook Town), striker Bryan 'Pop' Robson, winger Geoff Allen, and a young defender from Northern Ireland called David Craig.

All of these boys would have remarkable careers, mostly with Newcastle United. One or two of them would finally be counted among the finest servants in the club's history – who could argue with Craig's total of 406 games in 16 years, while collecting 25 Northern Irish caps? One was Scottish and one was Irish: the rest were Geordies. All of them signed professional terms with United within months of Harvey's arrival. It was clear to the educated eye that here was a harvest of home-grown talent to rank alongside the produce of the 1940s.

But they were not quite, in 1962, old enough and experienced enough to take over the first team. Harvey had also to buy. Here he proved less extravagant than Stan Seymour and more modest than Charlie Mitten, but more selective than either. Joe Harvey was not about to throw money around, although he insisted that despite the financial losses of recent years 'the board backed me all the way on the transfer market'. Perhaps that was precisely because he was not looking to splash out £50,000 on the likes of Denis Law.

Joe Harvey's successes in his 13 years as manager of Newcastle were based on the honest, what-you-see-is-what-you-get, fiercely irreproachable character of his playing days, coupled with a hitherto unsuspected ability to recognise skill. His attitude towards skill as a captain had usually been along the lines of: skill is all right, but it needs motivating. Harvey was too subtle and intelligent, however, to assume that motivation simply meant shouting at other players. Once when Ernie Taylor was having a bad day, Harvey patiently waited for the little forward to make one decent pass. And then the captain stood with his hands on his hips, shaking his head in astonished disbelief, and said: 'You know, Ernie, there's not another man in the bloody game who could pass a ball like that.' Taylor swelled with pride, and normal service was resumed.

After the vanities and eccentricities and strange ambitions of the Charlie Mitten era; after the vicious brawling between McKeag and Seymour, Honest Joe Harvey was made to measure. 'He took what he'd shown us on the pitch into the manager's office,' said Jackie Milburn, 'and added that special ingredient so vital to a boss: the ability to spot and sign real talent. Joe had two sides to him, the tongue-lasher and the lifter of sunken spirits. Such qualities are called "man-management".'

Harvey firstly pruned the squad of such remnants of the old days as Ivor Allchurch and Alf McMichael. He immediately bought the inside-forward Dave Hilley from Third Lanark, and the 27-year-old balding half-back Jimmy Iley from Nottingham Forest. Then in December 1962 he went for a centre-forward whom Harvey himself had earlier sold from Workington to Bolton Wanderers. Ron McGarry was an unaffected goalscorer who talked as quickly and as powerfully as he shot. He was a changing-room character with no pretensions to the finer arts of football. 'These lot are thoroughbreds,' he would say of the opposition. 'I'm an amateur, but if I can't play I might as well frighten the opposition to death by talking.' McGarry became famous not only for his goals but also for his calling cards – he would hand out little bits of printed pasteboard to opponents in the players' tunnel just before matches. They read: 'Ron McGarry. Have Goals – Will Travel'. He was as good as his word. In his five years with United he netted 46 goals in 129 games.

Harvey kept on adding carefully to his squad. In April 1963

the forward Willie Penman was bought from Glasgow Rangers, but United finished the 1962–63 season only in seventh place in Division Two. It was closer, but still not good enough. Harvey found himself spending hours on the phone to his old friend Jackie Milburn, who was in similar trouble in East Anglia, having taken over the new England manager Alf Ramsey's aging team at Ipswich Town; whereas Harvey had a First Division club sinking down the Second Division, as Milburn put it, Jackie had 'a First Division club with a Fourth Division team'.

But at least Newcastle – unlike impoverished Ipswich – had a little bit of money to spend. In the close season Harvey splashed £37,000 on the Welsh international half-back Alwyn 'Ollie' Burton, and rather less on the Walsall left-winger Colin Taylor and the Hearts goalkeeper Gordon Marshall. Shortly after the start of the new season the manager added to his haul by bringing back an old team-mate – Ashington lad Bobby Cummings, who had played with Harvey in the mid-1950s before being transferred to Aberdeen. Harvey brought him back to Tyneside in October 1963, and in November paid Nottingham Forest £20,000 for the hard-tackling 20-year-old Trevor Hockey. That same month he controversially swooped for the ageing ex-England international Stan Anderson of Sunderland. Anderson left Roker Park with mixed feelings – the club which he had served for 13 years was just about to be promoted back to Division One – but Harvey instantly made him captain of Newcastle United in place of Dick Keith, who was promptly sold to Bournemouth.

Surely the stage was set for a burst at promotion. If so, Joe Harvey's brave new squad disguised it well. On 4 January 1964 they suffered what Harvey himself described as 'the worst reverse in the history of the club'.

It was an FA Cup third-round tie. United, having suffered a bad series of early-winter league results, were looking for a good cup run to restore confidence. They got just the opposite. Bedford Town of the Southern League arrived at St James's Park on a roll: unlike Newcastle, they had just enjoyed a string of successes. And they continued that run of successes by knocking Newcastle United out of the FA Cup by 2-1. Joe Harvey left the ground, in his own words, 'ashen-faced'. 'It never pays to shout too loud in football,' he philosophised. 'It's a very small step from hero to mug.'

Only one team was promoted to Division One from the North-east in April 1964, and it was Sunderland AFC. But Newcastle started the 1964–65 season in blistering form. Harvey, his rebuilding almost complete, could do little but pick his team, put it on the field, shout loudly from the dug-out for 90 minutes, and hope that the boys would find a way out of that famously impenetrable maze that is the English Second Division.

They did so. By the Good Friday of 1965 Newcastle United had been top of the Second Division for a month. There were four league games to go. United had 52 points, second-placed Northampton Town were on 51, and third-placed Bolton Wanderers were on 45 with a game in hand.

Only Bolton could cheat United of promotion. As far as Harvey was concerned, they might well do it: 'It was Bolton I feared most. They had the bravest centre-forward in Britain, Wyn Davies.' They were due on Tyneside on 16 April, Good Friday, and three days later on Easter Monday Newcastle were due to play the Lancastrians at Burnden Park. The Good Friday game, therefore, was one of those make-or-break league matches. If Bolton drew or won, they would make up valuable ground on the Geordies, and face Newcastle at home three days later with an immense psychological advantage to present to their 60,000 fans. But if Newcastle won they would be nine points clear of Bolton, and Wanderers would just have four games left – Newcastle would be, in other words, home and dry.

Sixty thousand squeezed into St James's Park. 'I had that special spring tingle again,' remembered Joe Harvey, thinking of his own promotion decider as a player at Newcastle 17 years earlier. 'I had been manager for three years, we had been four years in the Second Division. Yet another of those emotional Tyneside matches. Promotion again the prize. This time Bolton stood in our way.'

Stop Wyn Davies, Harvey told his defenders before the game,

'and you will win promotion'. But for 45 minutes Bolton looked like seizing the points. Davies, the centre-forward that Harvey feared so much, caused havoc, twice seeing goal-bound attempts cleared off the line. Then centre-half John McGrath crashed into the Bolton striker and Davies had to leave the field. 'I cannot say that I was broken-hearted when he taken off,' said Harvey. 'Certainly it made all the difference. I made mental notes that come what may this Welshman must play in my team.'

In the absence of Davies the Newcastle half-back line of Anderson, McGrath and Iley was free to assert itself, and shortly into the second half Willie Penman pounced in a crowded goalmouth to make it 1-0. Jim Iley then moved forward from left-half to finish the scoring – and clinch United's return to Division One – at 2-0. Newcastle drew the return at Bolton three days later 1-1, and drew their two remaining league fixtures. Northampton Town never took the opportunity to make up ground, however, and United were promoted as Division Two champions for the first time in their history, with 57 points from 42 games. They scored a respectable 81 goals (Ron 'Have Goals, Will Travel' McGarry was top scorer with 16 of them), but it was the defence which clinched it by conceding only 45. Marshall, Clark and McGrath played in every league fixture; Anderson missed just one; Craig missed just two; and Iley missed four. They were the best, Harvey knew, in Division Two.

Would they be good enough for Division One? With his youngsters coming of age, Harvey was reluctant to spend too much money on new players to ease the transition into the top flight. He fancied two of the Bolton players who had worried him so much in 1965: Davies, of course, and the inside-forward Francis Lee. Lee, though, would not leave Lancashire because of the business commitments which would soon make him a millionaire (and eventually give him the wherewithal to purchase Manchester City).

Davies was an odder fish to catch. Deeply suspicious of the directors of football clubs (the story was put about that early in his career he had been promised money which never material-ised), he frustrated all of Harvey's early advances. Newcastle's offer of £70,000 was apparently accepted by Bolton, but Davies could not agree on his own signing-on fee. Newcastle had shuffled through their first season back in Division One, where they finished 15th, and were two months into the 1966–67 season when Joe Harvey and director Wilf Taylor picked up the phone to Bolton once more.

They did so on the tail end of some worrying early league scores, and a series of knock-backs from other players. Aston Villa's big striker Tony Hateley had escaped them, and an offer of £100,000 for Queen's Park Rangers' brilliant pairing of Rodney Marsh and Roger Morgan was refused by the west London club.

But Bolton Wanderers, in the October of 1966, were still prepared to sell Wyn Davies . . . for £85,000 now, and only if the player could agree terms. The board agreed the new price. (At 2002 rates, it amounted to about £1,000,000. Footballing inflation being what it was and still is, quite disconnected from the rest of the economy, that made Wyn Davies United's first million-pound player.)

So it was that Joe Harvey and Wilf Taylor found themselves with Davies in a Lancashire street looking for a public telephone box, from which the suspicious Welshman could telephone his widowed mother for advice. Many years earlier young Wyn had signed amateur forms with Wrexham without notifying his mother, and she had given him such grief for the action that he had never since taken any career decision without her explicit approval. Davies located the phone box, put his call through to another phone box close to the Davies family home in Caernavon, a passing neighbour answered it and went to fetch his mother, and Wyn Davies proceeded to discuss the matter in Welsh with Mrs Davies. Finally he put down the phone, emerged from the box, and told the two relieved Newcastle men, in English, that he would play for their team.

The next month, November, Harvey brought yet another player from Linfield in Northern Ireland, and goalkeeper Willie McFaul would prove to be yet another excellent Irish investment. Then, on 21 December 1966, Alan Suddick was despatched to Blackpool, who were in desperate trouble at the bottom of Division One, for £60,000 – and was given a £3,000 signing-*off* fee from Newcastle in thanks for all of his service, and because the club, which was by now chaired by the highly principled future chairman of the FA Lord Westwood, opposed signing-on fees and wished to replace them. That remaining £57,000 burned a hole in Harvey's pocket – he instantly used it to buy the midfield dynamo David Elliott from Sunderland, the winger Tommy Robson from Chelsea, and the centre-half John McNamee from Hibernian.

Sadly Wyn Davies did not turn out to be quite the goalscoring machine that Harvey had anticipated. At the end of his five-year spell he had collected almost exactly a goal every four matches in his 216 games. But his height, strength and much-trumpeted bravery did lay on a lot of goals for others, particularly Bryan 'Pop' Robson, but only once in five years was he the club's top scorer, and that was in 1967–68 when he grabbed just 12 of the club's miserly 54 league goals. Davies's great goalscoring triumph would come a year after that, and it would not be in domestic competition . . . but that is a future story.

In the first half of 1967 Newcastle showed more signs of missing Suddick than of gaining Davies, Elliott, Robson and McNamee. By March they were second bottom of Division One, with only Alan Suddick's doomed Blackpool beneath them. 'You're in trouble, aren't you?' a reporter asked Joe Harvey. He grinned. 'Wull not gan doon!' replied the Yorkshireman. Nor did they: two wins in the last two home games saw United safely into 20th place.

They were able, therefore, to relax and enjoy Jackie Milburn's testimonial match. This took place some ten years after the forward's departure, and was organised by the Supporters' Club. It took place on a wet evening in May 1967, and 45,404 Geordies paid £8,200 to watch the stars of past and present Newcastle teams, and some members of England's World Cup-winning squad of the previous year, lay on two exhibition matches. It was, said Milburn, 'one of the proudest moments of my life'. The size of the occasion so long after the man's retirement showed, as Joe Harvey commented, 'how much they thought of him'.

The last three years of the 1960s saw Newcastle United finish safely in the top half of the First Division. The fans could breathe again. But, comfortable as life might suddenly seem, something was missing, something quite identifiable. Newcastle United had traditionally fed upon a diet of passion and drama. The FA Cup had been the ideal tournament for this club, because the cup more than any other competition offered thrilling life and stunning sudden death: cut-and-thrust football which left the fans and players either exhilarated beyond expression, or nerve-dead with anguish. In the case of The Toon, it had more usually been the former.

But Newcastle had not so much as reached the semi-finals of the FA Cup since 1955, and they had done no better in its recently established poor relation, the Football League Cup. What was needed, said the fans of the late 1960s, was another cup run, another burst through the pack, another full-speed chase with winner takes all. They would get it, and in memorable style, but from an entirely unexpected source.

The Inter-Cities' Fairs' Cup – which would become the UEFA Cup in 1971 – had been established in 1955, in the same year as the inception of the European Cup. It was originally formed as a competition between those European cities which had staged trade fairs. Entry was therefore nothing to do with league achievements, many sides were composite teams, and the first tournament took three years to complete – the final in 1958 was between Barcelona and a London Select XI. Barcelona won the two-legged final 6-2 on aggregate. Jimmy Greaves, who had been almost unknown when London played their first-round game in 1955, scored in the first leg of the 1958 final.

By 1968, when Newcastle entered it for the first time, the Inter-Cities' Fairs' Cup had become an extremely popular and highly profitable club competition. Four English clubs were allowed to take part each autumn, according to their final league position the previous spring. But only one club from any given city was permitted entry. Newcastle United had finished tenth in Division One in 1967–68, but as two of the teams above them – Manchester United and West Bromwich Albion – committed themselves to the European Cup and the European Cup-Winners' Cup respectively, that reduced the number above them to seven. Luckily, three of those seven – Everton, Spurs and Arsenal – had finished below a club from their own city (Liverpool and Chelsea). So they were disqualified, and Newcastle United sneaked in through the back door.

British clubs had enjoyed scant success in the Fairs' Cup, although Birmingham City and Glasgow Rangers had followed London as finalists, and Leeds United were the current holders, having won it in 1968. British clubs had just begun to adjust themselves generally to European competition, with Celtic and Manchester United taking the European Cup and West Ham and Spurs the Cup-Winners' Cup.

But Newcastle United had never before played a team from the continent of Europe in serious competition. No Northeastern side had done so. Not one of Newcastle's players had any experience of such games. And in the first round, on 11 September 1968, they were drawn against Feyenoord – the Dutch giants who, in the last five seasons of the 1960s, would win their national league twice and finish as runners-up on the other three occasions. Feyenoord, who would not be out of the top two in the Dutch league for 11 consecutive years. Feyenoord who – most importantly – had been gathering experience of European competition since they first entered the European Champions Cup in 1961 (and had promptly announced their presence by dismissing the Swedish champions IFK Goteburg 11-2 on aggregate). It is a fair measure of this team's threat to point out that one season later, in 1969–70, as reigning Dutch champions they would enter and win the European Cup itself.

What hope had Newcastle's European virgins against the likes of Feyenoord? Plenty, as it turned out. The night of 11 September 1968 would not be quickly forgotten on Tyneside or in Holland.

That floodlit Wednesday evening in fact belonged to one young man. Geoff Allen, another product of the youth policy of the early 1960s and an England youth international, had found it difficult to break out of the reserves and into the first team. Now, having just celebrated his 21st birthday, he was holding down a position on the left wing, and was thrown in to tantalise the Feyenoord defence.

He destroyed them. After seven minutes he carved up Feyenoord on the flank and hit a low cross which Jimmy Scott, the right-winger who had arrived from Hibernian a year earlier, side-footed past Dutch international keeper Pieters Graafland for Newcastle United's first goal in Europe.

It was a classic European start, and the 46,000 crowd went wild as Allen ran loose down the wing, hitting the bar with a violent drive, and as Pop Robson, the new boy Tommy Gibb from Partick Thistle (who had just taken up his Newcastle right-half's shirt a month earlier), and Wyn Davies completed a 4-0 rout of the Dutch masters.

If United thought it was going to be that easy all the way, they were quickly – and fortunately – disillusioned a month later in Rotterdam, when Feyenoord laid seige to their goal and only heroics from McNamee, Burton and McFaul kept the score down to a 2-0 reversal. But United were through 4-2. Unfortunately, young Geoff Allen would never again play in a European match. Three weeks later he shattered his knee while playing against Nottingham Forest in the league, and his playing career was over. That game in Nottingham was only his 26th in the first team.

The injured Allen was replaced in that match by United's one permitted substitute: a tall 18-year-old forward called Alan Foggon. Foggon, who came from Chester-le-Street, was yet another youth-team product, and he ran out in Nottingham to join another 18-year-old who had come up through the ranks, Keith Dyson. Both Dyson and Foggon proceeded to score in the 4-2 defeat of Forest, and both were retained in the 12-man squad which faced Sporting Lisbon in the second round of the Fairs' Cup.

If Feyenoord had been a worrying prospect, Sporting were truly terrifying. Winners of the Cup-Winners' Cup in 1964 and

Portuguese champions in 1966, they were only prevented from dominating their country's football by the presence of their Lisbon rivals Benfica. But Newcastle travelled to the Stadium of Light in confident mood, and on a black, torrential and thunderous night Jim Scott gave them a lead which they held until the last minute, when an optimistic long shot came back off the bar and rebounded off McFaul's arm into the net.

Fifty-four thousand folk turned up at St James's Park three weeks later convinced that 1-1 would be enough. Away goals counted double in 1968, but this time they were not needed: Pop Robson took a Wyn Davies knock-down to volley home a sensational waist-high strike and seal the game at 1-0, and the two-legged tie at 2-1 on aggregate.

Newcastle the team and Newcastle the city were starting to enjoy this. The first leg of the third round took place in Spain on New Year's Day 1969. Newcastle travelled there to play Real Zaragoza, the Fairs' Cup finalists of 1966 and Spanish Cup-winners in the same year. Davies and Robson struck again to score the goals in a 3-2 defeat.

The crowd was up to 56,500 for the return, and they had hardly sat down before Pop Robson levelled the aggregate score, collecting a pass from Ollie Burton and smacking a 30-yarder past the Spanish keeper Nieves. Tommy Gibb made it 2-0 in the 28th minute with a header from a Robson corner, and when Nieves had to be substituted following a collision with Foggon the matter seemed settled. But in the 42nd minute Zaragoza scored the first European goal to be conceded in Newcastle, and all of a sudden the Geordie crowd had its first experience of European mathematics. The sums were elementary, really: one more Spanish goal without reply, and United were out. Luckily it did not materialise. The tie finished 4-4 on aggregate, and Newcastle were through on the away-goals rule.

As the fans trooped happily away and the players relaxed in the bath, a message got through to Wyn Davies that Ted Heath wished to see him. Something of a fan of the popular bandleader, Davies wandered upstairs to be introduced to a large, cheerful leader of the Conservative Party, who introduced himself to the puzzled Davies by explaining that he had enjoyed a fine seat in the middle of the stand.

'What about getting me one in the summer,' asked Davies.

It was Heath's turn to be puzzled.

'For the investiture of Prince Charles in Caernarvon,' the centre-forward explained. 'It's my home town, you know.' Such was the glamorous life of a football player in the late 1960s.

Joe Harvey still had time for the transfer market. In March he went to Greenock Morton in Scotland to buy a large Danish midfield player named Preben 'Ben' Arentoft. If Harvey was buying as much with Europe on his mind as anything else, he was to prove a wise man.

In the middle of March 1969 Vitoria FC Setubal of Portugal arrived on Tyneside for the quarter-finals. By now Newcastle's domestic season was all but an irrelevancy to the fans, which was as well, as they were out of the cups and in the middle of Division One.

The Setubal players arrived in a snowstorm. One of them, Jacinto Joao, astonished the 57,662 spectators by playing with woollen socks pulled over his hands. Two goals from Robson and one apiece from Davies, Gibb and Foggon clinched a 5-1 win and surely booked a place in the semi-finals. It was not quite all over, however. Only a Davies header kept United's nerves intact in a 3-1 defeat in Portugal in the second leg.

But they were through 6-4. 'It will be a remarkable achievement,' judged *The Times*, in an article celebrating Newcastle's return to cup-fighting eminence, 'if they now carry off the prize on their first entry into continental competition, where so much has to be learned by hard and often bitter experience.'

Three other British teams were in the semi-finals of European competitions: Manchester United in the European Cup; Dunfermline Athletic in the Cup-Winners' Cup; and Glasgow Rangers, who had just got past Athletic Bilbao to join Newcastle in the semis of the Fairs' Cup. Rangers, resentful second-fiddle to Celtic in the domestic competitions, and desperate to match their old rivals' European Cup win of 1967, were the opponents to avoid. So naturally, Newcastle – the 'back door' team who were suddenly the bookies' favourites – drew them in the semi-final.

A Fairs' Cup record crowd of 75,580 gathered at Ibrox for the first leg, which was given added spice when John McNamee, a former Celtic player, announced to the world that he would take care of Rangers' striker Colin Stein on one leg. Luckily, he did. Willie McFaul did the rest by saving a penalty.

St James's Park was jammed to its 60,000 capacity for the return on 21 May 1969, in a game which could be remembered as the cup-tie of three pitch invasions. United forced the play in the first half without reward, although Robson misdirected a point-blank drive in the 14th minute. Then came the first invasion. Wyn Davies found the Rangers centre-half pulling him down by the shirt. 'I got up,' he recalled, 'and grabbed Ron MacKinnon round the head and pushed him to the ground. The Rangers supporters didn't like that, and all of a sudden bottles came flying on the pitch. After the bottles came the fans.'

Early in the second half United forced a series of corners, and the fourth one in the 53rd minute resulted in Scotland international Jimmy Scott firing Newcastle into a 1-0 lead with a brilliant cross-shot. This time the Newcastle fans stormed onto the pitch to celebrate.

As a result of this second invasion the referee announced that he would take the players off the field if it happened again. So when Jackie Sinclair (yet another Scot, who had been bought from Leicester City 17 months earlier) collected a Davies nod-on to make it 2-0, the Rangers fans invaded the pitch once more in the hope of forcing an abandonment. Police with alsatian dogs cleared the playing area, however, and then guarded the visitors' Gallowgate end as the last ten minutes were played out in an atmosphere of bitter tension.

With Rangers gone, and Manchester United and Dunfermline both knocked out of their European semi-finals, the new boys Newcastle United found themselves the only British club in a European final in 1969. They would meet there Ujpesti Dozsa of Budapest in Hungary – 'Oopsy Daisy', as the Geordies would dub their opponents. Compared to Newcastle, Ujpesti had enjoyed an easy run to the final, having to beat off teams from Luxembourg, Salonica and Izmir as well as creditably defeating Leeds United in the quarter-finals – after which Don Revie had called them 'the greatest team in Europe'.

They were a formidable outfit. They had just done the league and cup double in Hungary, and, staffed by as many as seven members of their superb national team, were about to embark on a seven-year domination of the Hungarian league.

Another capacity 60,000 crowd paid record receipts of £42,000 to see the first leg of the Inter-Cities' Fairs' Cup at St James's Park on 29 May 1969. Everybody knew enough about European football by now to realise that the home draw was best played last. So for once, Newcastle played with caution. Not until the 63rd minute did they open the scoring – and they did it in style.

Tommy Gibb fired a free-kick towards Davies at the back post; the six-foot striker took it on his chest and smashed in a close-range shot which the Ujpesti keeper Szentimihalyi could only parry, and skipper and centre-half Bobby Moncur – up there for the fun of it – stepped in to score his first goal of the season.

Ten minutes later Moncur had his second of the game and of the season. This time he moved forward to play a wall-pass with Ben Arentoft and hit a low shot in by the far post. He could have had a third. Arriving in the box for another corner, he began to jog backwards to meet the outswinging cross – and smacked into a sickening collision with the incoming Wyn Davies. Davies got to his feet dizzily with no feeling in the side of his face. He was later taken to hospital, but the suspected fracture which would have kept him out of the second leg was not diagnosed. And as it turned out, Jim Scott made it 3-0 on the night with eight minutes to go, when Arentoft again popped up to release the right-winger.

It had been a physical campaign for big Wyn Davies. He had been hospitalised after the Feyenoord game with damaged shins as the result of not wearing shin-guards; his head was split open by Sporting Lisbon; he came away from the Rangers matches with a broken nose; and then Bobby Moncur gave him a black eye in the first leg of the final. 'I'm the centre-forward,' he philosophised, 'paid to take the knocks'.

Davies expected even rougher treatment in the second leg against Ujpesti Dosza. He had good reason for this: in the second half at St James's Park keeper Szentimihalyi had safely collected a cross, only to be barged heavily to the ground by Davies. 'The next thing I heard was the Hungarian defenders muttering "Budapest, Budapest!" I knew what that meant: "Wait till we get you out there".'

But in the first 45 minutes of the second leg of the 1969 Fairs' Cup final on 11 June – Joe Harvey's 51st birthday – the Hungarians did not need to resort to the rough stuff. They simply played Newcastle United off the park. Joe Harvey had sent his players out with instructions to play carefully, not to give the ball away . . . 'Give it away!' he would laugh. 'We spent the first half chasing shadows.'

By half-time Ujpesti had made it 2-0 on the night, 3-2 to Newcastle on aggregate, and but for four miraculous saves by McFaul the Hungarians might have turned the whole tie around in that magical spell.

'They pulled back two goals, and it might have been four or five,' Harvey admitted. 'I can still see the drawn faces of my players at half-time. Their heads were drooping – we were as good as out.'

David Craig would say that as those demoralised 11 foot-ballers trooped into their Budapest changing-room, dreading another 45 minutes against the Hungarian champions, they expected to be destroyed by Harvey's tongue. But, luckily, the great man-manager knew better than that.

'I haven't a clue how you're going to get one, and I don't much care,' he told his players. 'But score one you can, and you will. After that all our troubles will be over. Ujpesti will die.'

'With those words,' Harvey remembered, 'I went back to chain-smoking on the touchline – hoping and praying for a miracle.'

The miracle arrived right on cue. A minute after kick-off in the second half Newcastle won a corner. Szentimihalyi punched it out – straight to Jackie Sinclair, who clipped it back into the box where once again Bobby Moncur lay in wait to thrash the ball left-footed into the net.

That goal made it 2-1 to Ujpesti on the night, but 4-2 to Newcastle on aggregate. It was Moncur's third goal of the two legs. To put that statistic in perspective, in 341 other games for Newcastle, the centre-half scored only five more goals!

Newcastle were not finished. As Harvey had predicted, Ujpesti faded, and in the 50th minute Ben Arentoft made it 2-2. 'We grew and grew,' said Harvey, 'the Hungarians wilted . . .' Nothing could go wrong now for the manager. In the 68th minute he put on Alan Foggon for Jimmy Scott. Two minutes after taking the field Foggon hurtled for goal, brushed aside a couple of defenders and released a shot which Szentimihalyi could only push onto the crossbar, and Foggon, following up, gleefully smashed the rebound home.

That 3-2 win was not only Newcastle's first away win in the six marathon rounds of the Fairs' Cup; it also meant that unfancied United had, in the words of *The Times*, 'completed a staggering 6-2 destruction of Hungarian league leaders Ujpesti Dosza to win the Inter-Cities' Fairs' Cup'. For almost three decades afterwards it would remain the club's finest hour since the middle of the 1950s: a thrilling reminder, at the end of the swinging sixties, of the years when the rest of the footballing world feared Newcastle United, and Newcastle United feared nobody.

The years 1968 to 1971 were Newcastle United's European years. They did little in the league other than finish marginally in the top half of Division One, and the domestic cups were, on Tyneside, virtually non-events. In the whole of Joe Harvey's 12-year reign as manager of Newcastle United, the club which in the post-war years had made its name as a cup-fighting side, only once got beyond the fourth round of the FA Cup, and not until the fading months of Harvey's term of office did they get any further than the third round of the Football League Cup (which the League authorities had introduced in 1960 as a poor-man's challenge to the FA Cup).

But Europe more than compensated. Although United never won the trophy again, they re-entered in each of the following two seasons (the last two before the Fairs' Cup became the UEFA Cup). In 1969–70 they enjoyed a dazzling run to the quarter-finals at the expense of Dundee United, FC Porto and South-ampton, and were only eliminated on the away-goals rule by the eventual losing finalists Anderlecht. And the following year they beat Inter Milan in the first round, only to be dismissed from the second round by Pecsi Dosza in a penalty shoot-out in Hungary. It had been a great run. For some players this European spell provided the highlights of their career – Wyn Davies, for exam-ple, scored ten of his total of 53 goals (in 216 games) for New-castle in Europe. Never did the chorus echoing Bob Dylan's 'Mighty Flynn' – 'You've not seen nothing like the mighty Wyn' – echo down from the terraces more loudly than on those atmo-spheric floodlit European nights at St James's Park.

Harvey kept buying, of course, and rebuilding brick by brick. In July 1969 he celebrated his Fairs' Cup win by using some of the profit to buy from Luton Town a brash young striker, who had actually begun his career as a full-back, called Malcolm Macdonald. Macdonald's belief in himself was made clear from the first day of his arrival at St James's Park – he turned up in a Rolls-Royce. He had to wait until Pop Robson lost form (and was sold to West Ham in the February of 1971), and for Wyn Davies to be transferred (to Manchester City in August 1971) to assume the position that he desired: goalscoring king of New-castle. But then he did it in style, immediately scoring a hat-trick in his first home game against Liverpool, and subsequently netting 26 goals in the season.

The following month, August 1969, even more of that Fairs' Cup money went on buying the club's first £100,000 footballer, Jimmy 'Jinky' Smith, a Scottish inside-forward whom Jackie Milburn – by now a journalist on Tyneside – likened to Len Shackleton: a moody player who, when it suited him, 'could put the ball through the eye of a needle with his right peg'.

And the youth policy continued to pay dividends. In July 1970 Irving Nattrass from Fishburn signed professional forms, and within a year put on for the first time the number 4 shirt which he would wear for 275 games. In October Tommy Cassidy caught the boat from Coleraine. That close-season one of United's most consistent but unsung heroes, the winger Stewart Barrowclough, was signed from Barnsley. In August 1971 Terry Hibbitt arrived on a free transfer from Leeds, and never was a footballer better value. John Tudor came from Sheffield United the same year, and a month after Hibbitt's arrival, the defender Patrick Howard signed from Barnsley. It was an eventful 12 months.

But there were hints, throughout the early 1970s, of the major calamity which would end Joe Harvey's spell. On 24 January 1972 United drew Hereford United of the Southern League. The home tie finished a 2-2 draw, and Newcastle travelled to a tight, muddy pitch two weeks later for the replay. They were winning 1-0 a few minutes from time when a joiner called Ronnie Radford played a one-two in midfield with his Hereford team-mate Brian Owen. In Radford's words: 'When he gave it back I thought "ooh aye". I always liked a sudden dig. No rhyme or reason to it when your instinct sniffs a chance, is there? You don't think about it, nor look up to place it. Just head down and good contact. If it's on and you can see them white sticks, then have a go at getting it between them.'

That 40-yarder which screamed past McFaul put Hereford level at 1-1. In extra-time a substitute put Newcastle out of the cup, and cemented their reputation as the cup-fighting side which was prone to being knocked out of the cup by non-league teams (it has actually happened six times: three times in the 1890s, once in 1907 at Crystal Palace, by Bedford Town in 1964, and by Hereford).

The silver lining to the Hereford cloud was that a novice commentator named John Motson had been assigned the game by *Match of the Day*. 'Obviously,' he recalled, 'the game was made the main match that night . . . It turned my career, really. They saw that I could handle a big game and from then on I started to get better and better matches.' It was worth it, to set Motty on his way. Wasn't it?

In the following month another marker was laid. Newcastle travelled to play Bill Shankly's high-flying Liverpool in the league. As they walked down the players' corridor they noticed, yet again, the plaque of wood with 'This Is Anfield' carved upon it. Malcolm Macdonald saw Joe Harvey and Shankly standing beneath it. He pointed up at the plaque. 'There you are, Joe,' said Macdonald, 'I told you we were at the right place.'

Shankly wheeled round. 'You'll soon find out you're at the right place,' he growled. Liverpool won 5-0.

At the end of 1972 the legendary sportswriter John Arlott considered that Newcastle United were on the edge of yet another 'era of prosperity' in the great old club's history. Dismissing the Hereford defeat as an aberration, he pointed to the club's sound league position of eighth (they were to finish ninth) – and particularly to Malcolm Macdonald. 'He is essentially a goalscorer,' wrote Arlott, 'not simply a poacher ... Physically he is well equipped, powerfully built, a fast, tenacious straight runner, and with a shot not only strong but also, for one who throws his boot at the ball in the uninhibited fashion of a full-back, surprisingly accurate. His he ading is straightfor-wardly useful. His value in the air lies chiefly in the determina-tion which takes him to the ball.'

Supermac was goal hungry. Some sceptics noticed and dis-liked the habit of the new wearer of the number 9 shirt of claiming anything – deflections, own-goals, scrambles over the line, shots from other players which were already goalbound when Macdonald arrived on the scene to give them the *coup de grâce* – but nobody could resist his confidence. If he took the club half as far as he claimed he could, then Arlott was right: Tyneside was in for interesting times.

In 1973 Newcastle reached the final of the Anglo-Italian Cup, which was against Fiorentina in Florence. They were missing Macdonald, whom the FA refused to release from the England party which was due to play Poland in Katowice on 6 June, three days after the Anglo-Italian final. But no matter. 'In my years as player, captain, coach and manager of Newcastle United,' Joe Harvey told his footballers, 'I've never lost a cup final. I like it that way.' He did not lose that one. Tommy Gibb took the opportunity to relive his own personal European days of glory in the 35th minute when he slung over a cross from the right and the Fiorentina goalkeeper Superghi punched it into his own net. Nine minutes into the second half David Craig made it 2-0 with a rare and memorable goal: Terry McDermott set him away; he worked a one-two with Jinky Smith, and then the veteran full-back ran 35 yards to fire the ball under the unfortunate Superghi. Clerici made it 2-1 with ten minutes left, but United had won the minor trophy. Not many considered that Harvey had put out a hostage to fortune with his comments before the game.

After a bad-tempered series of league and League Cup games with Birmingham at the end of 1973, which concluded with Birmingham's Tony Want threatening to sue Jimmy Smith for a broken leg; Newcastle being knocked out of the League Cup; and Irving Nattrass being put out of the game for two months following a retaliatory tackle by the Birmingham boys, the FA Cup run of 1974 started breezily. In the third round Newcastle had yet another major scare against non-league opposition, when Hendon of the Isthmian League drew 1-1 on Tyneside, but the newly arrived Terry McDermott sealed a 4-0 victory from the penalty spot in the replay. Joe Harvey – who had dropped Jimmy Smith from the replay, despite Jinky's recent inclusion in Scotland's World Cup squad, because Smith 'doesn't seem to want to play, and I have no intention of playing him' – could breathe easy. An unrequested managerial record of three FA Cup defeats by non-league opposition had narrowly been avoided.

If not many other neutral observers were impressed, Leeds United captain Billy Bremner was. 'Joe Harvey could once again be lifting the famous old tin pot in a few months,' he announced. '[Newcastle] are a side that have rallied to the cause with tactics based on entertainment, skill and teamwork: the ideal basis in the cup.'

Others were just as prophetic. 'There will be an uprising on Tyneside,' Len Shackleton predicted to a passing journalist, 'if Newcastle don't get to the final this year.'

Scunthorpe United from the Third Division followed Hendon to the North-east to face this ideal cup-fighting side. They also drew 1-1 before two Macdonald goals and one from Stewart Barrowclough saw them off by 3-0 in Yorkshire.

Only in the fifth round – where United were competing for the first time since 1961 – did they begin to show some form. The draw was once more superficially favourable: West Bromwich Albion of Division Two, at the Hawthorns. And for once Newcastle made the divisional gap in standards show. West Brom were torn apart by some exhilarating attacking football before Jimmy Smith whipped over a cross from the right for Macdonald to steer home the opening goal with his head in the 30th minute. Barrowclough made it 2-0 shortly after half-time, and Tudor wrapped things up at 3-0 just before the finish.

And then, on 9 March 1974, came the hour of shame that few English professional football clubs were immune from in the 1970s. It came out of the blue. United had drawn Second Division Nottingham Forest at St James's Park in the cup sixth round.

After just 85 seconds Ian Bowyer headed Forest into the lead. David Craig made it 1-1 with a fierce left-footed drive in the 26th minute, but with Forest looking good value for their cup money, O'Kane put the Second Division visitors ahead once more just before the break.

The second half was played in a feverish atmosphere. Newcastle were reduced to ten men when centre-half Pat Howard was sent off. In the 56th minute David Craig barged Duncan MacKenzie in the box. As Forest's Lyall placed the ball on the spot, a kind of collective will thrilled through the Leazes End. Lyall thumped the ball home – and the invasion began. An estimated 300 fans ran onto the pitch. Referee Gordon Kew took the players off the pitch for fully eight minutes while the police restored order. 'It was exactly the same as a high-speed car crash when you are icy calm and your mind works twice as fast as normal,' he said later.

Then the game resumed, and the fight-back began. It was

simply extraordinary. Whatever was said later – and plenty would be said later – this was one of the great FA Cup recoveries. When he kicked the game off for the third time, referee Kew's watch showed 32 minutes to play and Forest leading 3-1. Ten minutes later, with the 54,000 crowd still humming madly, Macdonald was pushed in the back by the Forest keeper Barron, and McDermott made it 3-2 from the spot. Minutes after that Terry Hibbitt's cross found Tudor unmarked, and the forward's diving header hurtled past Barron. And in the last minute Bobby Moncur gave United a 4-3 win from a position which some considered to be offside, but 'with the crowd in that mood the linesman would not have dared put his flag up. He would have been lynched.'

The Forest manager Allan Brown said immediately: 'The Newcastle supporters put us out of the cup. We were playing at our best and then the game was halted, and that was the end of any concerted football.'

The draw for the semi-finals was made two days later, on Monday, 11 March 1974. It matched Newcastle against Burnley and Liverpool against Leicester City. But by then it was clear that the FA would have to reconsider the tie. Headlines such as 'THE FRIGHTENING FACE OF FOOTBALL' and 'FOOTBALL'S DAY OF SHAME' greeted their committee over the marmalade on Monday morning. Thirty-nine North-easterners were charged with violent conduct; 23 had been taken to hospital – two with fractured skulls – and 103 needed first-aid treatment at the ground.

'The Football Association,' demanded David Miller in the *Daily Express* 'must this morning put Nottingham Forest's name back with Newcastle's in the draw for the FA Cup semi-finals, if they have any real guts, any sense of fair-mindedness or responsibility to the dignity of the game they control.'

That was not a universal view. Some suggested that whatever else happened, football results should stand, and others that 'the real punishment for the Tyneside hooligan would have been for the match to have been abandoned at 3-1 and Forest awarded the tie'. There was a tightrope to tread. If games were always abandoned after pitch invasions, then almost any set of fans could finish a match when the scoreline favoured themselves. If replays always followed abandonments then fans could force replays when their team was losing. By playing on after the riot, referee Kew had at least achieved a result in a 90-minute game of football, even if the result went against the injured visiting team in the most extraordinary way.

On the following Thursday a four-man FA committee decided that the game should be replayed at Goodison Park on Monday, 18 March. As Patrick Howard's three-match suspension for his dismissal in the first tie did not begin until 19 March, he was free to play. This did not please Joe Harvey, who wanted to know why, if the result did not stand, the dismissal of Howard did. Nor did it please Allan Brown of Forest, who thought that he should have been given the tie. Nor Malcolm Macdonald, who got himself charged by the FA for bringing the game into disrepute by telling the TV cameras that his 'reaction is one of disgust, but not surprise'.

The first replay, as luck would have it, was a 0-0 draw. The tie, with its hungry media circus in hot pursuit, then progressed to Elland Road. There, after 12 minutes, the Forest midfielder Richardson feigned to run over a free-kick, swivelled and passed the ball back to Bowyer, who scored. Referee David Smith disallowed the goal and booked Richardson for ungentlemanly conduct. Twenty minutes later Macdonald for once broke free of Serella's attentions and whipped in a goal from the edge of the box. The game finished 1-0. It just had not been Nottingham Forest's cup-tie.

After all that, the semi-final at Hillsborough against Burnley, who were managed by Ashington man Jimmy Adamson, was a tea party. Twice in the second half Macdonald raced away from the Burnley defence to thump the ball home for a 2-0 win. If you believed the headlines, Supermac was a one-man show. It was a typically aggressive display which, several papers commented, put him in line for a long spell in the England number 9 shirt. This man, surely, could and would win the cup for Newcastle. *He* certainly seemed to think so.

Malcolm Macdonald would say later that 'Newcastle's immensely impressive unbeaten run of FA Cup finals at Wembley prior to their final against Liverpool in 1974 was the chief source of pressure exerted on the squad in the month leading up to the big match. Press, TV, radio, friends and relatives lost no opportunity to remind us of our tradition.'

Maybe so. The pressures certainly showed in the weeks before the match. League form slumped so dramatically that Newcastle neared the relegation zone (they would finish 15th, just two points clear of the bottom two), and Joe Harvey threatened to field a team of reserves at Wembley. Then Pat Howard fell out with coach Keith Burkinshaw, stormed out of a training session and failed to attend a pre-cup final photo-call.

Two weeks before the final United learned that as an extra punishment for the Nottingham Forest fiasco they would have to play all of their 1975 cup games on their opponents' grounds. Celtic cancelled a forthcoming benefit match at St James's for Tony Green, the Scotland international whose promising career on Tyneside had been cut short by injury after just 33 games in 1973. Then David Craig dislocated his elbow, and poor Stewart Barrowclough was dropped by the FA Cup final team. Pat Howard was selected.

All of which seemed suddenly irrelevant on 4 April 1974, as Newcastle United suffered their greatest humiliation in decades. This far outstripped the defeats by Bedford and Hereford. Tens of thousands of Geordies at Wembley, and hundreds of thousands of fans watching from afar, could hardly believe what happened to their side. The Liverpool strikeforce of Kevin Keegan and Steve Heighway inflicted the damage with three second-half goals (two to Keegan), but the difference in will, in aptitude, in class was apparent long before that.

The 'new Jackie Milburn', Malcolm Macdonald, had hardly a touch of the ball, and when he did he blasted it over the bar. The old Jackie Milburn, who was watching as a journalist from the stands (he was one of the few former players lucky enough to be there: true to form the club failed to invite its former stars), wrote later: 'It's not often I've been ashamed of the Magpies, but

I was saddened and shocked by the performance. Only the goalkeeper and the full-backs played. The rest were rubbish. Macdonald had been shouting from the rooftops as usual about what he was going to do but the only thing he did that afternoon was tie his bootlaces. It was awful. I could see Joe's [Harvey's] face and he was looking sicker with every minute.'

'We never got started,' was Harvey's verdict on this 3-0 hammering, 'and I can't understand it to this day.' He dreaded the return to Tyneside. The Newcastle fans had still been out-shouting the Liverpudlians when Emlyn Hughes went up to receive the cup, but that was for public consumption. Surely in private, back in the North-east, the team was in for a rough reception.

Not so. Tens of thousands greeted them off the train, and tens of thousands greeted them at St James's Park. It was as if the performance and the scoreline at Wembley had been reversed. 'Our supporters have moved me to tears on many occasions, most of them winning ones,' said Joe Harvey. 'But this time I knew they were entitled to show their anger, even disgust. They did no such thing. They gave us a heartwarming return which staggered me. I have never felt so humble.'

It was not quite the day a team died – although perhaps, in retrospect, it should have been. There were few immediate casualties. Bobby Moncur, that fine and inspirational captain, never kicked another ball for Newcastle United after the 1974 cup final, signing for Sunderland the following month. The rest stayed for at least another season, a season which saw New-castle get knocked out of the fourth round of the FA Cup, the fifth round of the League Cup, and finish 15th in Division One for the second consecutive year.

Immediately after the end of that season, in May 1975, the Newcastle board announced that they had accepted the resig-nation of manager Joe Harvey, a resignation which they had quietly demanded. He had been busy to the last, having just completed the signing of Mike Mahoney as replacement goal-keeper for Willie McFaul. A few months earlier, Harvey had said that 'Newcastle should have the finest team in the world.

God willing, I will live to see the day when they do.' Sadly, he would not. The Harvey era was over. The modern age had arrived in Newcastle, ten years too late some thought. Nobody expected what was to come. But what, on Tyneside, was new about that?

CHAPTER TEN

The Managerial Merry-go-round and the First Coming of Kevin: 1975–92

The board firstly failed to attract the Middlesbrough manager Jack Charlton. His credentials – apart from being one of the massed ranks of Geordie footballers Newcastle had failed to sign – were that he had just won the Second Division title by a mile with 'Boro, and taken them to seventh in Division One in their first season back in the top flight since 1954.

But Charlton told the go-between, his Uncle Jackie Milburn, that he was not yet ready for so big a job. And so, on 12 June 1975, the chairman of the board, Lord Westwood, announced that the new manager of Newcastle United would be Gordon Lee.

Lee, a 40-year-old former full-back with gaunt, cadaverous features (not unlike the headmaster 'Chalky' White in the Giles cartoons), had just taken Blackburn Rovers to the Third Division championship. His appointment was instantly controversial. There were squeals from Blackburn about illegal approaches (squeals which were deeply hurtful to Westwood, who had his eye on the chairmanship of the FA, and who instantly rebutted them. Nonetheless it was years before Blackburn, who threatened to sue over compensation terms, were mollified).

But Lee also announced that 'I will not be appointing a first-team coach. I will be doing the coaching myself,' and then promptly brought to Newcastle as first-team coach his assistant from Blackburn, Richard Dinnis. And then the new manager walked into St James's Park and stated that: 'There will be no stars on Tyneside,' which, as well as being a somewhat puzzling suggestion (surely the fans decided who was a star and who was not), was seen as the writing on the wall for Supermac.

(There was also a curious altercation behind the scenes, which did not come out until later. Gordon Lee happened to mention to Lord Westwood that he was utterly opposed to black footballers and would never sign one. Westwood was both surprised and offended, and asked Lee if this meant that if a certain internationally famous black soccer star was to become available to Newcastle – when retelling the story Westwood did not name this hypothetical star, but we presume him to have been Pele – Lee would not sign him? No, replied Lee, I would not.)

There were two immediate casualties. In July 1975, just a month after Lee's arrival, Frank Clark was given a free transfer to Second Division Nottingham Forest. Clark – the last of the local youngsters of the early 1960s – was no longer a youngster, having played 456 games for United since 1962. Joe Harvey had actually put the transfer of Clark in motion before he resigned, but the old retainer was still on Newcastle's books when Lee arrived and no attempts were made to reverse the decision. This outstanding full-back had much left to offer, and Geordie fans were left shaking their heads in dismay as he teamed up with Brian Clough at Forest and promptly became a member of the squad which won promotion to Division One, the league championship, and the European Cup, all in successive seasons. While Clark was gaining all of that glory, his old club was travelling in exactly the opposite direction.

A month after that, in August, Terry Hibbitt was also on his way. Lee's first words to Malcolm Macdonald, according to Supermac, were: 'Tell me about Terry Hibbitt. I understand he's a troublemaker.' The new manager's public justification for offloading the influential little midfielder was that there was no room in the same team for both Hibbitt and the sophisticated Scotland international Tommy Craig, who had arrived from Sheffield Wednesday at the end of 1974. The style of Hibbitt's departure became legendary at the club. On Wednesday, 27 August, United had just played their fourth match of the 1975–76 season, away at Derby County. After the 3-2 defeat Lee took Hibbitt to one side. The other players waited on the coach until, suddenly, Hibbitt appeared at the vehicle's door, grabbed his suitcase, said 'Goodbye, lads, I'm off to Birmingham,' and disappeared out of all of their lives until 23 September, when they travelled to Birmingham City and lost that one 3-2 as well.

Gordon Lee made signings, of course. While Hibbitt was settling down in the Midlands, Lee was (to the relief of the fans) agreeing a new one-year contract with Malcolm Macdonald, who promptly called him 'the most enthusiastic and ambitious manager I have known in football'. Macdonald would not hold that line for long.

And that same eventful August he met up at Scotch Corner with the Huddersfield Town striker Alan Gowling and convinced him, despite Gowling's nervousness about competing for a place with Macdonald and Tudor, to move to Tyneside for £70,000. (It was John Tudor who lost out of the equation, being given just seven more games for United before his sale to Stoke City the following September.)

Lee's 'no more stars' philosophy was based in his hunger to win Division One. In Alan Gowling's words: 'He used to say that cups were tin-pot trophies; for him, the league title was the supreme prize. And to win that you needed a team of 11 men, all of them 90-minute triers, as well as having the accomplishments which must go with the all-round effort . . . And he also made it clear that he had no time for the glamour-boys of the game – he wanted a team of 11 men without stars. That way, he believed, would real success be achieved.'

It was a kind of back-to-basics approach, and not everybody liked it. The United players under Duggie Livingstone and Charlie Mitten would have recognised the dismay of those under Gordon Lee, who 'once asked us to split into teams and hop towards the goal, left hand on our hip and the other hand holding the ball above our head. We then had to throw the ball against the bar and hop back again'.

'I couldn't work out,' said Malcolm Macdonald, whose training ground rows with Lee began almost immediately, 'whether Gordon Lee was being serious or just playing games.'

For a manager who had no interest in cups but devoted everything to league success, Gordon Lee's one full season in charge was a curiosity. Newcastle never strung two consecutive league wins together, and finally finished 15th in Division One – precisely the position achieved by Joe Harvey in each of his last two seasons.

But on 10 September 1975 they embarked upon an outstanding League Cup campaign. Alan Gowling had so far not scored a goal in the league, and as Macdonald had banged in eight in six games he was developing a complex about it. But Supermac was injured for the second round of the League Cup (First Division United had a bye in the first round), at home to Southport, and so the reserve striker Paul Cannell was brought in to partner Gowling.

Newcastle won 6-0. Gowling got four and Cannell two. You will score more in the season than Macdonald, Lee told Gowling. He did, thanks to 14 cup goals. (Macdonald finished as the top scorer in Division One with 21 strikes.) In the meantime Newcastle took off on an unexpected – but exhilarating – surge towards Wembley.

Second Division Bristol Rovers came next, and a Gowling equaliser in the second half ensured a replay at St James's, which a Tommy Craig penalty and a goal from Irving Nattrass clinched by 2-0. Then the stylish new talk of London, Queen's Park Rangers, were murdered at Loftus Road, Stan Bowles, Gerry Francis and all. Macdonald got his first and only goal of the campaign, and Mickey Burns and Geoff Nulty – two of Joe Harvey's last signings – completed a 3-1 victory.

An own-goal from Notts County's keeper Eric MacManus, who fumbled one of Malcolm Macdonald's celebrated long throw-ins, ensured United's passage from the fifth round on 3 December. Given United's poor league form and the obvious discontent among the club's various factions, there was talk before that fifth-round match of Gordon Lee's job being on the line if Newcastle lost it. If that was the case, he owed his extension to one of Supermac's little specialities.

The semi-finals of the League Cup were played over two legs. Newcastle had drawn Tottenham Hotspur, who promptly established a 1-0 lead in the first leg at White Hart Lane. Spurs then travelled north with some confidence on 21 January. It was misplaced. Fifty thousand Geordie fans turned out to see Gowling wipe out their advantage after just 150 seconds' play. Macdonald put his fellow striker away through the middle and, with the Tottenham players vainly appealing for offside, Gowling rounded Pat Jennings and stuck the ball away.

Fifty seconds into the second half Glen Keeley, who had been on the books since 1972 and was by 1976 United's third-choice centre-half, headed home a Tommy Craig corner, and with Newcastle asking questions that Spurs could not answer Geoff Nulty made it 3-0 on the night, 3-1 on aggregate, in the 65th minute, rounding off some good work by Craig and Tommy Cassidy. Tottenham defender Don McAllister pulled one back, but Newcastle were through to yet another Wembley final.

It was not the FA Cup, but it would do. The League Cup final against Manchester City on 28 February 1976 was an opportunity to make amends for the fiasco of two years earlier.

Unfortunately, United had chosen 1976 as the year in which to enjoy another good run in the FA Cup. Queen's Park Rangers and Coventry City had been put to the sword in third- and fourth-round replays, and Bolton Wanderers travelled to Tyneside for the fifth round on 14 February. A brace from Macdonald and one from Gowling ensured a thrilling 3-3 draw for the fans, and just for good measure Bolton's goalkeeper Siddall broke captain Geoff Nulty's jaw, putting him out of the League Cup final.

The FA Cup fifth-round replay on 18 February was drawn 0-0. On 21 February United travelled to Liverpool in the league, and two days later – the Monday before the scheduled League Cup final – they knocked Bolton out of the FA Cup at last in a second replay at Elland Road. It was their seventh FA Cup game in three rounds since January. And then they all went down with flu.

Forty-eight hours before the League Cup final only five of Newcastle's exhausted squad were fit enough to reach London. The rest travelled down in dribs and drabs, nursing injuries and influenza. Given the circumstances, a 2-1 defeat was almost creditable. Peter Barnes gave a confident Manchester City team a 1-0 lead; Alan Gowling slid in to convert a Macdonald cross to equalise before half-time; but just after the break City's Dennis Tuart scored with a sensational bicycle kick which bounced in at the bottom corner of Mahoney's goal. It was 2-1 to City, and a drained United team could find no way back. They retained their self-respect, however, forcing play up to the bitter end, but respect was all that they took away from Wembley in 1976. It was, at least, more than they had carried back to Tyneside in 1974.

And just to crown matters, United were knocked out of the sixth round of the FA Cup by Derby County seven days later.

In the close season of 1976 the Malcolm Macdonald crisis came to a head. On a summer tour of Majorca – a tour which included the striker – his future with the club was openly discussed among the squad. Incredibly, the managerial team of Gordon Lee and Richard Dinnis joined in these bar-room free-for-alls. It is as unpleasant a picture to imagine as it must have been for Macdonald to experience at the time. Lee and Dinnis had succeeded in creating their own clique within the club, and felt free to air the fact that Supermac had no part in their future plans. They found ready listeners. 'Some players,' Alan Gowling said later, 'felt that for too long they – or the rest of the team – had been living in Malcolm Macdonald's shadow. Up to that tour, perhaps this last group had felt that they were comparatively young and didn't have the experience to speak out . . . but alcohol tends to loosen tongues and gives people the courage to speak their minds.'

Where previously his fellow professionals might just have indulged themselves in a few witticisms about Malcolm's work-rate, and left it at that, suddenly the club's most valuable forward was the object of bitter resentment. He was letting everyone down. He was holding the club back. He would need to score not 30 but 40 goals a season if he was not prepared to track back and help the midfield. And Lee and Dinnis did not merely look on indulgently: they actively and openly assisted the prosecution in this people's trial.

Upon his return from Majorca, Macdonald decided to jump before he was pushed. He asked for a transfer. His 12-month contract was up, but it was pointed out to him that the small print gave Newcastle an option on another year of Malcolm Macdonald. He promptly refused to train, appealed to Lord Westwood, took legal advice, and prepared to fight in the courts. Westwood retreated from that prospect and sold the most consistent striker in Division One to Arsenal for exactly a third of a million pounds. 'I loved Newcastle,' said Malcolm Macdonald, 'until Gordon Lee took over.'

Rather then spend the money, Gordon Lee gave the local boy Paul Cannell his opportunity to stake a place alongside Gowling in the striking partnership. Cannell actually outscored Gowling with 12 goals against 11 in the 1976–77 season, but each of them was outstripped by their supposed provider, the converted centre-forward Mickey Burns, who netted 14 times. That was presumably what Gordon Lee meant by no more stars.

Newcastle had a good league season. They were knocked out of both cups early on, and despite a galling setback at Highbury in December when Malcolm Macdonald scored three times in a 5-3 Arsenal victory over his old club ('My own private dream come true,' he said), United were riding high in Division One as the New Year was born.

But Gordon Lee was already on his way out. On 29 January 1977 the Newcastle players trooped onto the pitch at Maine Road to meet Manchester City in the fourth round of the FA Cup. They lost 3-1, and on the Sunday Gordon Lee stayed in Lancashire for a meeting with the directors of Everton. On the first day in February he was introduced to the Goodison Park fans as their new messiah. Everton had reportedly raised his £12,000 per annum salary by almost 100 per cent. He left behind him a contract with 18 months unexpired, and few mourners. 'The trump card,' he said, 'is that my family are in Lancashire.' In the whole of his time at Newcastle he had never moved out of a hotel.

And then came player-power. One of this strange episode's leading figures, the university-educated Alan Gowling, explained later that under Gordon Lee 'there had developed a tremendous team spirit. His departure left the players in limbo for a little while. But we were all anxious about one thing – that the team spirit which had been fostered should not be allowed to crumble and fade away. Everyone was convinced that we were moving along the right lines.'

So Gowling, Geoff Nulty and Mickey Burns visited the home of Lord Westwood where, in the company of another director, Stan Seymour junior (Stan Seymour senior was ailing and had retired from the board in the previous April), the three players said that they would like the coach Richard Dinnis to become manager. They left Westwood's house under the impression that their host had agreed.

Three days then came and went, and Richard Dinnis – a teacher with a diploma in physical education who had never played professional football – was not confirmed as the new manager of Newcastle United. So the players issued a statement which publicly supported Dinnis. The board then bought a midfield player named Ralph Callachan from Hearts without consulting Dinnis. The players issued another statement, which informed the people of Newcastle that they had no confidence in the board of directors.

That very evening Richard Dinnis received a midnight telephone call from Lord Westwood, summoning him to the chairman's house. Once there he was given a contract which made him acting manager of Newcastle United until 30 June 1977. It was possibly the most damaging piece of paper Lord Westwood ever signed.

United's players, having got their way, certainly worked for Dinnis. 'All Dinnis did for the remainder of the season,' said the watching Jackie Milburn, 'was not get in the way.' Even so, plans by the directors not to renew his contract in June were scotched by the players muttering about mass transfer requests, and hoisting Dinnis shoulder-high after the last mediocre 3-2 home win over Aston Villa. Despite losing four of their final five matches they finished fifth in Division One and thereby qualified for the following season's UEFA Cup, the successor to the old Fairs' Cup which United had enjoyed so much at the turn of the decade. So Dick Dinnis was offered a fresh two-year contract as manager of Newcastle.

He would not see out the year. The UEFA Cup jaunt lasted precisely two rounds. Bohemians were beaten 4-0 on Tyneside after a draw in Ireland, and then in October and November SEC Bastia from Corsica, the eventual beaten finalists, knocked United out 5-2 on aggregate with wins at home and away.

Defeats though they might have been, those 1977 UEFA Cup nights came as blessed relief from the nightmare of the Football League. Newcastle had beaten Leeds United 3-2 at home in their opening game on 20 August 1977 – and then set off on a losing streak of ten successive league matches which took them like a plumbstone straight to the bottom of Division One. Jackie Milburn wrote later: 'Richard [Dinnis] was a lovely man who was a rank amateur. He was completely out of his depth and inevitably drowned.'

A win and two draws at the end of October and beginning of November took United's points haul to six from 14 games – and then they started losing again. Richard Dinnis did not really need to be pushed. He was more than happy to get away from the agony of it all. He left in November 1977, and he left Newcastle United almost certainly doomed to relegation before a third of the season's league fixtures had been played.

The board promptly telephoned the former England international Bill McGarry in Saudi Arabia, where McGarry was working as a coach. He left the Middle East immediately and arrived to attempt the impossible at St James's Park. McGarry was a rushed choice, but a deliberate one. As manager of Ipswich Town in the mid-1960s he had inherited a dis-illusioned, relegated side and taken it back into Division One. He had been a hard player, and cultivated the image of a hard manager – 'the most hated man in football', as he flatteringly described himself.

It was too late for him to do anything for Newcastle United in the remainder of 1977–78 – although it must be said that what little he did attempt, such as the purchase of the goal-shy number 9 Mike Larnach, was notably unsuccessful. United were relegated long before the season's end. They won just six league games out of 42 and drew ten for a total of 22 points. The only wonder was that Leicester City had played even worse for their 22 points, and pipped United to bottom spot in the division on goal difference. They had been knocked out of the FA Cup 4-1 by Wrexham of the Third Division. That was the team which Gordon Lee, Dickie Dinnis and their friends in the changing-room built. Frank Clark's Nottingham Forest, meanwhile, was winning the league . . .

Gowling and Nulty were sent on their way before the last rites had been read over Newcastle's First Division life. Bill McGarry's Newcastle settled down to an uneventful life in Division Two. In August 1978 he bought Peter Withe from Nottingham Forest, and for just over two seasons the tall striker, in company with the Blyth Spartans forward Alan Shoulder, provided a bit of entertainment in the pervasive gloom. The mood of the club was only worsened by the news, on Christmas Eve 1978, of the death of Stan Seymour, a man who, whatever the results of his actions, had devoted most of his adult life to furthering his local football club – and who, at the end of the day, had certainly edged the 'Mr Newcastle' title from William McKeag.

In August 1980 the first two home games of United's third season back in the Second Division attracted 17,000 and 13,000 spectators respectively. Ron McGarry was shown the door, Joe Harvey was asked to take control once more for a few days, and on 4 September 1980 a friend of Harvey's named Arthur Cox became Newcastle's fifth manager in six years. Things are as bad, Harvey told Cox, as when I came back as manager in 1962. In fact, things were arguably worse.

There was no immediate miracle. That came later. Two years later, on 19 August 1982. After stumbling about in the top half of Division Two for two further seasons after McGarry's departure, Arthur Cox invited the press to the Gosforth Park Hotel in Newcastle to report on 'the greatest signing in our history'. He then presented to them Kevin Keegan, twice European Footballer of the Year, the reigning Division One top scorer, and the son of a miner from Hetton-le-Hole. The former Liverpool, Hamburg, Southampton and England striker had put his name to a 12-month contract for Newcastle United. It was a make-or-break signing. Its function was simple: to galvanise the fans and the players, and thereby to regain the First Division. Promotion, the manager and directors had decided, could not be achieved without some hugely dramatic action and the psychological surge, the booster-rocket burst of confidence, which that would provide. If it worked, it would be cheap at any price, let alone the £80,000 which United offered the 31-year-old as a basic wage for his first year. 'Yes,' said Keegan to the press in the Gosforth Park Hotel, 'promotion is on.' And behind the screening curtains small boys began to chant: 'Kee-gan! Kee-gan! Kee-gan!'

Nine days later Newcastle kicked off their 1982–83 season with a home game against Queen's Park Rangers. The identical fixture in the previous season had attracted a disastrous 10,748 paying customers to St James's Park. On 28 August 1982 a capacity 35,718 people showed up to see Newcastle win 1-0 with a goal from . . . Kevin Keegan. That was why they had bought him. For his goals, of course, but also because without his sustained pulling power a football club the size of Newcastle United simply could not have survived.

United missed promotion by two places and three points at the end of that season. With three points awarded for a win since the previous year, that meant they had been one victory off the pace. Fortunately Keegan renewed his 12-month contract. And by 1983 Arthur Cox had found his settled team. Its defence was just adequate, and halfway through the season it was given a coating of class by the former Queen's Park Rangers sweeper Glenn Roeder. Its midfield was typified by David McCreery and Terry McDermott in his second spell with the club – two hard-working, ball-winning and ball-using footballers, the first a much-capped Irish international, and the second the current English Footballer of the Year.

And those two exceptional footballers were expected to serve one of the most exhilarating forward lines in the whole of Britain. On one side of Keegan Arthur Cox put the lad from Tow Law Town who had famously been rescued from a sausage factory in 1980, the 'king of the swaying hips', as his French fans would later call him, the brilliant Chris Waddle.

On the other side he put another North-eastern footballer, a 22-year-old who had started his career with Carlisle United, had been spending the summer with the Vancouver Whitecaps and was half expecting to sign for Manchester United until a September day in 1983 when his manager at the Whitecaps, the former Leeds and Ireland player Johnny Giles, told him: 'Newcastle would like to sign you.' Peter Beardsley was almost another Geordie who got away: it is thanks to Arthur Cox that he did not. He jumped on the plane to Heathrow and, while sitting with his wife in the departure lounge there, the shy Beardsley saw the great Kevin Keegan stride through and catch the same connecting flight to Newcastle. Beardsley signed for United on 20 September 1983; four days later he was substitute at Barnsley; and a week after that he took up the first-team jersey that he would wear as a matter of right until the very last months of his two glorious spells with Newcastle United.

Keegan got the most league goals, of course: 27 to Beardsley's 20 and Waddle's 18. But it hardly mattered, it was the irresistible variety that stuck in the mind. Those three footballers would be together for just seven and a half months of Newcastle's long history, but the impression that they left was enough to feed a lifetime of dreams. Keegan's speed, courage and ruthless opportunism; Waddle's astonishing sleight of foot; Beardsley's quick brain and breathtaking impertinence; and the ability shared by all three of them to make a football talk, to attempt things which no United forward line had tried since the Shackleton – Milburn – Pearson combination of 1948.

From being starved of success and quality, Newcastle's fans suddenly enjoyed a feast of football. They did not take the Second Division title. Their defence – the weakest part of the team, for in Beardsley's words, 'Arthur's [Cox's] idea of the perfect game would be a 5-4 victory' (a philosophy which perhaps rubbed off on his top scorer and future employer) – held them back. 'We always felt we had to score three goals to win a game,' Keegan would say. But although United finished in third place in Division Two in May 1984, they qualified for that last promotion spot by ten clear points.

There was no doubt about who was the driving force. Later in his illustrious career Beardsley would rate the 32-year-old whom he partnered on the pitch for less than eight months as the best footballer that he had ever played with – 'Not only did he score goals but he had the knack of being just where you needed him when you needed him.' Keegan returned the compliment: 'It didn't take me long to realise that Arthur had unearthed a diamond,' he said.

Halfway through the season, on St Valentine's Day, 14 February 1984, which was also his 33rd birthday, Keegan announced that he would retire from football at the end of that campaign. He would 'kick the last competitive ball of my career in a Newcastle shirt'. Three days earlier United had dropped a disappointing three points at home to Grimsby Town. Four days after the announcement Keegan travelled with the squad to Manchester City for a crucial away fixture with another promotion contender, and shared the goals with Beardsley in a vital 2-1 win. Newcastle did not lose another league match for two months and nine games. They clinched promotion on 7 May with a 2-2 draw at Huddersfield.

The last match of the season then became a celebration and a farewell. Brighton and Hove Albion travelled to Tyneside to join in with 36,415 Geordie fans. The script was, of course, already written. After 20 minutes Waddle hit the post and Keegan snaffled the rebound. He had played his part. Brighton briefly showed signs of departing from the plot by equalising, but Waddle put everything back on course by heading home a Keegan centre to make it 2-1. Five minutes from time Beardsley decided to score the best goal of his career. It came after the little man had to scramble to rescue a bad pass from Keegan (who was noticing?). He then got to his feet and chipped the ball delicately over the the huge figure of the advancing Joe Corrigan.

And then the helicopter descended, and Kevin Keegan was returned – for the moment – to the generous sky from which he had fallen less than two years earlier.

He was immediately followed out of door by Arthur Cox. The newly successful manager had been quibbling for months with the board over his own contract and the amount of money which would be available to buy new players for the First Division. That much had been fairly public knowledge: nobody seriously expected that Cox would follow his principles all the way out of Newcastle to accept an offer from Derby County.

When he did so, Jackie Milburn finally got his man. Jack Charlton had moved on from Middlesbrough since Milburn's last approach to him as an unofficial representative of his old club back in 1975. He had left the hot seat at Sheffield Wednesday a year earlier and had been enjoying 'a year off', which for Charlton meant angling, television work, angling, public appearances and more angling. He was opening a double-glazing factory in Consett in May 1984 when his older relative contacted him and said: 'Hey, Jack, we're short of a manager – do you fancy it?'

This time Charlton was open to persuasion. He met the directors – Stan Seymour junior and Gordon McKeag, son of Willie, who had by now effected a family truce and were running the club between them – on a McKeag family golf course in County Durham, was told that he could spend £200,000 on new players, and took the job. 'Take it from me, Peter,' said Milburn to Beardsley, 'he'll be the best thing that's ever happened to this club.'

Jack Charlton lasted for 15 months. He was employed to keep United in Division One, and for a season he did just that, although the club hardly covered itself with glory. After a start of three consecutive wins which put Newcastle at the top of Division One for the first time since early in the 1950–51 season, the team stuttered and declined to an eventual 14th spot.

And after the exhilarating up-and-at-'em soccer of the Arthur Cox era, many players such as Beardsley and Waddle found Charlton's tactics frustrating. In retrospect it is possible to see there the early cultivation of the ideas which Charlton was to use with such sensational effect in the Irish national team. As such, his year at Newcastle is of great interest to soccer historians and theoreticians. But, at the time, Waddle, Beardsley and most of the fans were bored and confused by the manager's instructions to full-backs Anderson and Brown to lob the ball over the forwards for them to chase, and not to pass to feet. Obsessively defensive, insistent upon stopping the opposition rather than starting Newcastle, loud and persistent in his criticism of players – such as Beardsley – who departed from the official playing line, Jack Charlton was not overly popular in some areas of St James's Park.

But what finally did for him was the sale of Chris Waddle. The Gateshead lad had enjoyed a magnificent season, fully relishing the top division and winning the first of his England caps. He was a prime target for other clubs. To Newcastle's long-suffering fans, convinced as ever that their club should be a buying club and not a selling club, Waddle was the perfect example of a footballer who should stay, if United were ever to do anything in the game.

'I don't think Jack broke his back to keep him,' said Beardsley later.

'I tried very hard to keep Chris Waddle,' insisted Charlton. Whoever was right, Waddle went to Tottenham for £590,000 at the end of the season. He was the first of the big local departures of the 1980s. The second and the third would hit progessively harder, but Waddle's going hurt. During a pre-season friendly against Sheffield United early in August a section of the 6,000 crowd barracked Charlton. At the final whistle he walked down into the home changing-room, announced: 'That's it. I don't need this. I'm off,' and left the club. He had a chat with the sympathetic Joe Harvey in the former manager's chief scout's office by the car-park, and he packed up his things and left for a colourful managerial career far away from the demanding, critical, outspoken people of the North-east of England.

The stunned directors, looking a full First Division season in the face without a manager, had little choice but to give Willie McFaul the job on a provisional basis. As least he was unlikely to walk out on them – Willie had been serving quietly and competently behind the scenes as an assistant coach since he hung up his goalkeeping gloves in 1975. He had seen managers come and seen them go, and now he took the opportunity to become Newcastle's seventh manager in ten years. He would at least last longer than some, but it would not be an altogether happy reign.

Jack Charlton may have been made slightly more sanguine about Chris Waddle's departure by the fact that he had an interesting replacement coming up through the ranks. Charlton had watched the 17-year-old Paul Gascoigne perform one or two feats of astonishing virtuosity for the youth team as it progressed to lift the FA Youth Cup for the second time in the club's history, with a 4-1 aggregate win over Watford in the April and May of 1985. At the end of the 1984–85 season the boy had been given two appearances as substitute, and then offered professional terms. With no less an authority than Jackie Milburn, who was bowled over by his first sight of Gascoigne, proclaiming the lad as a genius who was certain to replace Bryan Robson as captain of England, Willie McFaul blooded Gazza immediately.

Gascoigne's emerging genius and Beardsley's maturing brilliance secured an unimpressive Newcastle United team in the First Division for two more seasons. It was not so much their goals – although they could be crucial enough, and Beardsley certainly doubled as a main striker when necessary – as their inspiration, and the promise that their continued presence gave to St James's Park that there was a bright future waiting to be seized.

When Beardsley went to Liverpool in July 1987, the club and its supporters were struck a disproportionately fierce blow. They were losing not only a great local footballer, but also hope and belief. Beardsley himself said as much. His boyhood hero, the Liverpool manager Kenny Dalglish, was prepared to pay £1,900,000 for him, but he had not been straining to leave Tyneside. He was finally prompted away from the place by the realisation that time and trophies were passing him by . . . 'I was beginning to feel envious of the players and teams who were almost guaranteed to win the game's top honours . . . I wanted desperately to do that at Newcastle but I felt the club was not as hungry as I was.'

That terrible condemnation of his home-town team was not published until many years later, when he was back at an utterly changed St James's Park. But it was sensed at the time – and by some, it was stated. Alex Ferguson attempted to buy Beardsley for Manchester United that summer, and was rejected. 'Still,' Ferguson informed the world, 'when I look at how their club is run I pity their fans. I feel sorry for our supporters not having the championship for 20 years, but their fans have even more to complain about.'

The Machiavellian Ferguson would normally be no authority on the condition of other football clubs, but in this instance his verdict was difficult to dispute. Even when Newcastle did splash into the transfer pool, the result was too frequently embarrassing. His old team-mate Malcolm Macdonald, who was trying to establish himself as an inter-continental agent, persuaded McFaul to invest in a Brazilian named Mirandinha to fill the Beardsley gap in the close season of 1987. He turned out to be a sulky, ill-tempered failure with, as the writer Ian Hamilton put it, 'a repertoire of muttered curses and black looks'. (He was also comparatively cheap. At £575,000 from Fluminense, Mira cost just over a quarter of the sum received for Beardsley. The board did not have the class to go for a vastly expensive flop.)

Hamilton watched Gascoigne and Mirandinha struggle to connect in their one season together. 'When Mirandinha was unmarked,' he summarised perfectly, 'Gascoigne tended to ignore him, preferring instead to set off on an intricate, inventive and usually doomed run into the heart of the enemy's defence. When Mirandinha was marked, or merely unavailable, Gascoigne liked to zip classy first-time balls into spaces where the Brazilian should have been but never was.

'For much of the game, Newcastle's exotic foreigner was to be seen standing in the opposition's 18-yard box, hands on hips, eyes raised in exasperation to the heavens. Sunshine he was not.'

Nonetheless, Newcastle performed creditably in that season. Paul Goddard and Michael O'Neill gave sterling support to Roeder, Gascoigne, McCreery and Mirandinha, and the club finished eighth in Division One: their best placing since the latest promotion.

Then the inevitable occurred. Gascoigne had been making noises about leaving throughout the second half of the season. Convinced that United had exploited him in the early days of his career by paying him only £85 a week; unhappy with the occasional barrackings from the terraces; tempted by the southern riches which Chris Waddle was enjoying; and above all convinced like Waddle and Beardsley before him that Newcastle lacked ambition, that the club's only desire was to stay in Division One and avoid bankruptcy by selling off playing staff occasionally – convinced of all of those things he turned down a new contract and went to Spurs for a British record fee of £2,000,000 (plus £125,000 a year to himself: roughly twice what Newcastle had offered him to stay).

This time the fans knew it was serious. Their club was going nowhere. Rightly or wrongly, much of their immediate rage was turned on Gascoigne himself. Astonishingly, the second Saturday of the 1988–89 season scheduled Tottenham to play Newcastle at St James's Park. It was United's first home game of the session, and Tottenham's first away. When Gascoigne ran onto the park he was bombarded with hundreds of frozen Mars Bars (one of Paul's admitted weaknesses) which some Thatcherite entrepreneur had smartly put on sale outside the ground. Whenever he touched the ball – whenever he approached the ball – he was booed, and chants of 'Fattie', 'Judas' and 'Yuppie' went up. He could not take it. Who could? After 75 minutes he was substituted, jeered all the way to the tunnel, and smuggled out of the stadium.

Newcastle United and Tottenham Hotspur drew that game on 3 September 1988. Thereafter their fortunes diverged. Tottenham, Waddle, Gascoigne and all, floated to sixth position in the league while Newcastle plummeted to the bottom of the table and stayed there.

It was a decline as fast and irreversible and humiliating as that of 1977. The only consolation to be gained at the season's end was that Jackie Milburn had not lived to see it. The old hero, the chain-smoking centre-forward, the best-loved man in the North-east of England, died of lung cancer on 9 October 1988. Soon there would be a statue immortalising him in the middle of the town. In the short term there were the crowds silently acknowledging his passing, and the accolades from all across the land. 'It is very difficult,' Jack Charlton would write, 'to imagine Newcastle United without Jackie Milburn.'

In May 1989 Newcastle were demoted once more from Division One of the Football League. They had in fact been assured of relegation long before May. They finished bottom of the table, nine points short of safety. Willie McFaul had left months earlier, in October 1988, after just one win in the first two months. Jim Smith arrived in December to inherit a doomed football team.

Smith's changes included such masterstrokes as getting rid of Mirandinha, signing as his replacement an unromantic figure named Micky 'Sumo' Quinn (who promptly hit four goals against Leeds United in his first game, bagged a total of nine in his first five matches, and finished the season with 34 league and cup goals; Mirandinha had managed 22 in twice as many matches), and bringing back Mark McGhee for his second spell with the club.

They resulted in an immediate revival of hope. 'Geordies,' the much-mourned Jackie Milburn had once commented, 'are a resilient race.' The supporters steadily flocked back as Smith seemed likely to steer Newcastle towards promotion. A late run of six consecutive league wins in March and April 1990 pushed

Newcastle into third place in Division Two, five points below the automatic promotion spots, but comfortably qualifying for the play-offs for promotion.

These play-offs, which had been used in the early years of the Football League but abandoned in 1898 after Stoke and Burnley were accused of conniving in a draw to keep Newcastle out of Division One, had been reintroduced in 1987. In 1990 four Second Division clubs played each other at home and away in a small knock-out competition: the winner filling the one remaining promotion place to Division One.

Newcastle were drawn to play-off against Sunderland, who had finished four places beneath them. In two ill-tempered collisions the Wearsiders drew 0-0 at home but beat United 2-0 on Tyneside. Just to make matters worse, Sunderland then lost to Swindon in the final play-off at Wembley, but were later gifted the promotion spot when Swindon were found guilty of making illegal payments.

Less than a year later, in March 1991, with United out of that season's promotion battle, the honest and capable manager Jim Smith decided that he wanted no more of the ferocious infighting which was once more raging behind the scenes at Gallowgate, and left for the gentler climate of Portsmouth. He was instantly replaced by Osvaldo Ardiles, the little midfielder who had distinguished himself with Tottenham and Argentina, and who had taken over at Swindon.

It did not take long for Ossie to make an impression. By 1 January 1992 United were bottom of the Second Division. They had 19 games left in which to avoid relegation to Division Three. The club had never been lower.

In December 1991 a millionaire local businessman named John Hall had finally, at the end of a long campaign which was to change utterly the structure of the club, its ownership, and its ambitions, become chairman of Newcastle United. On 5 February 1992, after the United defence had just conceded a further nine goals in two matches, Sir John Hall invited the press to the Newcastle Breweries Visitors' Centre for a special announcement concerning the future of the club.

CHAPTER ELEVEN

THE SECOND COMING: 1992–97

It was of course Kevin. The rumours had suggested as much. The main element of surprise in this quasi-dramatic announcement came not from the fact that Keegan was returning to Tyneside. Most footballers praise their home fans, wherever they may be. It is very much in their interests to do so. But when Keegan had rhapsodised about Newcastle and its supporters and what they deserved from their football team, he was being more genuine than most. He seriously believed – as did, for that matter, Alex Ferguson, most of the English press, and the supporters themselves – that the Geordies had been appallingly exploited and under-served for 40 years and possibly more.

If Keegan was to go into football management, therefore, it was more likely to be at Newcastle than anywhere else. The problem was: Keegan had repeatedly insisted that he did not want to become a manager. If you read that I am about to take over a football club, he had said, laugh along with me. And in the eight years since that helicopter had arrived on the pitch at Gallowgate to spirit him away into the ether (in fact, to a celebratory club dinner in Newcastle centre) Keegan's resolve had shown no signs of flagging.

He was a rich man. He had no need to work again. He was apparently happy. And whatever his qualities as a footballer and as a television pundit, Keegan had no experience whatsoever of coaching or of management. 'You hope and you pretend,' he would say of his first months in the job, 'you know what you're doing.'

As it turned out, he did know what he was doing. In *Geordie Messiah*, his definitive account of the Keegan years at Newcastle, Alan Oliver presents a fascinating table of managerial achievement at St James's Park since 1893. Analysing all home and away league and cup matches played by Newcastle United under different régimes, Oliver unearths some stunning statistics.

His chart proves beyond dispute what the fans knew in their hearts – that Kevin Keegan, as well as presenting to the world the attractive, exciting team which neutral commentators praised and occasionally condescended towards, was also the most successful manager the club has ever had, not in trophies but in cold statistics: in numbers of wins and draws achieved. Nobody else approached the 71 per cent of home games which were won by Keegan. And only Stan Seymour, with 34 per cent of his away games won, came close to Keegan's 40 per cent of victories in that category.

In total, Keegan won 55.4 per cent of his 249 games as manager of Newcastle United, drew 20.1 per cent, and lost just a quarter of them – 24.5 per cent. George Martin and Duggie Livingstone (the first of whom also took a Second Division team back to a good spell in the first, and the second of whom enjoyed those good cup runs in the mid-1950s) come statistically second and third overall – but a long, long way behind the maestro.

(Oliver's table also clears up – on paper, anyway – the debate about who was Newcastle United's worst manager. Naturally, the wooden spoon is hotly contested between Charlie Mitten, Richard Dinnis and Ossy Ardiles. Dinnis lost most matches: 50 per cent of his total. Mitten lost 44.1 per cent of his games, and Ardiles 39.1 per cent. But Mitten had at least won 39.2 per cent, whereas Dinnis had won only 31.6 per cent, and Ardiles 21.7 per cent. The only way to decide who was the all-time worst, therefore, is to treat all of those matches as league games and award the three managers points. As two of them were working in the era when just two points were awarded for a win, we shall extend this to all three of them – which actually does Ardiles a favour, as he won so few games and drew as many as he lost. Reducing all their games in charge to a mean average of 100, then, Mitten won 95.1 points; Ardiles – saved by all those draws – won 82.5 points; and the worst manager in Newcastle United's history, Richard Dinnis, won just 81.6 points, or an average of 0.816 points per game. Kevin Keegan, by contrast, won 130.9 points from his mean of 100 games, or an average of 1.309 points per match. Before hanging the anorak back up again, however, it may be worth pointing out that Charlie Mitten's and Richard Dinnis's matches were in the First Division, and Ardiles's were in the Second, and that if we offer them all three points for a win Dinnis and Ardiles swap positions and Ossy – with that appalling record of winning just a fifth of all his games – finishes bottom of the table.)

The task facing Keegan on 5 February 1992 was more severe than that which had confronted Joe Harvey in 1962, Arthur Cox in 1980, or Jim Smith in 1988. Of those three, only Harvey inherited a side which was in danger of slipping out of the Second Division – and thanks to Norman Smith that danger had, by 1962, largely evaporated. What was more, Harvey had discovered to his horror that Newcastle's Second Division gates had fallen below 30,000. The last home game before Keegan took over (a 4-3 defeat by Charlton Athletic) had attracted just 15,663 customers.

They flocked back, of course, to the court of King Kevin. Three days after taking the job he sent his side out at St James's to play Bristol City, and almost 30,000 roared them to a 3-0 win. It was far from plain sailing. Keegan had agreed to do the job for just three months, to try and get the club out of trouble, but at times he showed signs of wondering exactly what he had taken on. Terry McDermott willingly travelled up from Liverpool to assist him, but within weeks the two men were driving south once more, this time apparently for good.

They returned, and Newcastle United were saved from the ultimate indignity – and inconceivable financial problems – of Third Division football by four points thanks to two wins in their last two games.

Keegan and McDermott left Newcastle, their job done. 'I've had three great months,' said McDermott, 'loved every minute of it. I just thought I'd get back on with my life. So, I've told everyone it wasn't going to come off and then, two days later, Kevin's phoned and said: "We're going back, pal! We're going to change that club round!" Back we went and signed three-year contracts.'

And the party could begin. Keegan would make something of a habit of beginning football seasons like a sprinter off the blocks, but the start of that 1992–93 promotion season was in a class of its own. With the new majority shareholder Sir John Hall looking on with avuncular pride, they raced away. After 11 matches Newcastle United had collected the maximum 33 league points. As about 80 points were reckoned as the target for promotion, they could be said to be almost halfway there with less than a quarter of their fixtures played. David Kelly – one of the few welcome inheritances from Ardiles – continued his rich run of goalscoring form, assisted as the season progressed by Paul Bracewell, John Beresford and Robert Lee. Gavin Peacock, who since his purchase by Jim Smith in 1990 had lived and played through all of the storms, revelled in the joyous roll of success. And in March 1993 Keegan made one of the emblematic signings of his régime when he paid Bristol City £1,750,000 for a young striker who had earlier been rejected by Arsenal, Andrew Cole.

They hardly faltered. United finished as they had started, with five straight wins. They clinched promotion with three games to go and the title with two games to go. Andy Cole was allowed to start each of the last 11 games, and in them he scored 12 goals. Newcastle United were back at the top on their own terms.

They were just in time, because in fact United did not gain promotion to Division One in 1993. They went up to the FA Premier League, which would soon be renamed the Premiership. The difference was more than just titular. It was the culmination of the long power struggle between the Football Association and the Football League. The FA won, and football had suddenly divided into two nations: the haves and the have-nots. The Premier League attracted the big money from television, from sponsorship, from the direct sale of club goods which prestige encouraged, and from gates (which were simultaneously increasing in net bulk everywhere, while declining as a portion of the big clubs' income). The clubs of the old Second Division – which was quickly renamed the First Division in this brave new looking-glass world – while still allowed access to the top flight through promotion, were truly poor relations: ragged wannabes with their noses pressed up against the plate-glass window.

Writing in 1995, by which time it was possible to digest the implications of the revolution which had convulsed English football, the actor and author Tom Watt said: 'Everyone's aware of which way the wind's blowing. As the richer clubs try to cut the dead wood away, widening the gap between themselves and the rest as each season passes, the rush to jump across and join them has become a stampede.'

It had in fact become for many a stampede for life itself. Thanks to that magisterial promotion season of 1992–93, Newcastle United had no need to join the cut-throat battle. They were in at the birth of the Premiership. As a direct consequence they were able to reinstate themselves in their proper role: as one of the five or six leading football clubs in Britain. In the Premiership anything was possible. Away from it, almost nothing was.

In September 1993 Peter Beardsley returned. The board did not support Keegan's bid of £1,350,000 for the 31-year-old, largely because it broke an established policy of only purchasing footballers with a resale value. But Keegan had his way, and his second great emblematic signing was made. Newcastle had not enjoyed a good start to their first season back, winning just two of their first eight matches. But Beardsley and Cole clicked instantly. In what were supposed to be the twilight years of his career, Beardsley rediscovered a partnership similar to the one which had enjoyed all those years before with Kevin Keegan himself. Two shy men, one of whom hated training and the other who was fanatical about it, Cole and Beardsley never hit it off personally. But on the field they shared 55 league goals.

As Newcastle stormed to third place in the Premier League, Andy Cole topped the goalscoring charts with 34 (three ahead of a certain Geordie named Alan Shearer, who was banging them in for Blackburn Rovers while nursing a latent love of his home-town team). That was two short of Hughie Gallacher's 36 league goals in 1926–27. But Gallacher was restricted to only three cup games that season, in which he scored three more times, raising his total to 39. Andy Cole had six cup games in 1993–94, and bagged seven strikes in them, making his league and cup total a new record of 41 goals. (Overall there was ultimately no real question about who was the greater. When Cole left he had scored 68 goals in his 84 games: a strike-rate of 0.81 goals a game. Gallacher netted 143 times in his 174 appearances: a strike-rate of 0.82, marginally superior and maintained over four and a half rather than just one and a half seasons.)

Third place in the Premiership meant European football in 1994. The first round UEFA Cup game against Antwerp on 13 September came just as United were putting together another barnstorming start to a season, winning their first six league games to stride clear at the top of the league. They scored 22 goals in those six games with a cavalier style of attacking football which simply took the Premiership by surprise.

Over in Belgium, it also caught Antwerp on the hop. Presumably expecting the usual stuffy English visitors intent on nothing but keeping the score respectable for the second leg, Antwerp were rocked by a 52-second diving header from Robert Lee, who promptly added another in eight minutes, and then saw Scott Sellars make it 3-0 before half-time. Lee completed his hat-trick in the second half, and Steve Watson wrapped up the tie at 5-0.

The dangerous flip side to Keegan's new football philosophy was shown in the first leg of the second round, when despite three United goals Athletic Bilbao were allowed to score twice and – away goals being what they are in Europe – give themselves the cushion to edge a 1-0 win in Spain: 3-3 on aggregate meant that Newcastle went out on the away goals rule. UEFA did not award points for entertainment.

In the middle of January 1995 Keegan, walking a tightrope as though it were a six-lane highway, accepted a £7,000,000 offer from Manchester United for Andy Cole. It was a deed of breathtaking confidence. He was selling English football's leading striker to the league champions and his club's greatest rivals. He would be reminding, he knew, a huge support made sensitive by decades of decline of their club's recent craven history of selling rather than buying; of going for the money and running; of patching up the monthly accounts by sacrificing the team's long-term future. Keegan had only his reputation and his character behind him as he faced the irate fans in front of television cameras on the steps of St James's Park. Trust me, he said, trust me.

He was right, of course. Things would change, but in the beginning it appeared almost as if Andy Cole had deliberately been sent to sabotage Alex Ferguson. The one-touch predatory striker who had fitted perfectly into Newcastle's hell-for-leather scheme of things, broke down at the sharp end of Eric Cantona's philosophical tactics – and as often as not, he broke down Manchester United's moves as well.

And Newcastle were £6,000,000 and Keith Gillespie to the good. It was more than mere genius, it was somehow blessed. And Keegan, riding the wave of success and goodwill, just kept on upping the ante. Warren Barton was bought for £4,000,000 in the close season. Les Ferdinand, the striker whose goals had single-handedly kept Queen's Park Rangers in the top division for the previous two seasons, arrived on Tyneside in return for another £6,000,000. David Ginola, the French forward whose partnership with George Weah had thrilled British watchers of the previous season's European Cup, crossed over from Paris St Germain for a laughable £2,500,000.

'When I looked around the dressing-room,' said captain Peter Beardsley of the 1994–95 season which was about to begin, 'and saw just how many top-class players we had at the club now, and compared it to the situation during my first spell at Newcastle, I could only marvel at the giant strides the club had made in the past three years.'

It is possible now to see that third full season of Kevin Keegan's reign as the little man's final throw. He wanted the Premiership title; he wanted it on his terms alone; and here – before any disillusion set in, before over-familiarity produced weariness – was his chance. It was also the last full season of his three-year contract.

They went for it, no doubting that. If the Newcastle of the previous two seasons had been attractive in a kind of unaffected, surprising, boy-next-door way, this team, stuffed with multi-million-pound glamour and glossy thoroughbred quality from its base to its glittering apex, was the real thing. 'Of all the strikers now clamouring for attention in the Premiership', wrote Ian Ridley in *The Independent* in October 1995, 'Ferdinand looks the most complete English example. His pace matches Robbie Fowler's, his shooting Stan Collymore's and his control surpasses Andy Cole's. Not even Shearer can match his heading ability and astonishing hang-time in the air.'

'He can cross like a dream,' glowed Amy Lawrence of David ('Dah-veed,' insisted Keegan) Ginola in the magazine *FourFour Two* in November, as United topped the league. 'Dribble past opponents at will, and drift in for the odd wondergoal . . . If things don't work out, Ginola's swoonworthy looks mean he can always find work as a model.' (He did.)

On 22 January 1995 Newcastle United were 12 points clear at the top of the Premiership with 54 points, against Liverpool and Manchester United's 42 points each. All three teams had played 23 games. Kevin Keegan was still not finished. In February he bought the Colombian international Faustino Asprilla from Parma for £7,500,000, and David Batty from Blackburn for £3,750,000. What did Keegan want to win? The world?

Then it began to curdle: horribly, steadily, before the eyes of the country like a slow death. The bare facts are cruel enough. By 13 April that 12-point lead had dissolved. Newcastle had taken just 13 points from ten games, while Manchester United had lifted 31 from 11 matches. Alex Ferguson, whom Keegan had pledged himself to defeat, was top of the Premiership with 73 points against Newcastle's 67 points.

But those facts are only the skeleton of the tragedy. They do not tell of the match of the century, the 4-3 defeat at Anfield when the lead changed hands three times – the final deadly occasion being in the last minute when Collymore shot home from close range. And they do not tell of Keegan's furious defence of his signings and of his tactics. 'I'm not going to ask Ginola and Asprilla to defend,' he said. 'I want to challenge people to play us.'

In the meantime Newcastle's travelling support, at Anfield and at Blackburn if not at Leeds, looked on ashen-faced and stricken, heads bowed into shaking arms, as yet another three points were stolen from them. 'He told *The Times*, "Newcastle fans say, 'Let's have a great game' first, and then, 'Let's win'." The pictures of those distraught faces, after a truly great game, contradicted him in spades,' wrote Joe Lovejoy of Keegan in the *Sunday Times*.

'We'll carry on playing this way or I'll go,' responded Kevin Keegan. 'I don't know any other way.'

Keegan immediately offered his resignation at the season's close, when the title was finally lost. It was rejected. Instead he was given a ten-year contract. Perhaps that was a mistake. His failure to win the title in 1996 was the true curtain-call on Kevin Keegan's drama at Newcastle United. What followed was simply a swansong. The season of 1996–97 hit operatic highs and lows before, halfway through its scheduled plot, it collapsed in a riot of dischord.

It began with the fantastic £15,000,000 signing of Alan Shearer, the Blackburn Rovers and England striker who had topped 30 goals in each of the three previous Premiership seasons, and whose goals had almost won his country the European Nations Championship in the summer. That purchase took Keegan's expenditure on footballers to a total of £62,000,000.

It progressed from there to a miserable 4-0 defeat by Manchester United at Wembley in the Charity Shield, which brought back unhappy memories of 1974, and to a shaky start to the league programme which saw United in 14th spot after three matches.

Then they surged, as brilliantly and irresistibly as ever, straight to the top of the league with five consecutive victories. When Manchester United travelled to Tyneside on 20 October 1996 they were journeying into the heartland of the league leaders. When Newcastle's Philippe Albert strode forward in the second half of that league match to float a sensational chip over the head of Peter Schmeichel and complete Newcastle's 5-0 victory, he was doing rather more than taking vengeance for Wembley. He was suggesting to Alex Ferguson's men that this time, surely this time, their run was over.

But the king was tired. The strain and stress which he had long subdued was rising inside him. A 1-0 defeat at Blackburn on 26 December was nothing desperately serious, Newcastle were still in sixth position after it. But Keegan once more asked to be released. And once more he was refused.

On 8 January 1997 he gave it all up. This time he could not be denied. 'I feel,' he said, 'I have taken the club as far as I can and that it would be in the best interests of all concerned if I resigned.'

Jackie Milburn's resilient Geordies were tested this time. A stricken city hummed with rumours of city suits forcing Keegan's departure in preparation for the club's stock-exchange flotation (rumours which the maestro seemed to confirm five years later when he returned to St James's for a cup tie with his new club, Manchester City, saying: 'I think that everybody knows by now that I never wanted to leave here') . . . and then, inevitably, with rumours of his replacement. Two Englishmen abroad, the Geordie Bobby Robson (one of the men who got away: Robson had actually played against United for Fulham in that astonishing FA Cup-tie on 28 January 1956) who was managing Barcelona, and John Toshack at Deportivo of Coruña.

In the end it was neither Robson nor Toshack. Kenny Dalglish got it. The man who had won league championships with Liverpool and Blackburn Rovers arrived at Gallowgate on 14 January 1997. The dream team of Keegan's wonderland began steadily to unravel. Peter Beardsley, the player whom Keegan had predicted picking for another decade, was relegated to the substitutes' bench. David Ginola, hearing the beating of the wings of departure, drifted into semi-obscurity.

Ginola would go at the end of the season, along with Les Ferdinand – who left for Tottenham in the same July week that Alan Shearer collected an injury which would keep him out of action for months. 'A week ago we had three world-class strikers,' mused Dalglish. 'Now we have one.' The one, of course, being the steady, dour, dependable Faustino Asprilla.

Those three musketeers left Newcastle United in as strong a position as ever the old club had been. A collection of victories in April and May of 1997 had all led to one particular match. On 11 May 1997 Stewart Pearce led relegated Nottingham Forest up to Tyneside. Pearce, who would himself shortly sign for Dalglish, was playing for nothing but his immense pride. Newcastle United were playing for the big win which could give them second place in the Premiership, and – under new conditions of entry – a place for the first time in their history in the European Champions' Cup.

The capacity crowd which had jammed the stadium for four seasons, and which was making the directors and investors itch for a new ground to do them justice, to accommodate them all, streamed up the hill once more.

They saw a Shearer shot cleared off the line before Tino Asprilla ran through the defence to make it 1-0. They saw Asprilla set Ferdinand on his way to make 2–0. They saw Ferdinand steam in from the right to collect his second of the game and 21st of the season. They saw Shearer head home a free-kick to make it 4-0 before half-time. They stood and applauded as Peter Beardsley came on as substitute, making his last appearance on the rectangle of land by Newcastle's Gallowgate which has hosted association football since the

1880s. They saw Robbie Elliott make the final score 5-0 with a shot from outside the box. They heard, along with Kenny Dalglish and his players, that Liverpool had failed to win, and Arsenal had won but not – unlike Newcastle – by enough goals.

Second place in the English League. A place in the major European competition. A 5-0 win at home. A full house on a sunlit afternoon. Somewhere up above, Frank Watt was smiling.

CHAPTER TWELVE

BRINGING BOBBY BACK HOME:
1998–2002

❖

There is sex and there is sex, and Ruud Gullit's sexy football – at least as he attempted during his short spell on Tyneside – was a schoolboy's clumsy fumble.

With one notable exception, the Dutchman's year at the helm veered between hell and high water. That exception – and it was truly remarkable – was that he took Newcastle United to the final of the FA Cup for the second year in succession. The club had achieved this feat before, of course, but in 1951 and 1952 they won both matches. In 1998, as we have seen, they lost the first one, and in 1999, despite a marginally better performance, they also lost the second, 2-0 to Manchester United. The one-time undisputed masters of Wembley had, it seemed, become the crumbling old stadium's whipping boys. In Lancashire and north London a new joke made the rounds: 'What goes to the Cup final every year but is never used?' sneered our rivals. The answer was no longer the losing side's ribbons. The answer was now Newcastle United.

It was a bitter enough jibe, but read carefully (by anybody who had a mind to do so) it contained a germ of consolation. The implication of the joke was not that Newcastle United were beyond help, or a complete laughing stock, but rather that Newcastle United were not 'being used' – they were turning up at the party and then failing to do themselves justice. They were simply not performing on the stage which once had been their second home.

That was a managerial problem, and Ruud Gullit was not the manager to solve it. A player of extraordinary brilliance in Holland and Italy, he had segued with alarming ease into management at Chelsea, winning the Stamford Bridge wide-boys the FA Cup before going the way of all those who cross Ken Bates in south-west London. Gullit learned the hard way that Bates was unprepared to offer million-pound contracts to managers and found himself out on the seat of his stylish pants looking for another job.

The position he found was Kenny Dalglish's recently vacated billet, but his appointment was a mistake for both parties. It is possible in retrospect to criticise the United board for that strangest of football vanities: blind over-ambition. Few men in modern soccer came equipped with better or more glittering credentials than Dalglish and Gullit. Few men would ever be more seductive company for an impressionable club director. Few, however, if one probed beyond the glamour and the reputation, had more hidden complexities, more little vanities and prejudices and fatal susceptibilities.

In Dalglish's time at Newcastle these traits manifested them-selves in a bizarre desire to keep his old friends in work; a desire which led to John Barnes and Ian Rush being given the run of St James's Park as a retirement home. In Gullit's reign they boiled down to two fatal weaknesses. One was a total incomprehen-sion of the will of the north-eastern football fan, and – more damagingly – an obstinate refusal to attempt to comprehend that passion. And the other (not unconnected) was his adaman-tine inability to work with Newcastle United's talismanic players: Rob Lee and – infinitely greater – Alan Shearer.

Ruud Gullit rated neither of these two servants. Why he and Shearer fell into dispute is not difficult to analyse. Both are strong-willed and stubborn men, both considered themselves to be more valuable to their club than the other, and both felt it necessary to gain the upper hand. It just so happened that Gullit had the aces, because he picked the team. It also happened to be true that if Gullit played those aces in a losing hand he would lose his place at the table.

A more flexible character than Gullit would have realised that 25 August 1999 was not the perfect date upon which to demonstrate his unique vision for the future of Newcastle United. The club had experienced its worst league start in decades, losing the first three matches and drawing the fourth at home to Wimbledon, 3-3. In the course of those four games United had conceded 11 goals. The fifth game was against Sunderland, in Newcastle.

Sunderland were newly re-promoted and, unlike the Geordies, they had experienced a happy beginning to their season. They did not expect to win the Premiership, but that was not their main ambition. Their main ambition was to finish above Newcastle United in the table.

Did Gullit recognise the significance of this fixture? Had he read the first editions of this book, *The Toon*? Had nobody told him that for a century Newcastle managers who lost at home to Sunderland became, by and large, as welcome in the city as anthrax? Did no friendly colleague edge the Dutchman to one side and suggest that while losing to Sunderland might just about be survivable – it had happened before – losing at home to Sunderland after dropping the most popular footballer on Tyneside was the equivalent of swallowing arsenic?

If they did, he ignored them. Shearer was dropped. The brilliant young Kieron Dyer gave United a 1-0 lead at half-time. Then disaster fell on Ruud Gullit's dreadlocks. Sunderland's much-vaunted striking duo of Niall Quinn and Kevin Phillips struck twice in the first ten minutes of the second half to take the three points back to Wearside. United would not be the last side to be bushwhacked by Quinn and Phillips, but such details hardly figure on Tyneside. Dreadlock wigs – until recently a major fashion accessory in the town – were binned from North Shields to Hexham. Five days later United travelled to Old Trafford where they were swamped 5-1 (four of them coming, most painfully, from Andy Cole) – the era of Gullit's sexy football was comprehensively over.

Newcastle had tried before to attract Bobby Robson to the managerial hotseat but they hadn't reckoned on his integrity. Despite being appallingly treated and sidelined by Barcelona, Robson refused to break his Catalonian contract, and Dalglish got the job at St James's. By early September 1999, however, Robson's circumstances had changed and the 67-year-old maestro joined, for the very first time, the club of his youthful dreams.

Robson had come home. Born in Langley Park, County Durham in 1933 he had been one of the boys who got away. Signing as a teenager for Fulham, he become a highly respected England half-back and enjoyed a lengthy spell as manager of Ipswich Town before following his East Anglian predecessor Alf Ramsey into the England manager's job in 1982.

Under Robson, England enjoyed their best World Cup since 1966, reaching the semi-finals in Italia '90. A piece of extraordinary buffoonery by the Football Association, who told him that his contract would be up at the end of that summer no matter how well England performed, led Robson – by now in his late 50s – into the most successful continental career of any English club manager. In less than ten years he won the Dutch league twice with PSV Eindhoven, won the Portuguese title twice with FC Porto and won the European Cup-Winners' Cup with FC Barcelona. His contract with Barca finally expired and Robson enjoyed a second flirtation with Eindhoven before grasping with open arms and enormous satisfaction the one club job to which he had always aspired: the managership of Newcastle United.

At last the board had got it right. This was not only a Geordie; this was a Geordie who happened to be the most eminent working English manager of the day. On 3 September 1999 he walked into what could charitably be described as a difficult situation. Newcastle were second from bottom in the Premiership. They had one point from six matches. They had not won a single competitive game in 13 (and had actually contrived to lose to Scottish minnows Livingston in the pre-season friendlies). It had been 20 matches since United had managed not to concede a goal.

To add to the new manager's problems there was little or no money for new players. The continuing mystery of Newcastle United was that the club not only played in the richest league in the world, it was also one of the three richest clubs in that league. Any table of affluence put the outfit from St James's Park comfortably in the top ten of the world's multi-millionaire soccer aristocracy. Yet this loaded soccer club had failed to win a domestic title since 1955.

The board did have one excuse to offer Robson in 1999. The ground itself was being expanded to a seating capacity of 52,000. Premiership football guaranteed that capacity would be filled at every home game. In time, therefore, it would pay off. But in the short term, Robson was told, the coffers were dry.

But he took the job, the job that all of his 50 years in professional football had drawn him towards, and the result was almost instantly electric. After losing his first match 1-0 at Chelsea, CSKA Sofia were beaten away in the first leg of the first round of the UEFA Cup. Shearer was back in the side, and on 19 September Sheffield Wednesday came to call. Legends are made of what happened on that Sunday afternoon. United won by 8-0. The feat of maintaining a second successive clean sheet and of winning their first domestic match in 15 attempts was eclipsed by another detail. Alan Shearer, Ruud Gullit's least favourite striker, scored five of the eight goals. In the following three matches he would claim another five, and he did not stop scoring until the end of the season. Robson was doing something right.

He nipped and tucked, the bus-pass manager, selling and signing frugally and cannily, consolidating his team in the Premiership. Within 18 months he was ready. His slender squad of beautifully organised talent found itself halfway through the 2001–02 season on top of the English Premiership.

It was parsimony which eventually let them down. Robson, too wise an owl to deceive himself or anybody else, knew and said as much. Those tight purse-strings meant that injuries to such players as Dyer and Craig Bellamy – injuries which would be compensated for in a properly equipped major European football club – fatally weakened the 14-man outfit of the 2002 Newcastle team.

Despite all these difficulties Robson still managed to lead United into Europe, and once again this continuing saga closes on a note of optimism. It will be short-lived optimism unless the purse-strings are loosened and a squad is assembled which can cope with 50 or 60 top-flight matches in the course of a season. The 52,000 fans who fill that glorious new stadium on every available opportunity not only deserve that reward, they are paying for it. It is time – and it has been time for 46 years – that they received their due.

CHAPTER THIRTEEN

BOBBY IN DOUBT: 2002–04

'It's a funny thing,' said Sir Bobby Robson shortly before 5.00 pm on 15 May 2004. 'Ranieri finished second, and he's been sacked. Ferguson finished third and they say he's past it. Houllier's finished fourth, and they say he should be sacked. We've finished fifth, and they say I'm not good enough. That's the nature of the game today, isn't it – win, win, win. You've just got to win.'

The name of the game had more truly become: win, win, win – and qualify for the European Champions' League. Bobby Robson was of course speaking at Anfield, where a 1-1 draw with Liverpool in the last game of the season (coupled with the aforementioned Alex Ferguson doing his friend Sir Bobby a good turn by beating Aston Villa) had just given Newcastle fifth position, and the consolation UEFA Cup place for season 2004–05.

The Champions' League had slipped from their hands three nights earlier in a rocky, roller-coaster of a 3-3 draw with Southampton on the south coast. Ambitious Premiership clubs should not score three goals and merely draw. Many of the large contingent of Geordies at Southampton that night were left reflecting that if Jonathan Woodgate had been present when James Beattie seized on an uncleared cross, or when Leandre Griffit ran through to score Southampton's third, Newcastle would have left St Mary's with a win.

It had been a strange two years, which left the once impregnable Bobby Robson's job apparently under threat. Newcastle United had continued to win plenty of games without winning – or even getting very close to – a single trophy.

There had been one unimpeachable signing, and that was the 23-year-old Woodgate, a Middlesbrough-born central defender of international class who arrived in the transfer window of January 2003 for £9 million from Elland road as part of the Leeds United clearance sale.

Woodgate's last two years in Yorkshire had been unhappily mired in a lengthy court case surrounding an ugly racial incident, and he celebrated his arrival at St James's Park by holding up the shirt and announcing: 'I'm black and white now.'

Then he promptly set a pattern by getting injured. He missed the disastrous first two months of the 2003–04 season following a double hernia operation. In that August and September Newcastle managed to slip out of the Champions' League at the hands of Partizan Belgrade, and collect just two Premiership points from their first five matches.

Alan Shearer's winning goal against Southampton on Tyneside put them back on track – and that was also typical. But Shearer's scorching Indian summer and Woodgate's return could not disguise the fact that Bobby Robson was obliged to trim his 'Rolls Royce' wages bill.

Newcastle were between £50 and £60 millions in debt, which cost £4.5 millions a year to service. Seven players were put out on loan – most notably Lomano Lua-Lua, who displayed his gratitude in February 2004, just three weeks after moving south, by scoring Portsmouth's crucial equalising goal against Newcastle. .

Nobby Solano was sold to Villa for £1.5 million, and Carl Cort to Wolves for £2 million. On the credit side, Michael Bridges and Lee Bowyer followed Woodgate north from Leeds, one on loan and the other a free transfer. But the stark fact remained that since Darren Ambrose arrived from Ipswich in the spring of 2003 for £1 million, Bobby Robson had bought not a single new player. And three of the stars for whom he had earlier splashed out a combined £23 million – Laurent Robert,

Hugo Viana and Titus Bramble – had yet to display their full worth.

The club was not in crisis – how could it be, with 52,000 clamouring at the gates for every home game? But Newcastle needed a trophy. A 7-1 aggregate hammering of Mallorca, followed by a gritty, powerful display by Alan Shearer and the Newcastle crowd to knock PSV Eindhoven out of the quarter-finals, saw United as the last British team left alive in the semi-finals of the 2004 UEFA Cup. Thirty-five years after the glory days of 1969, it seemed a familiar old piece of silverware might be beckoning.

Marseilles were drawn in the semi-final. And Jonathan Woodgate got injured again. Drogba made hay. The club was left jousting for next season's European places. Defeat at Manchester City and a home draw to relegated Wolves put the Champions' League in doubt, long before that visit to a rejuvenated Liverpool.

Chairman Freddie Shepherd (basic wage £668,920) announced that 'The next Newcastle United manager will be a Geordie.'

Steve Bruce of Birmingham City was born within the Tyneside borderline. But Alan Shearer was, at the end of the 2003–04 season, just 12 months away from completing his coaching ticket and hanging up those worn old boots. And Sir Bobby Robson remained the most famous living Geordie of them all. If the grand old man could only, in his own words, win, win, win.

CHAPTER FOURTEEN

TRIUMPH AND DISASTER

The years between 2004 and 2010 were the most tumultuous in the long history of Newcastle United. They began with the club riding high. It then sank low. It teetered on the brink of disaster. It finished the decade in triumph and with the possibility of redemption.

In those six years United had eight different managers. Bobby Robson was sacked in August 2004 after just four games of the new campaign. 'It was a shock,' he said. 'I was bewildered. We had qualified for Europe and were looking forward to the new season.' His crime had been to finish 5th, 3rd and 4th in the Premiership in the previous three seasons. Newcastle United would not again reach those peaks for the rest of the 2000s. Robson managed 255 United games between 1999 and 2004. He won 119 of them, drew 64 and lost 72. Within a very short time that would look like a record to dream about.

Sir Bobby was replaced by Graeme Souness. A Scottish international who had made his playing reputation with Liverpool, Souness's only consistent managerial successes had been at Glasgow Rangers in the duopoly of the Scottish First Division. He had moved from there to Liverpool, where he managed in three years to win one FA Cup Final against Second Division Sunderland. Souness went from Merseyside to Galatasary, with whom he won one Turkish Cup; to Southampton where he won nothing; to Torino where he lasted four months; to an equally barren spell at Benfica; and then in 2000 to Blackburn Rovers.

Having taken the Ewood Park club back up to the Premier League he managed a series of respectable but trophyless seasons. The offer from Newcastle arrived in time for Graeme Souness to jump before he was pushed out of Blackburn.

It was difficult to know what Freddie Shepherd imagined he was getting from his new manager in 2004. By then the Scot had been a manager for 18 years at seven clubs in five countries, and it was clear to most observers that in the higher levels of football, Souness talked a better game than he walked. 'First thing Monday morning, after a weeks' gardening leave,' wrote a reporter who probably echoed the Newcastle chairman's fantasies, 'Souness will be introduced to those United players, a precocious bunch whose indiscipline and ambivalence towards the ambition of the club brought about Robson's reluctant departure. They are long overdue a good clip around the ear. In Souness, Shepherd has found someone who is not afraid to deliver that blow.'

The blow was quickly landed. The pugnacious Welshman Craig Bellamy, who had formed a productive goalscoring partnership with Alan Shearer, was predictably one of the first to fall out with his equally aggressive Scottish boss, and was banished to Glasgow Celtic. Laurent Robert, Olivier Bernard and Jermaine Jenas quickly followed him out of the door. Newcastle made the quarters of the UEFA Cup and the semis of the FA Cup but finished in the bottom half of the Premiership.

The job in the close season of 2005 was clearly to reinforce the defence and find a replacement for the 34-year-old Shearer. Graeme Souness spent tens of millions in that quest. He gave his former club Glasgow Rangers £8,000,000 for the French central defender Jean-Alain Boumsong, who had gone to Scotland on a 'Bosman' free transfer just a few months earlier. The deal attracted the attention of the police and the Stevens Report into football corruption. Boumsong lasted two seasons at St James's Park before being sold to Juventus for less than £4,000,000.

But the signature signing of the Souness reign was that of Michael Owen. Real Madrid were paid a club record fee of

£16,000,000 (a million more than Alan Shearer had cost ten years earlier) for the 25-year-old England striker in August 2005. It should have been the deal of the decade. Owen and Shearer were the most dangerous English goalscorers of their generation.

In the event, it turned out to be the signing which typified the last years of Owen's career and the next five years of United's existence. Owen – who had depended since his precocious teens on rapid turns and bursts of formidable speed – suffered injury after injury. No sooner had his signature been put on the contract than a thigh strain ruled him out of the start of the 2005–06 season. That set the tone. When he played, Michael Owen still scored goals. But in four seasons with Newcastle United he played only 79 matches, hitting the net 30 times. Seven-and-a-half goals a season was a poor return on £16,000,000.

United finished seventh in the Premiership in 2006. Graeme Souness had been sacked in February. More notably, Alan Shearer retired at the end of the season. He had won not a single trophy during his extended swansong at his hometown club, but he signed off as Newcastle's record goalscorer with 206 strikes in 395 games. Satisfactorily, his 206th and last goal was against Sunderland. The sheet-metal worker's son from Gosforth became a Deputy Lieutenant of Northumberland, a Freeman of Newcastle upon Tyne and an Honorary Doctor of Civil Law of Northumbria and Newcastle Universities. Oh, and a member of the Order of the British Empire. 'When I was a young boy,' he said, 'I wanted to play for Newcastle United, I wanted to wear the number nine shirt and I wanted to score goals at St James' Park. I've lived my dream and I realise how lucky I've been to have done that.'

Graeme Souness was replaced by Glenn Roeder. A stylish and respected defender with the club in the 1980s, Roeder had gained some managerial experience in the lower leagues and under Glenn Hoddle with England, before becoming first a coach and then manager of West Ham United. He was an Essex boy, but he did not have a happy time in east London: the

Hammers were relegated and Roeder contracted a brain tumour. He was sacked in 2003, and in 2005 went to Newcastle as youth development manager.

After Souness's dismissal Glenn Roeder, with Alan Shearer as his assistant, enjoyed a golden early spell as caretaker manager at St James's Park. The club was lifted from the relegation area to seventh position, and in May 2006 he was given the job permanently.

Or as permanently as managers got at Newcastle in the 2000s. Roeder lasted almost exactly a year as permanent manager. The club won a strange, semi-technical European trophy in the form of the C-level Intertoto Cup, and occupied the top half of the table until the last few games of the season, when a bad run of just one win in ten games finished them in 13th place. Roeder was hampered by the departure of the irreplaceable Alan Shearer, by an unprecedented number of injuries to senior players (not least Michael Owen, who played three matches in the whole campaign after being injured while playing for England in the 2006 World Cup Finals), and by the board's refusal to invest in major talent. A decent man who was given an impossible task, Glenn Roeder was fired in May 2007.

It was not Roeder's fault, argued one commentator. The malaise lay elsewhere in St James's Park. 'Ultimately the reason that Newcastle have underperformed has been that the board have badly managed the club. Despite pouring money in, there is a sense in which the club has been a vast popularity project for directors. They seem to have seen their role as representing the fans to the manager – and not shielding the manager in times of crisis. Indeed the directors have too often been led by short term enthusiasms – often taking decisions behind managers' backs ... because of perceived popularity gains to be made. The Board ultimately have held Newcastle back.'

The board itself soon went. Shortly after appointing Sam Allardyce as manager, the Hall family sold their shares to a businessman named Mike Ashley. Freddie Shepherd subsequently also sold his holding to the same buyer. The Hall/Shepherd era ended in July 2007. Newcastle United was withdrawn from the stock exchange and became a private holding. At a cost to its new owner of around £135,000,000, the Mike Ashley administration began.

Mike Ashley was a 44-year-old sporting goods multi-millionaire. Previously known as a publicity-shy recluse, he promptly contradicted the image by acting as no other owner of Newcastle United or any other major English football club had ever behaved. Ashley installed Christopher Mort, a corporate lawyer, in Freddie Shepherd's old chairman's office – and then Ashley himself, who was Buckinghamshire born and bred, proceeded to apply for full membership of the Toon Army.

The wealthy middle-aged entrepreneur appeared to be attempting a second adolescence. He spurned his own director's seat, joining the fans in the stands wearing a team shirt. He watched the Sunderland derby at the Stadium of Light from the away end in his black-and-white stripes. He ostentatiously drank beer during matches.

He and chairman Mort negotiated Sam Allardyce's departure after the big midlander had spent half an unsuccessful season in the job, winning just eight games out of 24 in the first part of the 2007–08 season. Instantly, like any other besotted Newcastle United fan, Ashley re-appointed Kevin Keegan as manager.

The third coming of King Kev was an avoidable mistake. It was a move made more from sentiment than considered judgement. The Keegan who had played two seasons for Newcastle United in the early 1980s had been an experienced international footballer relishing the twilight of his career in the company of several excellent younger team-mates, playing against Second Division opposition and enjoying the adulation of an adoring Geordie crowd.

The Keegan who became United's manager in 1992 was then fresh from an eight-year break from football. He returned to the game like a hurricane. All of his characteristic drive and enthusiasm, coupled with eight years watching and analysing English professional football from his armchair, made him a new force in management which his opponents, at least initially, could neither understand nor contain. As was noted earlier, despite winning no trophies but the Division One (old Division Two) title, he became the most successful results-based manager in Newcastle's history. He did it all with uncompromising flair. And of course, he signed Alan Shearer.

But the Kevin Keegan who returned to the manager's chair at St James's Park in January 2008 was a different man. The signs of his future erratic behaviour had been on the Gallowgate wall in 1997, when he decided in the middle of the season that 'he no longer wishes to continue in football management at this stage in his life.' Eight months later he became 'Chief Operating Officer' at Fulham FC, and took over as manager there in 1998. With his trademark burst of irresistible energy Keegan took Fulham out of Division Two and into the top flight. He then became the manager of England in 1999 – only to walk away from that job the following year, saying 'I have had all the help I have needed to do my job properly, but I've not been quite good enough.' In 2001 he took over at Manchester City, and also guided them out of the second tier into the first, before announcing his decision to retire not only from City but from all football management in 2005.

So when Kevin Keegan sensationally agreed to return to St James's Park early in 2008, his career pattern was clear. As a manager his drive and exuberance convinced everybody – his players, his employers, the media, and even himself. But it was short-lived. Those qualities, coupled with investment in good players, were enough to lift an affluent club out of the second tier of league football. But he lacked the depth, the tactical wisdom, the mental toughness and ultimately the confidence to manage teams at the highest level. As he was essentially an honest man, he was quick to accept his failings and to walk away. But he was also in love with football and could not resist returning time and again to give it another try . . .

So when in January 2008 Kevin Keegan announced 'It's nice to be home. I'm delighted to be back' and signed a three-and-a-half year contract, only the most optimistic Geordies – of which there are tens of thousands – expected him still to be on Tyneside in 2011.

He lasted eight months this time. Early in September 2008 a protracted dispute with Christopher Mort and Mike Ashley resulted in King Kev leaving Newcastle United, probably for the last time. There were arguably good reasons for his 2008 departure, which were unrelated to his own abilities. Ashley and Mort had recruited the former Wimbledon and Millwall hard man Dennis Wise to Keegan's managerial team. Wise was always too much of a latterday cockney version of Keegan's old adversary Billy Bremner for Kevin to love. When Keegan said in his resignation statement that 'a manager must have the right to manage', he was alluding to the unwanted interferences of Director of Football Dennis Wise. Matters were brought to a head when Wise saw on the internet video site YouTube the midfielder Ignacio González playing for Valencia, and signed the Uruguayan on loan against Keegan's wishes (González played two matches for Newcastle United). But it was difficult to avoid the conclusion that if Dennis Wise had not upset the Keegan applecart, something else would have pushed him. Kevin Keegan was, ultimately, too sensitive a flower to bloom perennially in the harsh climate of the English Premier League.

Among all this chaos, which resulted in passionate fan protests at a 'cockney mafia', Mike Ashley putting the club up for sale and the owner feeling suddenly afraid to sit even in the directors' box at St James's Park, it was perhaps remarkable that Newcastle sustained a mid-table league position in the top flight. The succession of managers had signed some useful players. Those players may not have been sure who was selecting them from one week to the next, but even without consistent direction they were good enough to win as many games as they lost. After a shaky start Obafemi Martins was proving his worth upfront, in the occasional company of Mark Viduka and Michael Owen. At the back, Shay Given had developed into one of the finest goalkeepers of his generation.

So when Joe Kinnear took on the manager's job, supposedly as a ten-week holding operation while Ashley sold the club, he held a decent hand of cards. A former Republic of Ireland international with a solid managerial record at Wimbledon and Luton Town, Kinnear was an interim manager who could have been much more. At a time of economic recession Mike Ashley failed to find a buyer for Newcastle United, and Kinnear's contract was extended until the end of the 2008–09 season.

It would be the most traumatic season for many years. Joe Kinnear made some promising signings, bringing in the experienced Danish forward Peter Lovenkrands, the accomplished midfielder Kevin Nolan from Bolton Wanderers, and the England under-21 international defender Ryan Taylor from Wigan. The last transfer was a classical case of 'if you can't beat 'em, sign 'em up.' Ryan Taylor was emphatically not a goalscorer. He netted just six times in 56 appearances for Wigan. But four of those goals came in four games against Newcastle in 2007 and 2008.

On the debit side, the long-serving Shay Given was sold in January 2009 to Manchester City for almost £6,000,000. The loss of Given, who would be described as 'one of the five best goalkeepers in the world' by his future Manchester City manager Roberto Mancini, could have been catastrophic. Luckily one of the most extraordinary Newcastle United players of all time was there to replace him.

Steve Harper had been a Newcastle player for longer than Shay Given. The Easington boy signed at St James's Park from the Wearside non-league side Seaham Red Star as a teenager in 1993. But as understudy first to Pavel Smicek and Shaka Hislop, and then to the apparently irreplaceable Given, Harper did not make a first team debut until 1999. He had lengthy periods on loan to several lower division sides, and extended spells in the first team during Given's injuries in 2007 and 2008 before his moment arrived after the transfer window of January 2009, when Shay Given left.

Steve Harper, at the age of 34 years and in his 16th year at Newcastle United, became first-choice goalkeeper. In the previous 16 years, Harper had played only 72 league games for Newcastle. But the north-easterner would not let his club down. In the first half of the 2008–09 season Shay Given conceded 37 league goals in 22 games. In the second half, Harper conceded 22 in 16 matches. They were playing against similar opposition in similar circumstances behind a similar defence, but Given picked the ball out of the net 1.7 times in each game, whereas Harper kept it down to an average concession of 1.4 per match. He may not have been a better keeper than the Irish international, but the disaster was not Steve Harper's fault.

It was the fault of dysfunctional executive management and its malign effect on a team which was, player for player, too good to be relegated. An avalanche of misfortune hit the club in the first months of 2009, and the executive was unable to cope with it. In January Newcastle United was disappointingly, but not tragically, hovering in around 12th place out of the 19 Premier League clubs – four places above the relegation zone. They still fell into most pundits' category of a team which was just about strong enough to stay up.

In February Joe Kinnear was hospitalised for a heart bypass operation. The former first team coach and Kinnear's assistant manager, Chris Hughton, became yet another stand-in manager at St James's Park. It was a baptism of fire for Hughton. A series of abject draws and defeats saw the club slump quickly into the relegation zone. In a move of pure desperation, on April Fool's Day 2009, Alan Shearer was made manager, Iain Dowie assistant manager, and Dennis Wise left the club. Shearer won just one match while in charge. On 24th May 2009 Newcastle United lost 1-0 to Aston Villa and were relegated in 18th place to what was by then called the Championship, but which Hughie Gallacher and Jackie Milburn would have known as Division Two. 'I am feeling raw inside,' said Alan Shearer, the inheritor of their goalscoring mantle, as his team dropped out of the top division in English football for the first time in 16 years.

Mike Ashley had not been able to sell a Premier League club in an international recession, and he could find no satisfactory buyers for a Championship outfit. The summer months of the 2009 close season echoed with rumours of one consortium or another preparing to offer upwards of £80,000,000 for a football club with as much potential as any in western Europe. But after a series of aborted negotiations, Ashley took the club off the market once again.

It was altogether a strange, unpromising pre-season. There was no full-time manager, just the unassuming Chris Hughton holding down a temporary post. Newcastle were thrashed 6-1 by lowly Leyton Orient in a warm-up friendly. It may have been a blessing in disguise. 'Getting tonked 6-1 was a shambles, but brought a few things to light,' said Kevin Nolan. 'It showed who wanted to be here and who didn't . . . The media frenzy was ridiculous. Reports saying we were going to do another Leeds sort of spurred us on. We promised each other we're all going to be together and nobody is going to break the bond as players and staff.'

A week before the start of the season Sir Bobby Robson died. The man who had been so badly mistreated by his hometown club five years earlier, and whose continued presence at St James's Park might have forestalled much of the trouble which followed his departure, succumbed to the cancer which he had nobly battled since 1992. Of all the tributes, that of UEFA president Michel Platini was best phrased. 'He will be remembered not only for his playing career,' said Platini, 'and his outstanding managerial career at both club and international level, but also because he was a truly warm and passionate human being.'

On 8th August 2009 Newcastle's Championship season began with a 1-1 draw with West Bromwich Albion at The Hawthorns. After that, Chris Hughton's team took off.

The great club servant Shola Ameobi got the season properly underway with all of Newcastle's four goals in two home wins over Reading and Sheffield Wednesday. Four more consecutive victories followed, and by the end of August Newcastle were sitting on top of the Championship. They would stay there for almost all of the rest of the campaign, and would never slip out of the top two promotion places.

The ghosts of two of the clubs better managers were laid to rest in six days at the end of September and beginning of October. In the league match at Ipswich Town which Newcastle won 4-0 – both sides wore shirts commemorating Bobby Robson. And on 2nd October an employment tribunal awarded Kevin Keegan £2,000,000 in damages for his 'constructive dismissal' a year earlier.

On 27th October, following a 2-1 win over Doncaster Rovers that put the club back at the top after a brief slide into second place, Chris Hughton was appointed permanent manager until the end of the season. It was no more than he deserved. Hughton made his way to the top job by the back door. But the quiet, intelligent, dedicated Irish international and former Tottenham full-back would prove to be the solution that the directors had failed to spot, perhaps because he was quietly dedicated and had been right in front of their eyes for almost two years.

Then the boys got down to work. 'Even players were saying [the previous few years] was like being in EastEnders,' said Kevin Nolan. 'What we've tried to do is close ranks and bring it back to being a football club. You can look back to when the club last went up in 1993 and mistakes were made from then until 2009 and some of them were major, major mistakes, whether it was transfers or behind-the-scenes . . . We now have a management . . . They allow us to manage the dressing room but if Chris comes in and says "no, that's not right, this is what we do", then that's it. It's finished, no matter what we say. When Chris wants something he gets it. He is a great manager, a great fella. Make no mistake, they manage, we just play.'

Hughton depended largely on English players, with three crucial north-easterners in Steve Harper, defender Steven Taylor and top scorer Andy Carroll. Fabricio Coloccini added uncompromising Argentine power and Jose Enrique gave penetration to the defence, and Peter Lovenkrands offered art and experience to the forward line.

It was all too much for most of the rest of the Championship. West Bromwich Albion and then Nottingham Forest nipped at the heels of the club without ever seriously threatening Newcastle's dominance of the division. St James's Park was occupied in most home games by upwards of 40,000 loyal fans – attendances that almost all Premier League clubs would envy

– rising to 47,000 and 48,000 as promotion grew closer, and topped off with 52,000 celebrating the Championship title at home to Ipswich on 24th April 2010.

Newcastle United's average home gate in 2009–10 was 43,388. That was not only the biggest in the Championship by a country mile; it was also bigger than all but three Premier League clubs – Manchester United, Arsenal and Manchester City. The average Premier League attendance in 2009–10 was 34,154. The average Championship crowd was 17,959, and would have been much lower but for the presence in the division of Newcastle United.

Playing in the second tier of English football, Newcastle attracted more regular fans than did the high-flying Chelsea, Liverpool, Aston Villa, Everton, and every other Premier League team but the three mentioned above. They were, in short, the fourth best supported club in England.

That emphasised once again the old and festering contradiction. How could a football club that big, with such obvious potential to occupy a permanent place at the apex of world club football, so consistently under-achieve?

There are many answers and they cover the whole pyramid of the club, from peak to base. Newcastle United has been restricted by ownerships which have been egotistical, greedy, self-serving and ultimately too ignorant of the game of football to keep pace with the fast refinements and improvements to the sport at the end of the 20th century and beginning of the 21st.

The ownership's bafflement by what was going on all around them – in Manchester, London, Milan and Barcelona – was reflected in managerial appointments and player purchases which were inadequate, chaotic, and inspired by no consistent philosophy of how a top-level modern football team should perform. Those players then found themselves directionless and confused, reduced to trying as individuals to impress one short-lived team manager after another, and football is not a 100-metre sprint, not an individual's sport, but a team game which accumulates results over the best part of a year and relies upon the intimate cooperation and implicit selflessness of a dozen or more players.

The masses who sustained the whole edifice, the huge foundations at the base of the pyramid, rarely withheld their passionate support but grew impatient and angry with the performances and results. They could look at English football's attendance figures and justifiably wonder why their team did not reflect their loyalty. And the supporters' loud frustration fed the uncertainties of the players, the management and the ownership . . .

Newcastle United would play once more in the Premier League in 2010–11. The fans would certainly be with them. The manager and many of the players who returned them there had earned the opportunity to work at the highest level. For as long as he retained his asset the undistinguished owner, Mike Ashley, would hopefully take better advice and, having taken it, sit back and allow the team and the management a period of calm and security and investment. He was unlikely to be spotted in the crowd in a black and white shirt, drinking beer.

INDEX